IMAGES
of America

JEROME

ON THE COVER: In 1907, Ira B. Perrine's stagecoach delivered people and the mail from Jerome to the two-year-old town of Twin Falls 15 miles to the south. Starting from Jerome, the coach traveled south on to Blue Lakes Road, down off the north rim into the Snake River Canyon, across the river on the Perrine Ferry, then up the south canyon road to the rim, and on to Twin Falls A few years later, Perrine built the first Perrine Bridge in the canyon on the same ferry route.

IMAGES
of America

JEROME

Linda Helms

ARCADIA
PUBLISHING

ISBN 978-0-7385-9518-4

Published by Arcadia Publishing
Charleston, South Carolina

Printed in the United States of America

Library of Congress Control Number: 2012933467

For all general information, please contact Arcadia Publishing:
Telephone 843-853-2070
Fax 843-853-0044
E-mail sales@arcadiapublishing.com
For customer service and orders:
Toll-Free 1-888-313-2665

Visit us on the Internet at www.arcadiapublishing.com

This collection is dedicated to all the people who have lived, worked, visited, or wanted to visit the Jerome area, specifically including the volunteers at the museum. All these persons are essential to preserving the greatness of Jerome.

Contents

ACKNOWLEDGMENTS

This collection of images has been made available by the Jerome County Historical Society Museum. Many local persons donated their personal photographs permanently to the museum to be preserved and shared with others interested in learning about the beginning of Jerome. Certain images have been loaned for this project only and are noted as such individually. Special recognition is made to Clair and Virginia Ricketts for their foresight to begin the museum and publish some of the area's history in two books, *Then And Now In Southern Idaho* and *Shoshone Falls: The Magnificent Spectacle*. In some cases, caption information was obtained from the four historical supplements to Jerome's pioneer newspaper the *North Side News*: North Side Golden Jubilee (1907–1957), Bicentennial Edition (1976), The History of the North Side: The First 75 Years, and The History of the North Side: The First 100 Years. We are thankful to those editors for preserving our history.

Introduction

Even though people have traveled through this area for many years, beginning with Native American Shoshone, Blackfoot, and Piute tribes followed by the Wilson Price Hunt party, which included Pierre Dorian with his pregnant wife, Marie, and their four children; trapper Donald McKenzie; the Whitman and Spaulding missionaries; the Oregon Trail emigrants; and the Snake River Canyon gold-seekers, not many wanted to stay on the dry sagebrush desert.

This was the case until Ira B. Perrine, a newcomer himself to this area from the gold and silver mines in the Wood River area to the north, had a dream that the Snake River water could be diverted to canals above the canyon rim. In 1900, Perrine filed a claim on the waters at the Cedars, the area just upstream from where the Snake flows into a deep canyon for the next 50 miles. In 1905, his dream became a reality when the Milner Dam was built 30 miles upstream. Before this, the Upper Snake River was free-flowing from its beginning near Yellowstone Lake. The first dam on the Snake was built in 1901 at Swan Falls, located south of Kuna, Idaho (near Boise). The 500-foot-deep canyon near Jerome did not allow for irrigation of the land on the rim. Not only was the Milner Dam used for diverting irrigation water, it was the first of many in the upper Snake to convert waterpower into electricity. With the canals filling on the south side to the new town of Twin Falls, attention was turned to the north side in 1907. Without irrigation water and electricity, the towns in this area would not exist. The financiers were honored by adding their names to the area towns: Jerome Kuhn (Jerome), Wendell Kuhn (Wendell), Peter Kimberly (Kimberly), and H.L. Hollister (Hollister). A school was named for Paul Bickel, and the dam itself was named after Stanley Milner. Even Perrine had a community named for him, situated eight miles east of Jerome.

The William S. Kuhn family of Pittsburgh, Pennsylvania, along with other wealthy easterners, understood Perrine's dream. Their financing of the endeavors to make the desert bloom ensued. With the passing of the Carey Act and accessibility to reasonably priced land, thousands of people came to the North Side Tract to begin new communities. Many of the present residents have direct ties to these early pioneers.

In the fall of 1906, Jerome S. Kuhn and William S. Kuhn of Pittsburgh became interested in irrigation in Idaho. The Twin Falls Land and Water Company (named for two waterfalls in the middle of the Snake River, just a few miles east of Jerome) had filed a request to irrigate 155,000 acres of land north of the Snake River in an area known as Lincoln County. In the summer of 1907, Robert McCollum, Jerome Kuhn, and two other men rode in a horse-drawn wagon up the Blue Lakes Grade from Perrine's ranch in the Snake River Canyon. Looking for the ideal spot to form a new town, they traveled 10 miles northwest through the sagebrush desert of southern Idaho. At nightfall, they stopped to camp. The next morning, they awoke to a beautiful vista of not-too-distant mountains and decided this was the perfect spot. Their campsite became the crossroads of West to East Main Street and North to South Lincoln Avenue—the exact center of Jerome, Idaho. They organized the North Side Land and Investment Company to sell both town and country lots. Paul Kartzke was hired to erect buildings to establish the town, the first being his own home, then the State Bank building and the Lodging House and adjoining restaurant. In later years, Kartzke also constructed other buildings, including schools, churches, and the courthouse.

In anticipation of selling the land on September 30, 1907, the new town had a water well with piped water to businesses and residences, electricity, and telephone service, making it the first town in the area to have these amenities. The first business was the Boomerang Saloon, established in August 1907. The post office was officially established on August 24, 1907, with Adeline Becker as postmistress. The first public officials before the land drawing were notaries Harvey Hurlebaus and Samuel Champlain. Jerome became the center of agriculture, as many farmers and dairymen bought the surrounding land. Because of agriculture, the following businesses formed: farmers' grain elevators, lumber yards, hardware stores, and dairy supply stores along with the regular grocery, clothing, and general merchandise stores, and the Jerome Cooperative Creamery. Within the first few years, there was a brick schoolhouse, six churches, and many social organizations, such as the ladies' civic club, the Odd Fellows and Rebekah, and the Freemasons. The Kuhns felt that parks were important and donated two full blocks north and south on East Main Street, and several organizations planted trees and grass. Ball games, picnics, and holiday celebrations brought many people into the community. The downtown crossroads of Main Street and Lincoln Avenue were also the crossroads of State Highway 25 from east to west and US Highway 93 from north to south. (When Highway 93 was realigned four miles east of town, the road directly south of Jerome became State Highway 79.)

Over the last 100 years, Jerome has added a hospital, several doctors and dentists, and many churches, as well as nine different schools, five more parks, many clothing and variety stores, furniture shops, and car dealerships. Lawyers, real estate agents, and insurance agents found business within the city. Hotels, restaurants, saloons, snack bars, swimming pools, and movie theaters were added for recreation. At one point, there was a Tupperware manufacturing plant, Moore's Business Forms, and C.J. Marshall's potato processing center, and now Hilex Poly, a plastic bag manufacturing facility and the only plant of its kind in the western United States. Because of the many dairies near Jerome, more milk processing plants have sprung up. Thrift stores and antique stores occupy many of the historical buildings. One building has been the same insurance agency since 1908. For most of its life, Jerome has been a self-sustaining community. What started as an incorporated village became a town and now a city with over 10,000 residents. It is the county seat of Jerome County, with Eden and Hazelton residents coming to the courthouse and purchasing products and services and visiting with others.

After 1930, the streets running north and south parallel to Lincoln Avenue were renamed. In those cases, both names are given, with the current names in parentheses. The street names west from Lincoln Avenue are trees in alphabetical order, and the streets east from Lincoln are named for US presidents in alphabetical order. The avenues parallel to Main Street northward are consecutive numbered both east and west of Lincoln Avenue. The avenues south of Main Street are consecutive alphabetical names both east and west.

One

The Building of a New Community

With the promise of irrigation water for 155,000 acres of undeveloped volcanic soil for agriculture on the north side of the Snake River Canyon, a town was envisioned. As in most of the western United States at the turn of the 20th century, towns needed to be no more than 10 miles apart (the distance a team and wagon could go in one day) and be as self-sufficient as possible. Because of the foresight of its first settlers, Jerome still stands independent over 100 years later.

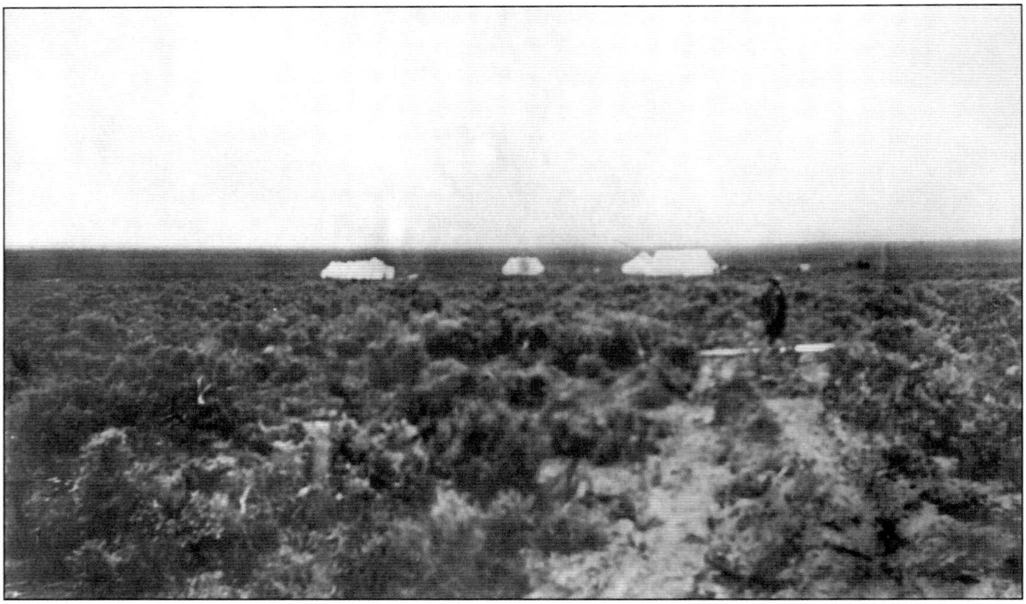

In July 1907, three tent structures in the middle of the sagebrush were the only indications of the future city of Jerome. One tent was the residence of R.M. McCollum and H.W. Hurlebaus, and another was the temporary residence of Paul and Jane Kartzke. Paul, a carpenter by trade, was under contract to build a bank, company building, and Lodging House. The man in the foreground is not identified.

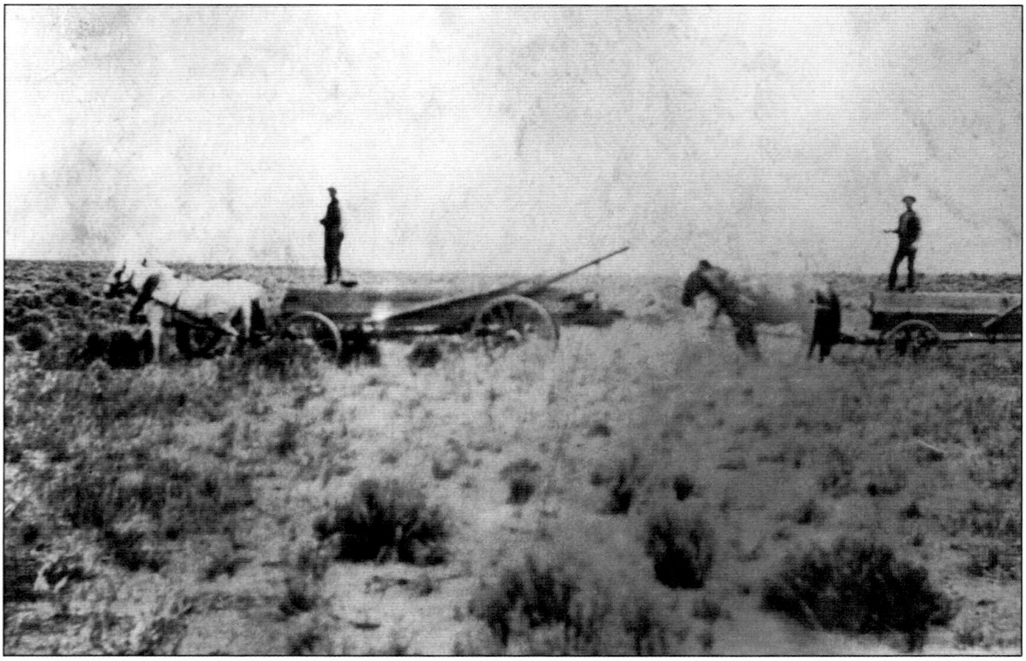

The first load of lumber arrived in Jerome by wagon, probably from the Wood River area 50 miles to the north, in July 1907. This was used as wall planking for the first tents and in the construction of the Kartzke home. Electricity, telephone service, and a city well were in place soon after, making Jerome the first town in the area to have these services before the official selling of lots on September 30, 1907.

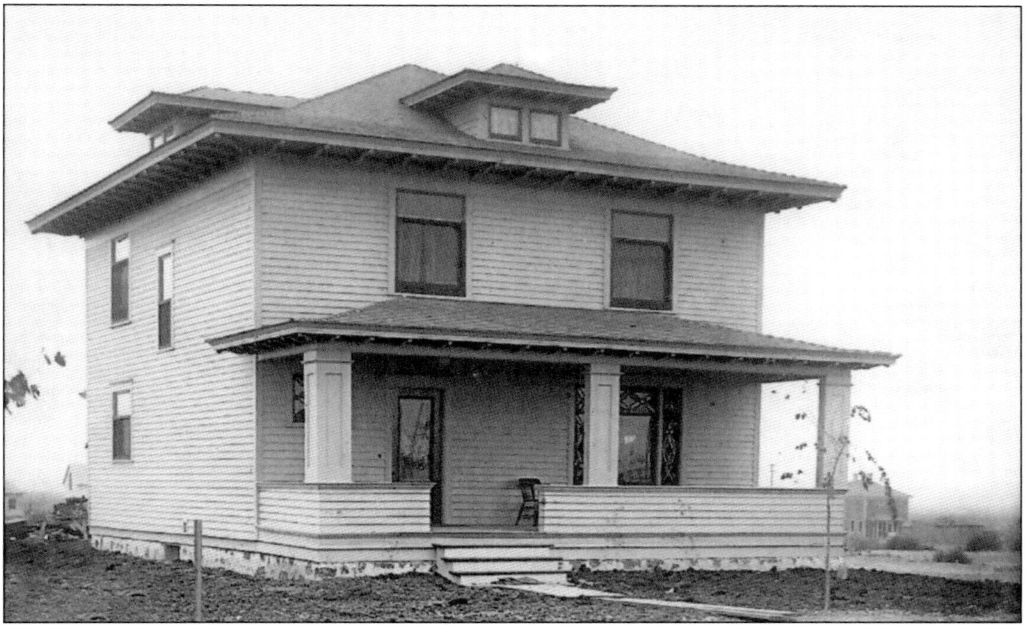

The Paul and Jane Kartzke home was the first building in Jerome. It was two blocks north of the center of town.

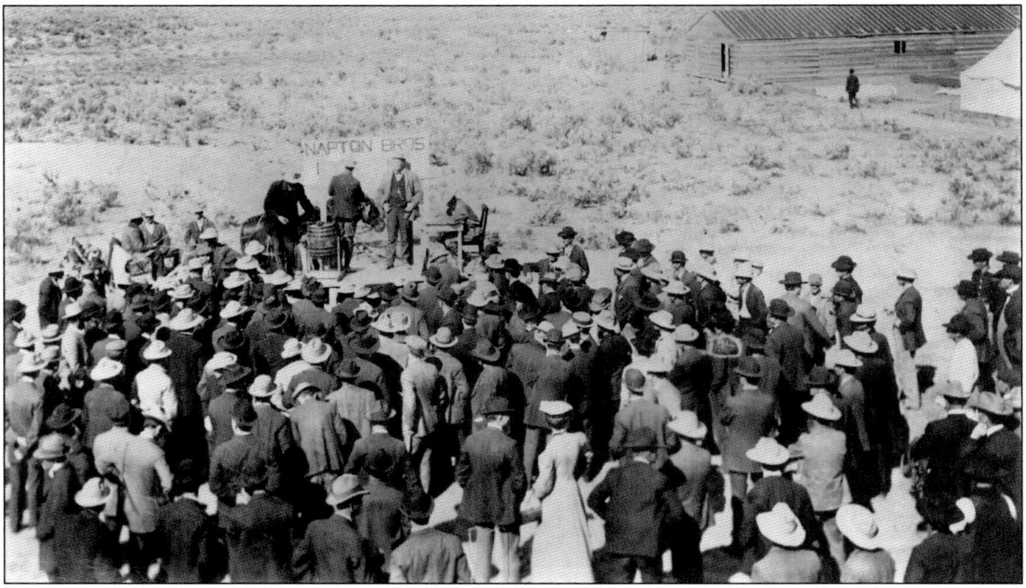

On September 30, 1907, over 1,000 people from almost every US state were present to bid on townsite lots. Each bidder received a number. The numbers were also written on wooden cubes, which were placed into a large milk churn. The first number pulled from the churn had first choice of land. Maj. Fred Reed and Robert McCullom were in charge. The next day, the country lots were sold, after which a total of 75,000 acres out of the available 150,000 acres had been sold for $2.04 million.

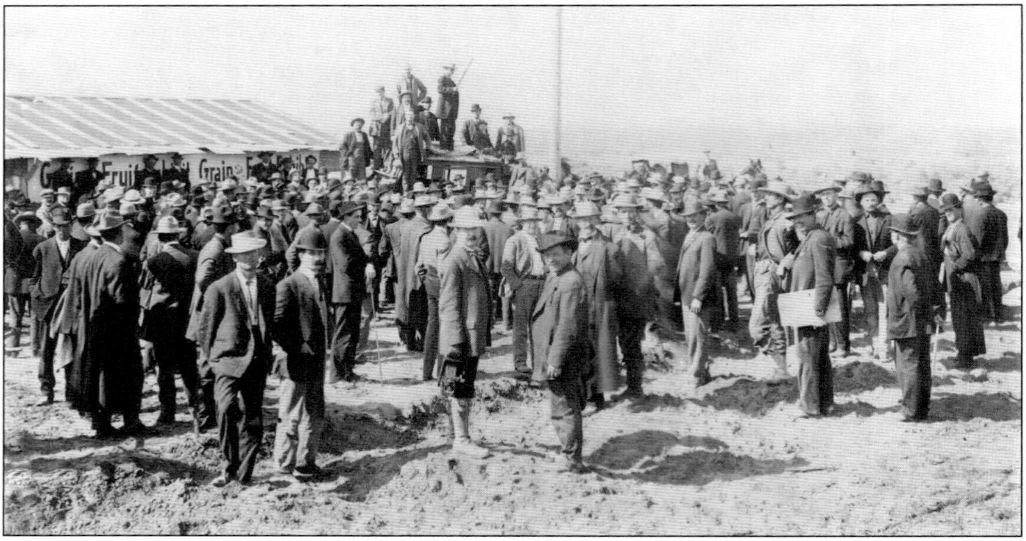

I.B. Perrine used this stagecoach as a platform to announce the land drawing on September 30, 1907.

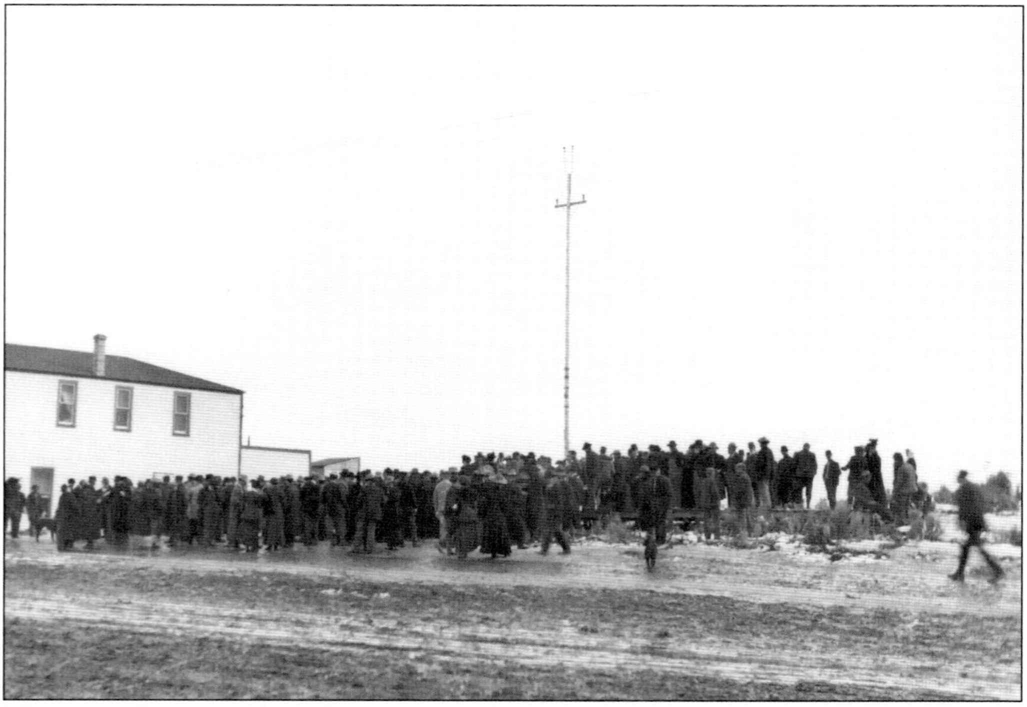

This is another view of people waiting for their names to be drawn in the land drawing on September 30, 1907.

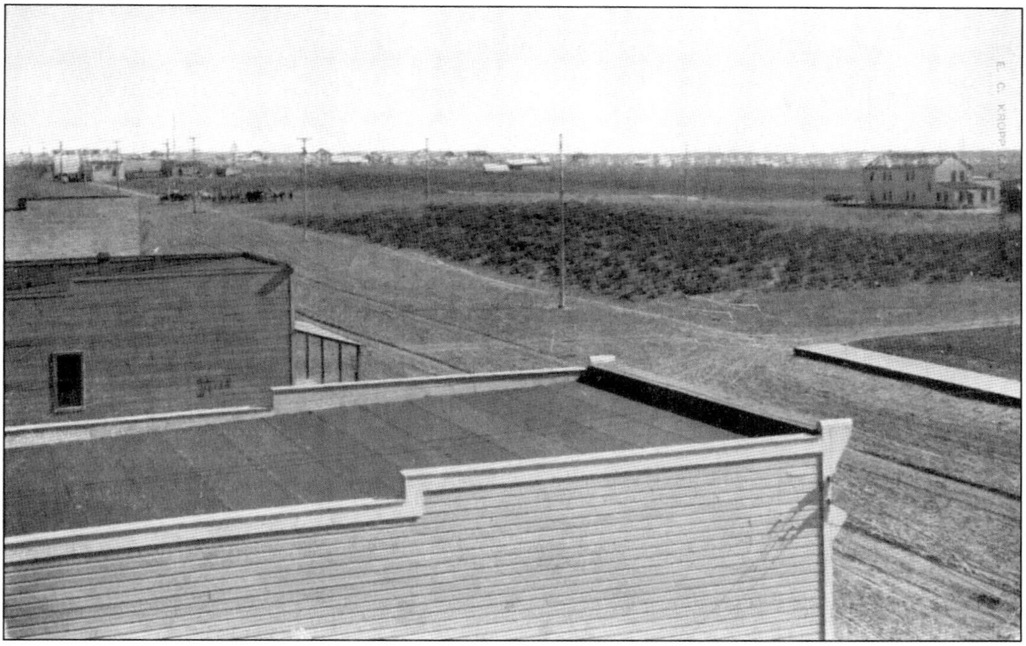

This rooftop photograph from October 1, 1908, shows Jerome buildings and homes. Note the cement sidewalk already in place.

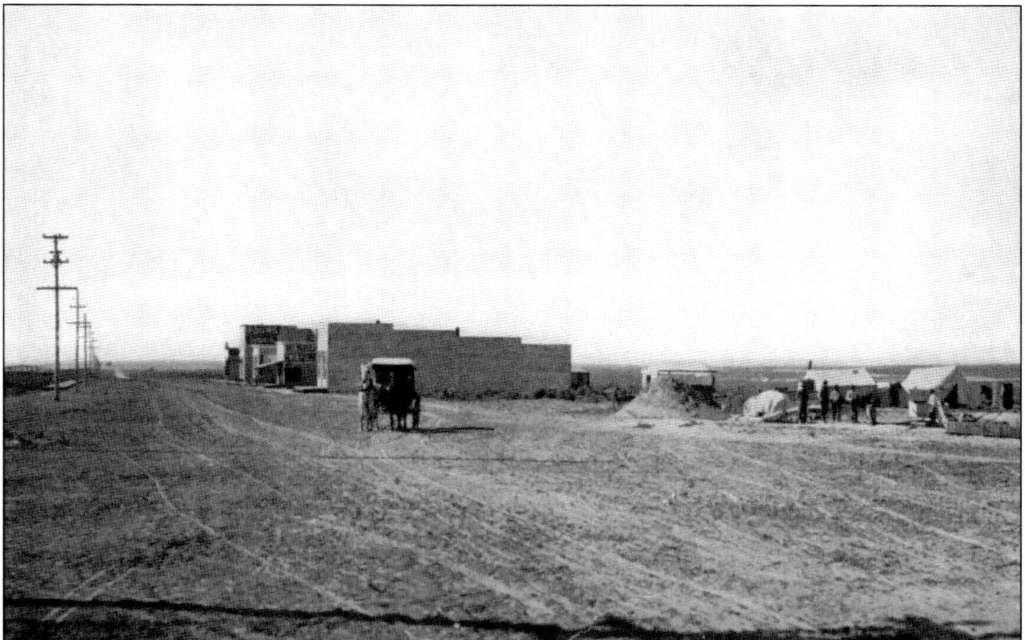

This image of Main Street, captured 15 months after the beginning of the town, shows the Lodging House with nearby drugstore, company house, and bank.

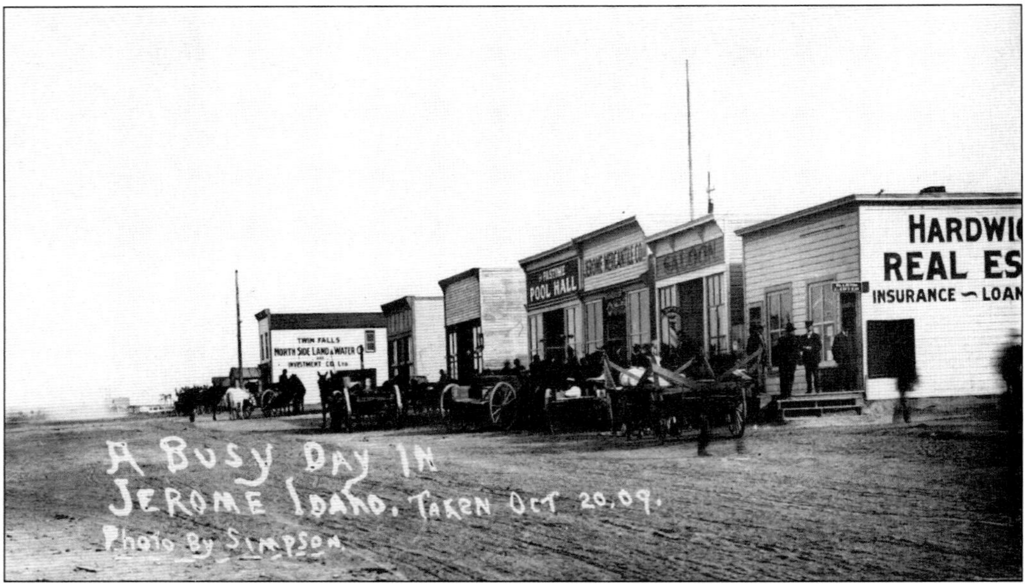

On October 20, 1909, a busy day in Jerome just two years after its founding, several businesses were in place. This image shows the south side of Main Street, looking east. The Twin Falls North Side Land and Water Company building was one of the first structures erected in the new town in the middle of the sagebrush desert. The town of Twin Falls, founded in 1904, was named for two waterfalls in the nearby Snake River Canyon. The city lots and outlying farmlands were purchased from this business. While men purchased land, bought insurance, obtained a loan, or enjoyed visits to the Pastime Pool Hall and the Saloon, with baths and barbershop, the women shopped at the Jerome Mercantile. Besides these buildings, several more had been erected on the north side of Main Street, east and west of this position, and on the crossroad Lincoln Avenue, which ran north and south.

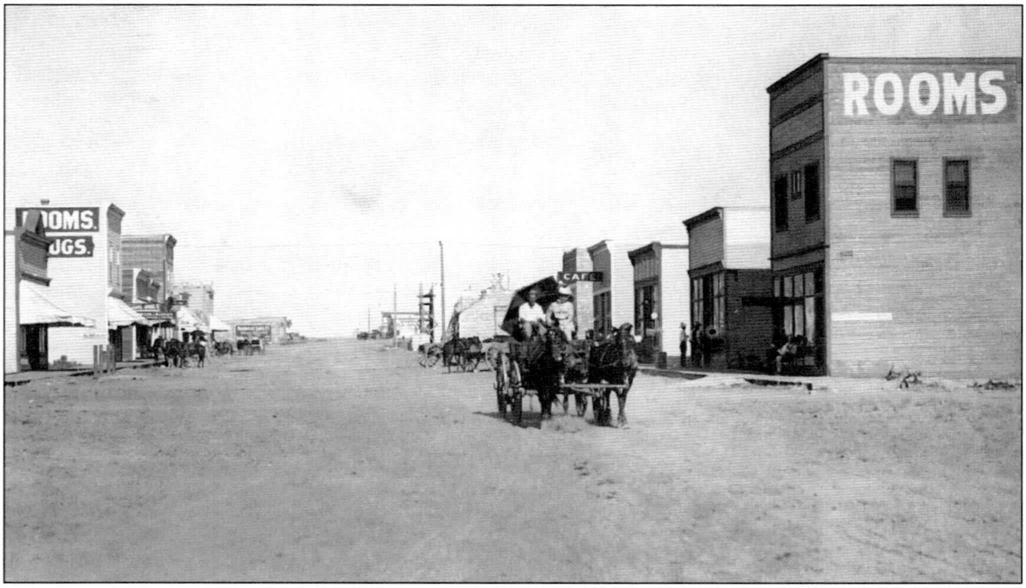

On Main Street, pictured in this 1909 image looking east, some of the buildings included, from left to right, a rooming house, a drugstore, an investment company, Haddock Real Estate, Hardwick Real Estate, a café, and another rooming house.

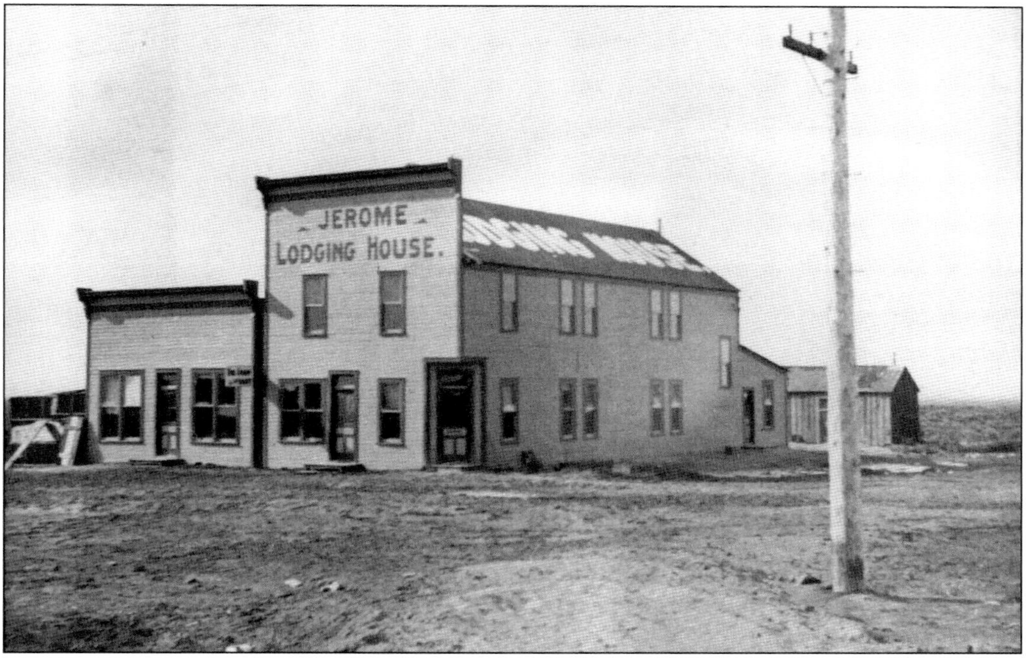

Jerome Lodging House and the adjoining restaurant are on the southwest corner of South Lincoln Avenue and West Avenue A. The upper story, which housed several apartments, burned in a fire in the 1970s and was removed; the main floor now houses Jerome Eye Center Optometrists.

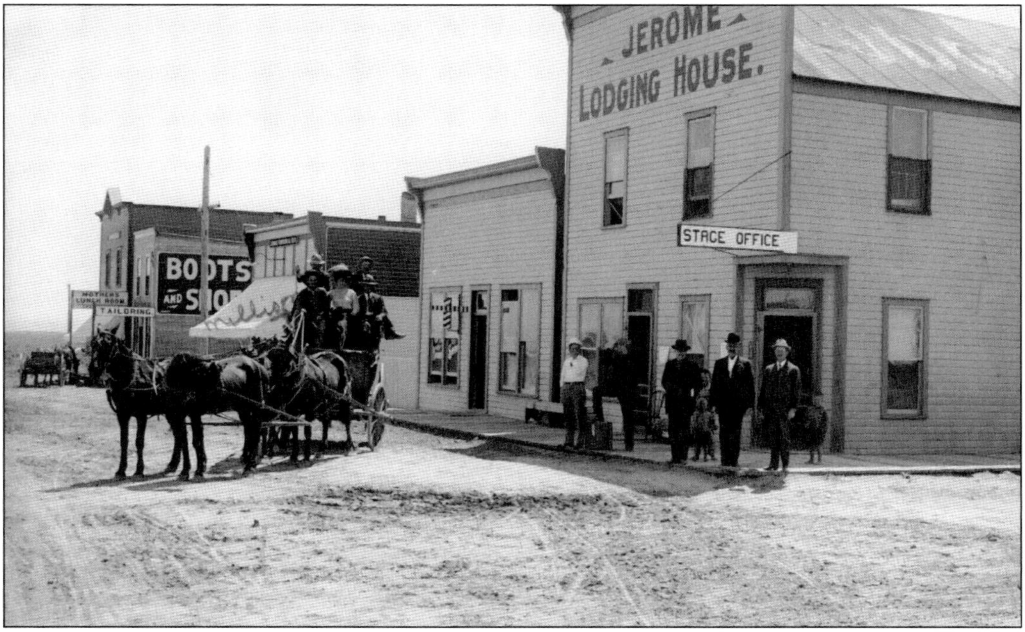

In May 1909, more stores were added to the west side of South Lincoln Avenue between West Avenue B and West Avenue A. Ira B. Perrine's Jerome stagecoach arrived at the stage office from his home at Blue Lakes Ranch in the Snake River Canyon, eight miles south of Jerome. From left to right, the buildings pictured housed Mother's Lunchroom, a store to buy boots and shoes and tailoring, Jerome Commercial Club, a millinery shop, a barbershop, and the stage office. The second floor of the stage building is the Jerome Lodging House.

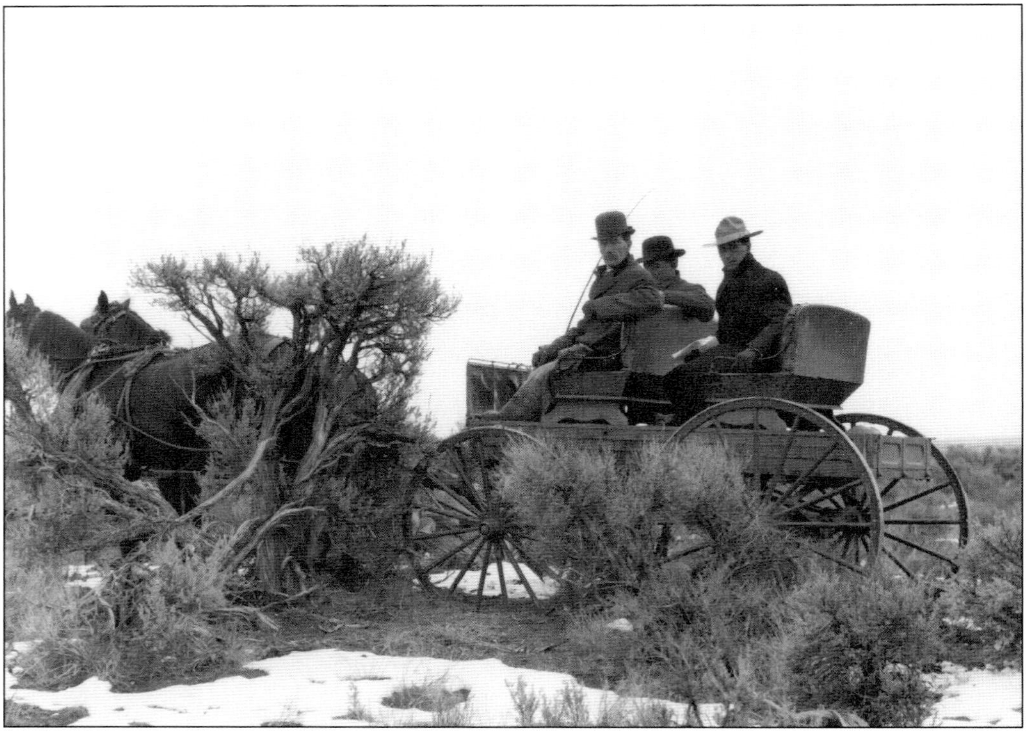

One way to measure a large amount of land in 1909 was to count the number of revolutions of one specific spoke of a wagon wheel after it has traversed it. Note the height of the sagebrush.

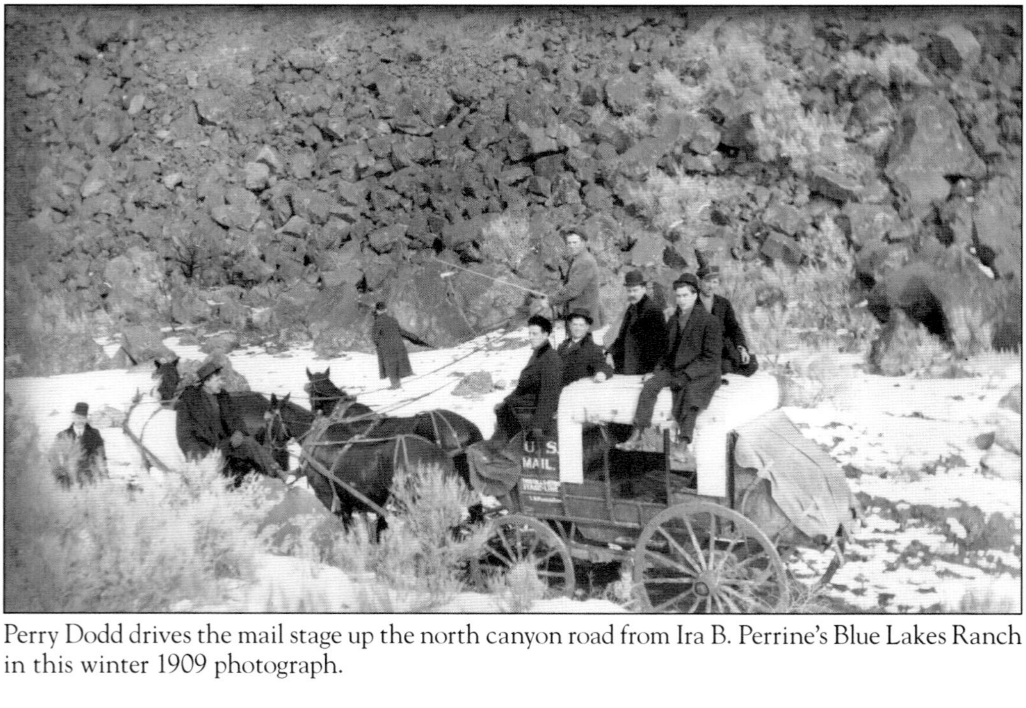

Perry Dodd drives the mail stage up the north canyon road from Ira B. Perrine's Blue Lakes Ranch in this winter 1909 photograph.

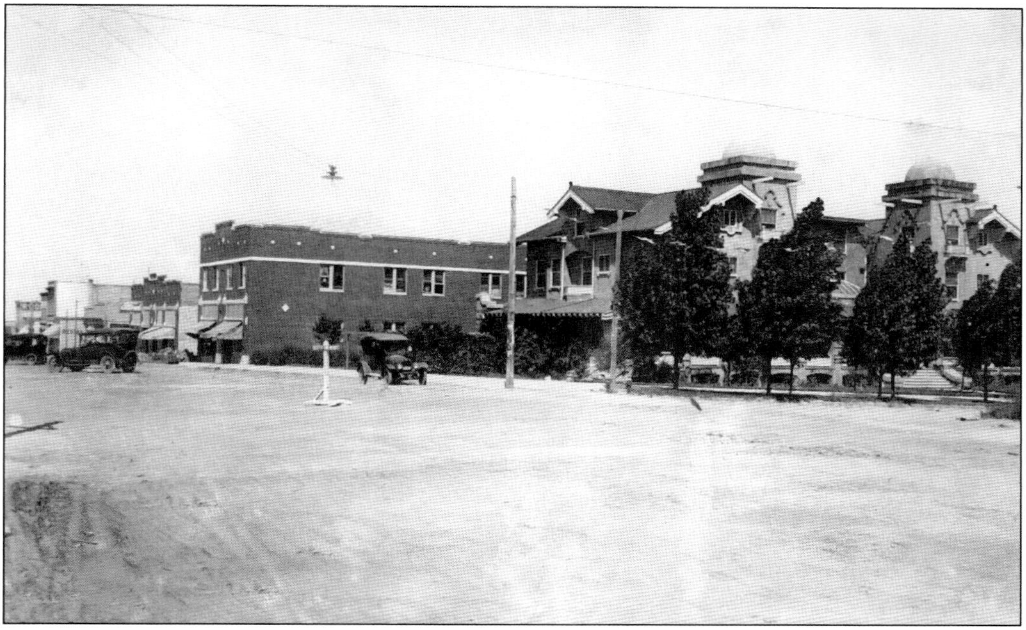

This early 1920s image of Northwest Main Street at the corner of Lincoln Avenue shows, from left to right, a rooming house, a restaurant, the Ford dealership, Dave L'Herisson's furniture store (he had moved into the new brick building across the street from his old building), and the North Side Inn. The sign in the middle of the crossroad states, "Keep to the Right" and identifies Lincoln Avenue and Main Street by the writing on the post.

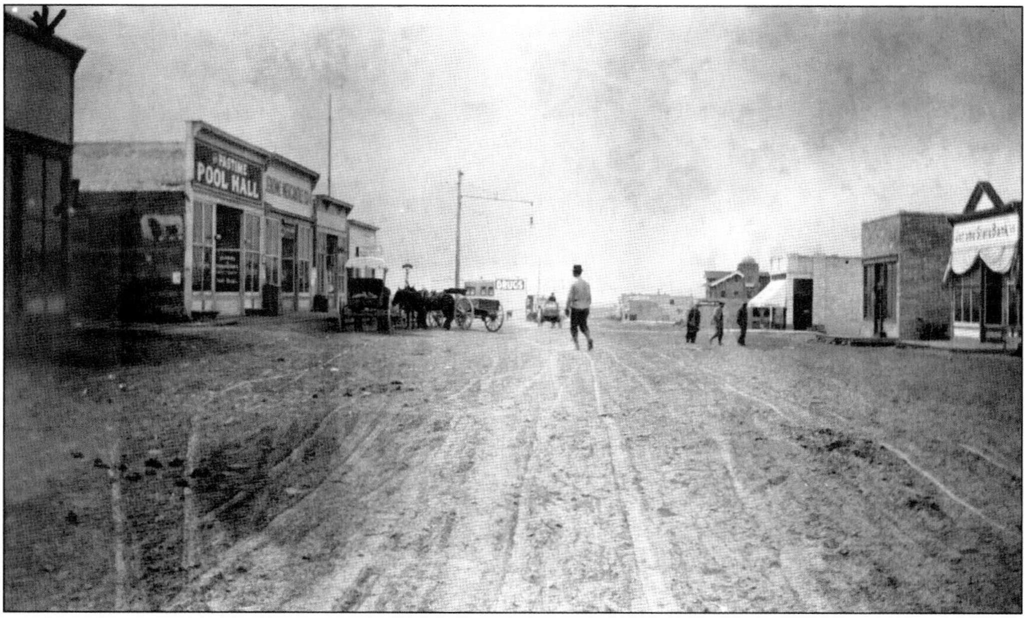

In this photograph of Main Street facing west, the first building on the left is Dave L'Herisson's furniture store and mortuary, followed by the Pastime Pool Hall and tobacco store. On the right side in the background, the North Side Inn with one of its roof domes is visible.

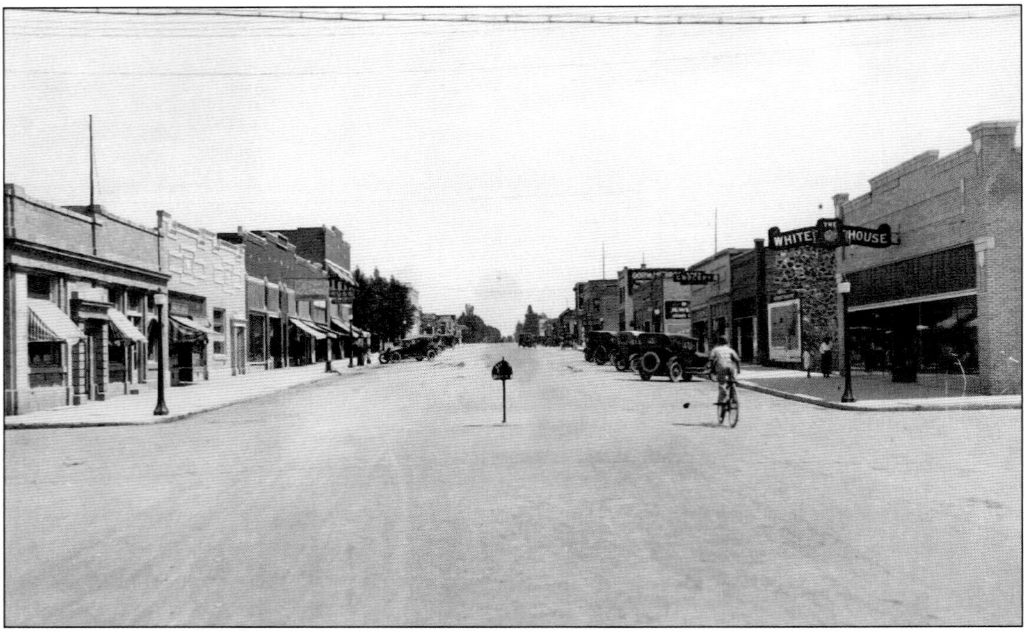

This photograph shows both sides of Main Street looking east from Maple (Alder) Street (one block west of Lincoln Avenue) to the North and South Parks at Elm (Buchannan) Street in the 1920s. The sign in the middle of the street at West Main and Maple (Alder) Streets states, "Keep to the Right, Drivers."

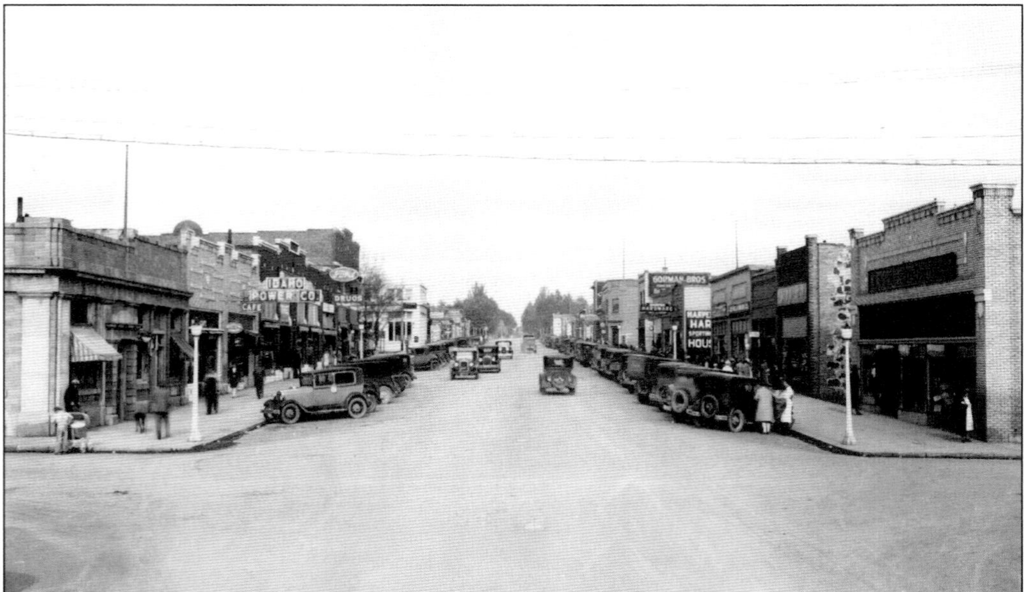

This photograph was taken a few years after the one above. The buildings are the same, but some of the businesses within them have changed.

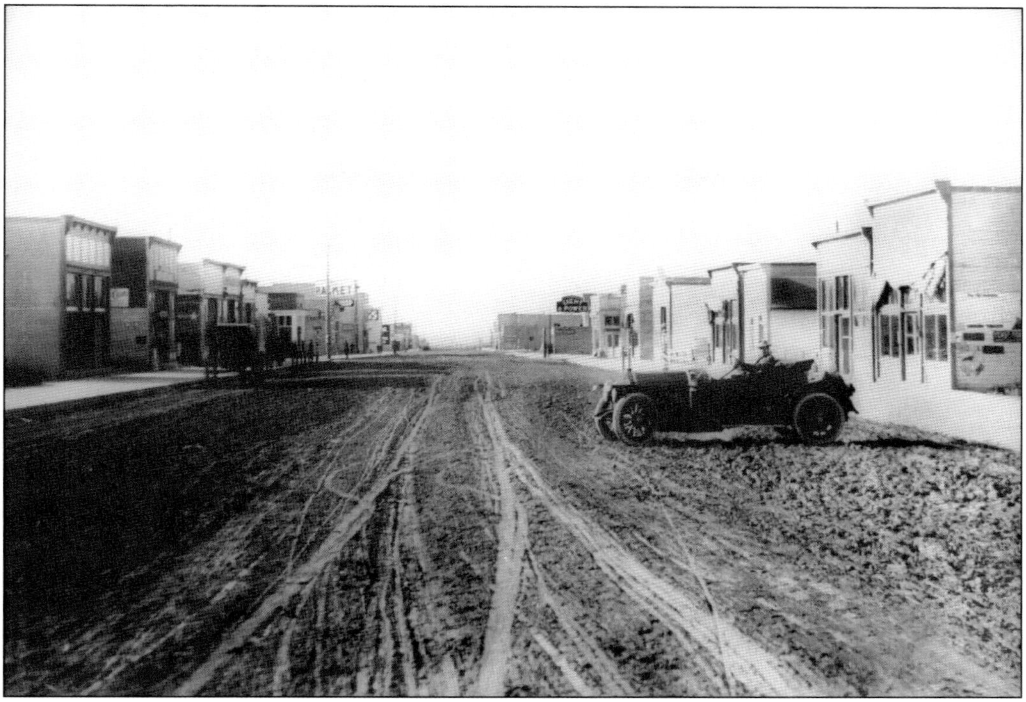

The first car in Jerome was a red 1910 Overland that belonged to Paul Kartzke.

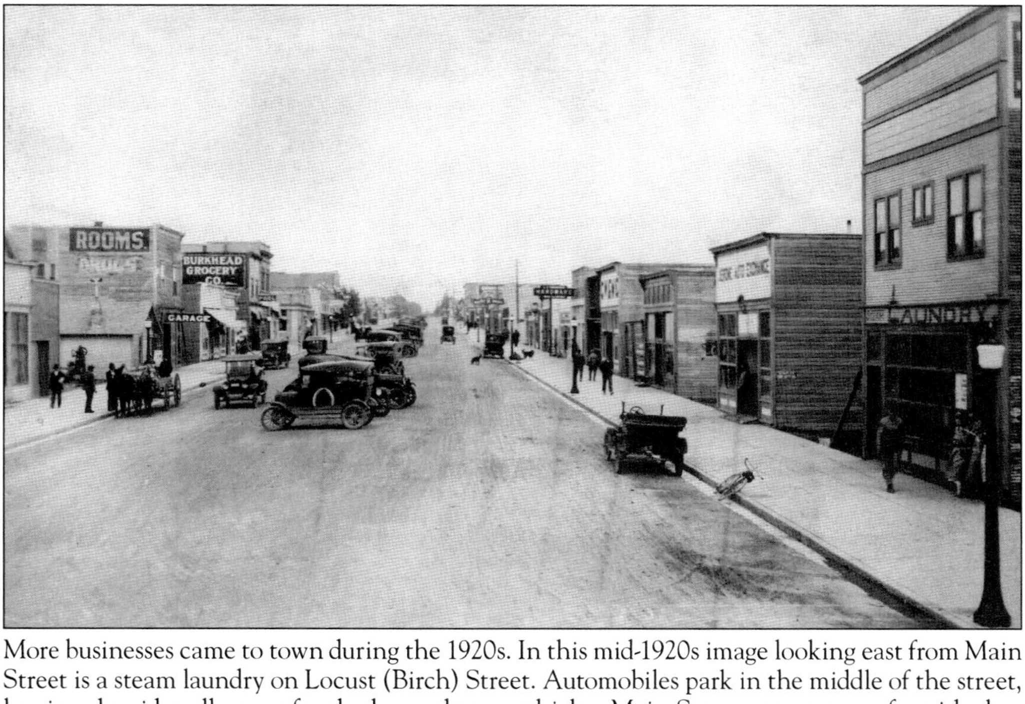

More businesses came to town during the 1920s. In this mid-1920s image looking east from Main Street is a steam laundry on Locust (Birch) Street. Automobiles park in the middle of the street, leaving the sidewalk areas for the horse-drawn vehicles. Main Street was pretty safe, with slow traffic. Note the bicycle leaning on the sidewalk and the two dogs in the middle of the picture.

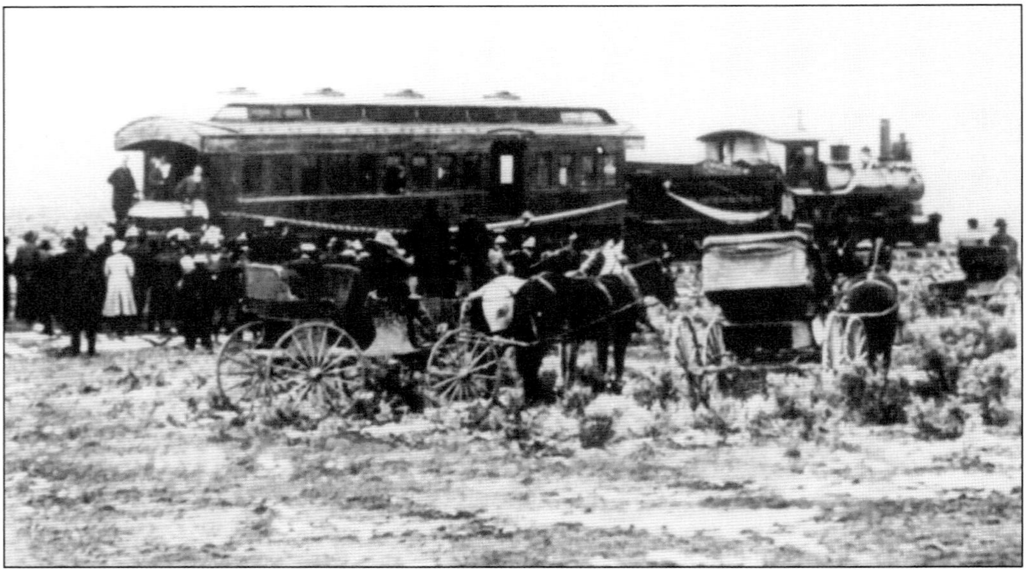

The first train came to Jerome on January 1, 1909. The Idaho Southern Railway was in operation 26 miles from Gooding, Idaho, to Jerome until July 31, 1916. The rail line was originally meant to be an electric trolley line between Milner, Idaho, and Boise, Idaho.

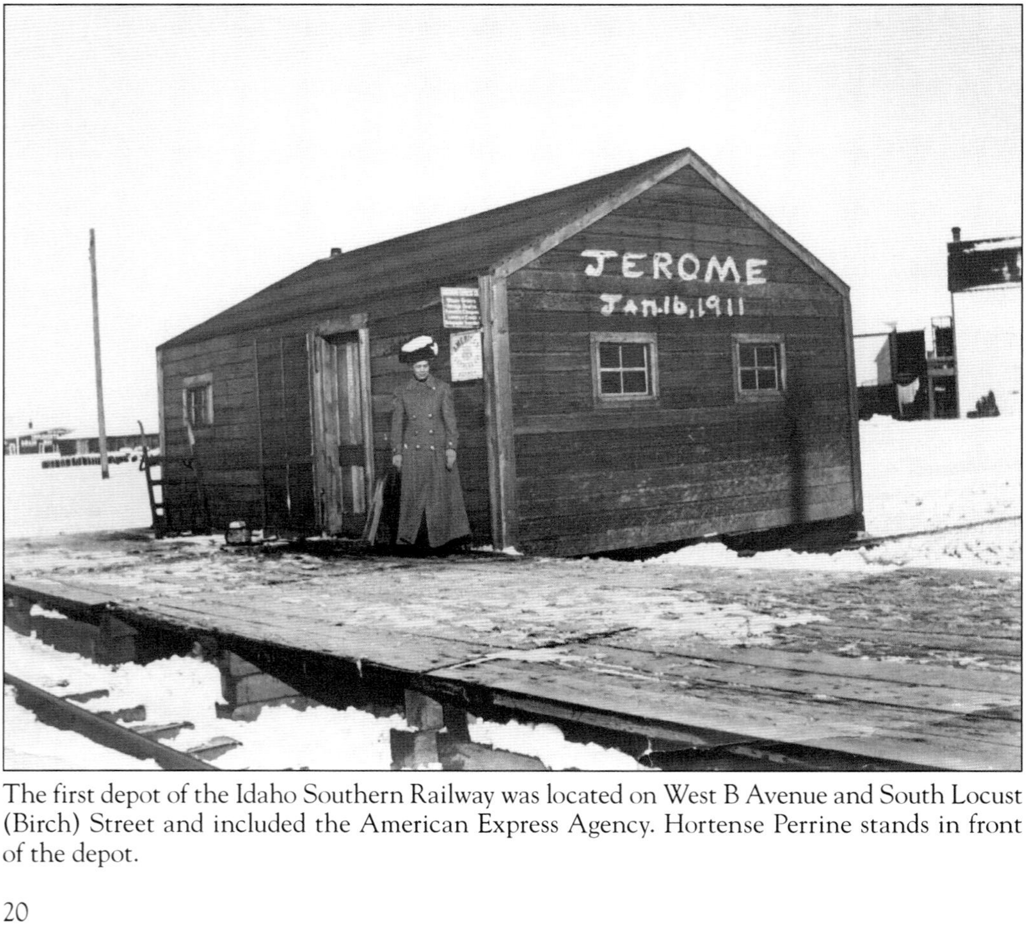

The first depot of the Idaho Southern Railway was located on West B Avenue and South Locust (Birch) Street and included the American Express Agency. Hortense Perrine stands in front of the depot.

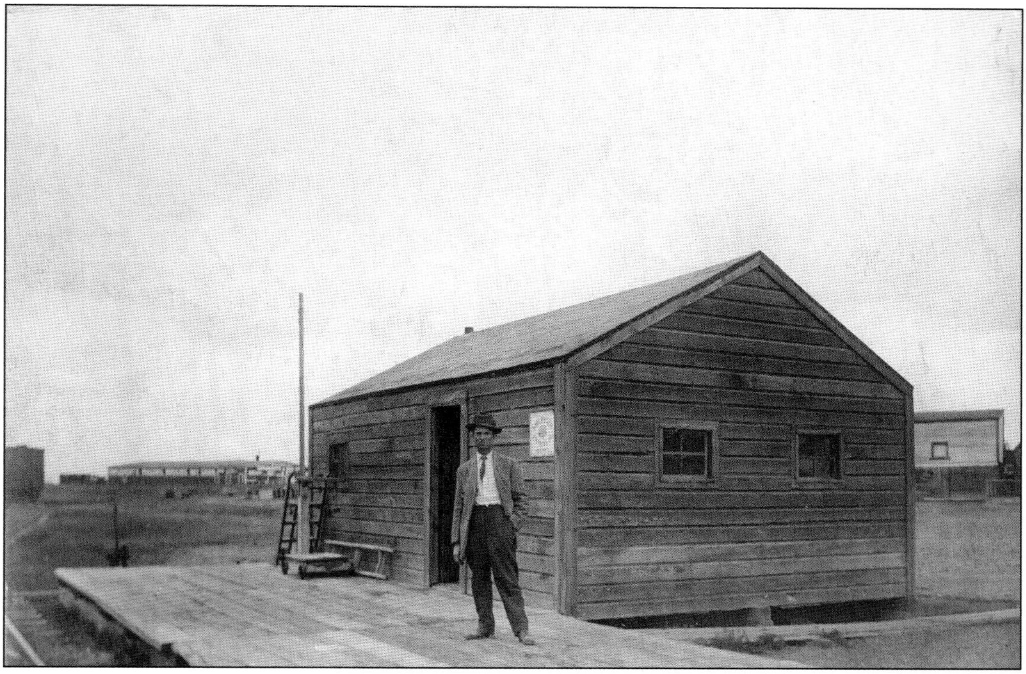

Joe Lawrence, an agent for the Idaho Southern Railway, stands in front of the depot on January 1, 1909.

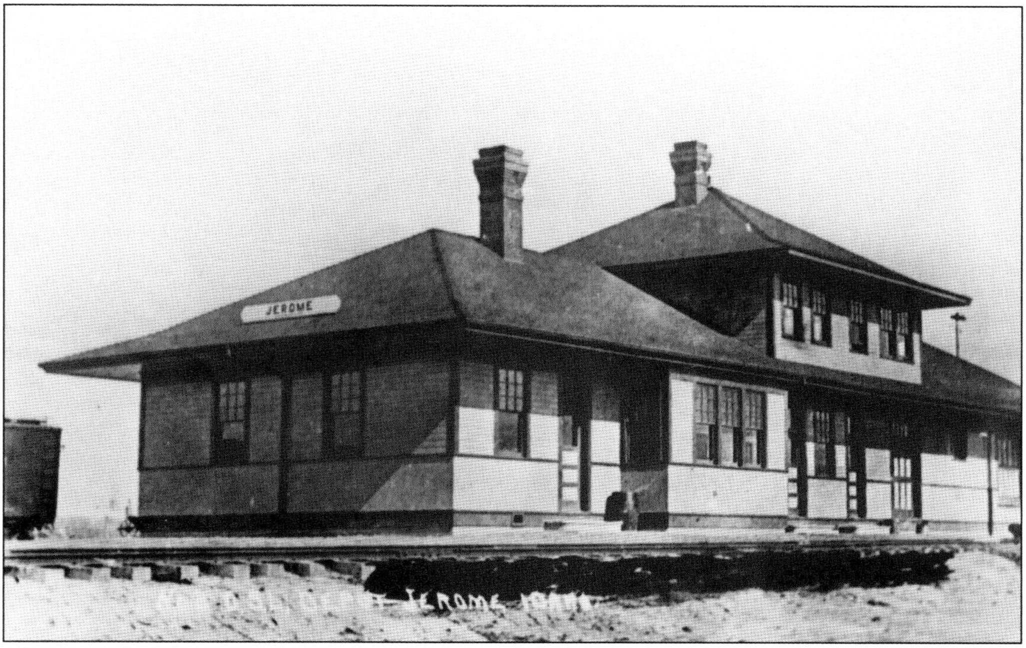

The second Idaho Southern Railway depot, built in 1912, was located almost one mile west of town. In 1911, the Oregon Short Line Railroad (OSL) was in competition and edged out the Idaho Southern. Then the OSL took over the rail line and the depot. In 1982, this building was moved to downtown First Avenue East to be used as a senior center. In 2009, a new structure was erected on North Lincoln Avenue for the Jerome Senior Center, and the Jerome County Historical Society Museum moved into the depot.

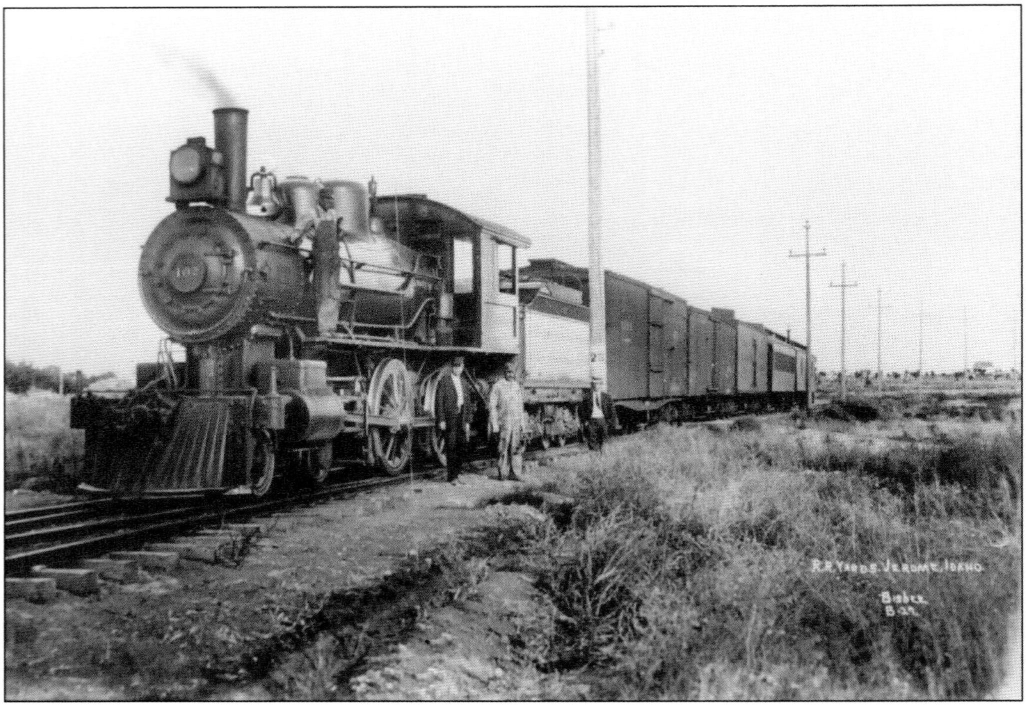

This Idaho Southern Railway train, engine no. 102, stopped at the depot west of town. The conductor and engineer are not identified.

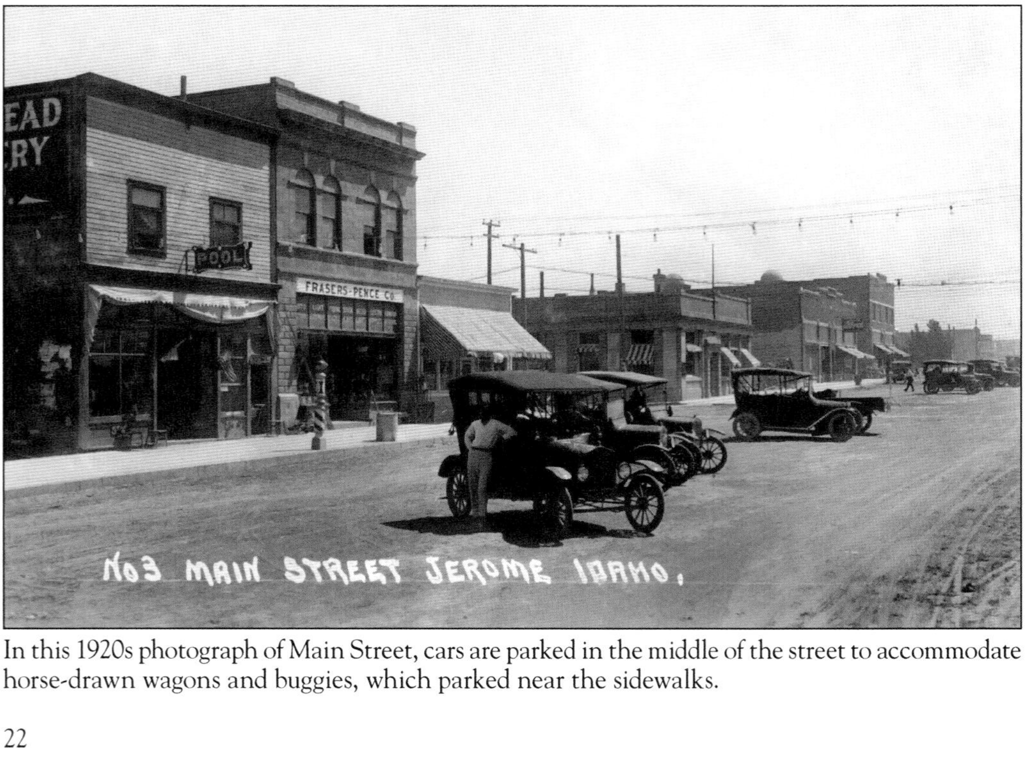

In this 1920s photograph of Main Street, cars are parked in the middle of the street to accommodate horse-drawn wagons and buggies, which parked near the sidewalks.

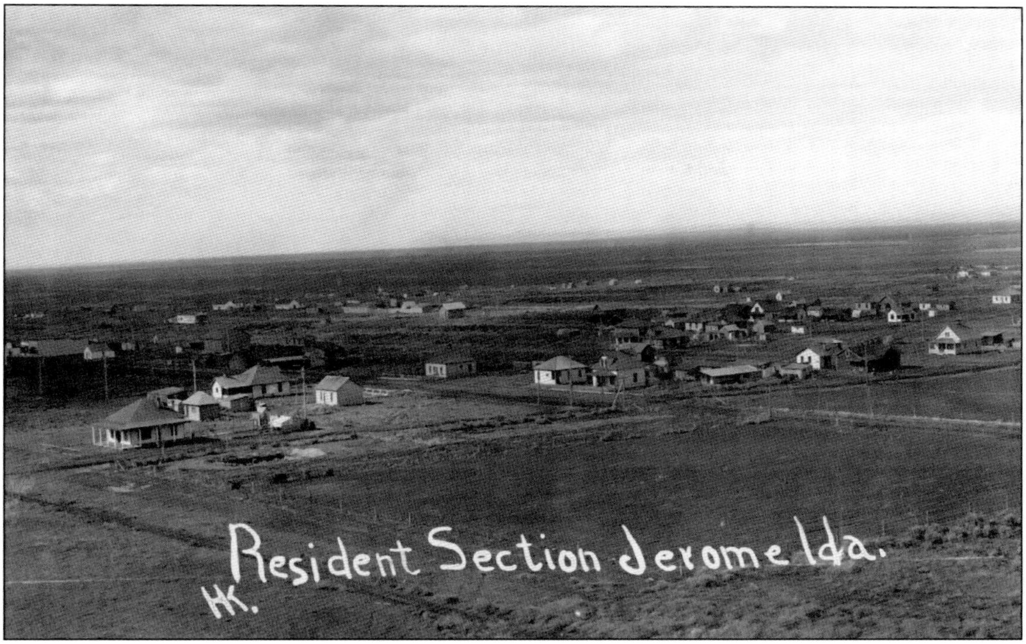

As the businesses grew predominately on Main Street and Lincoln Avenue, residents built their homes. Even though there is no date on this photograph, it was probably taken between 1910 and 1920. Some land is still in sagebrush.

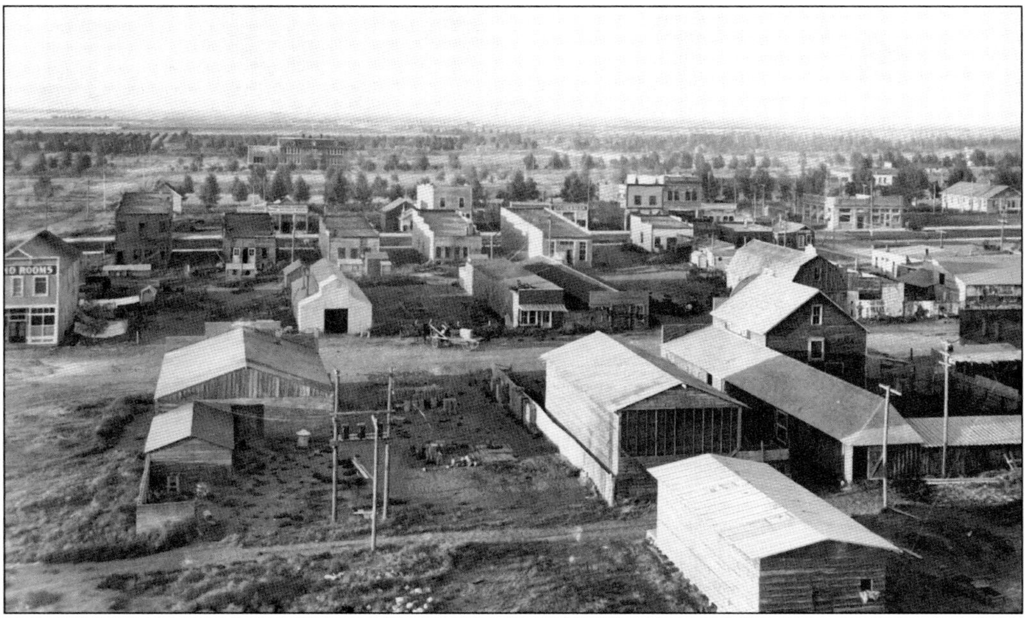

The warehouse district southwest of the center of town developed around the railroad track. In the distant background is the Lincoln School.

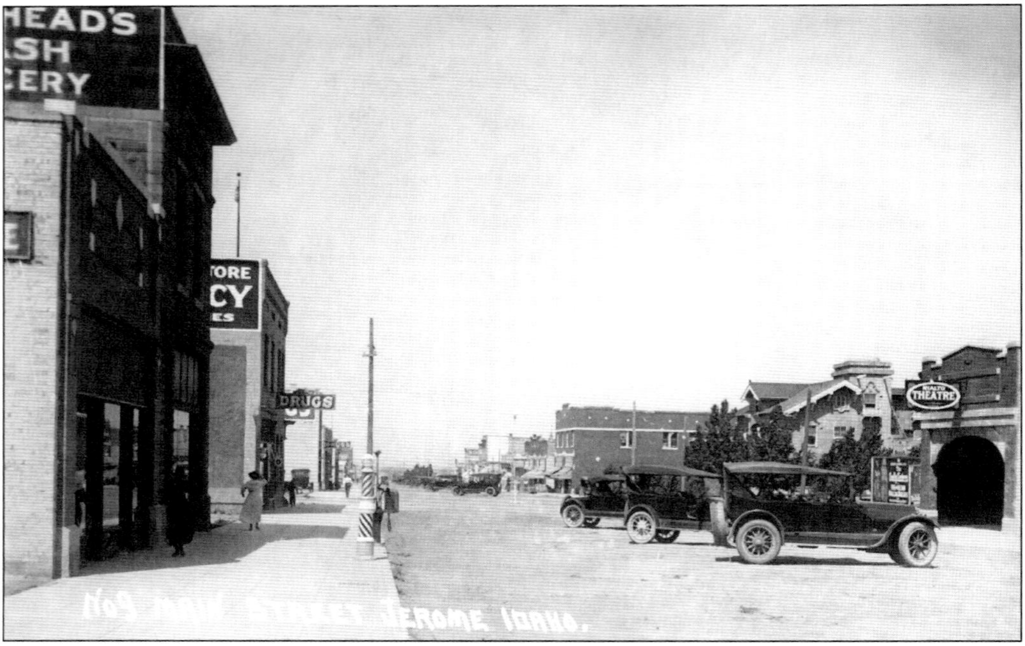

At the barbershop on East Main Street, a person could also get a bath, as stated on the top of the barber pole. All of these buildings, with the exception of two on the right, the North Side Inn and the Rialto Theatre, which have been demolished, still stand; however, they are now home to different businesses.

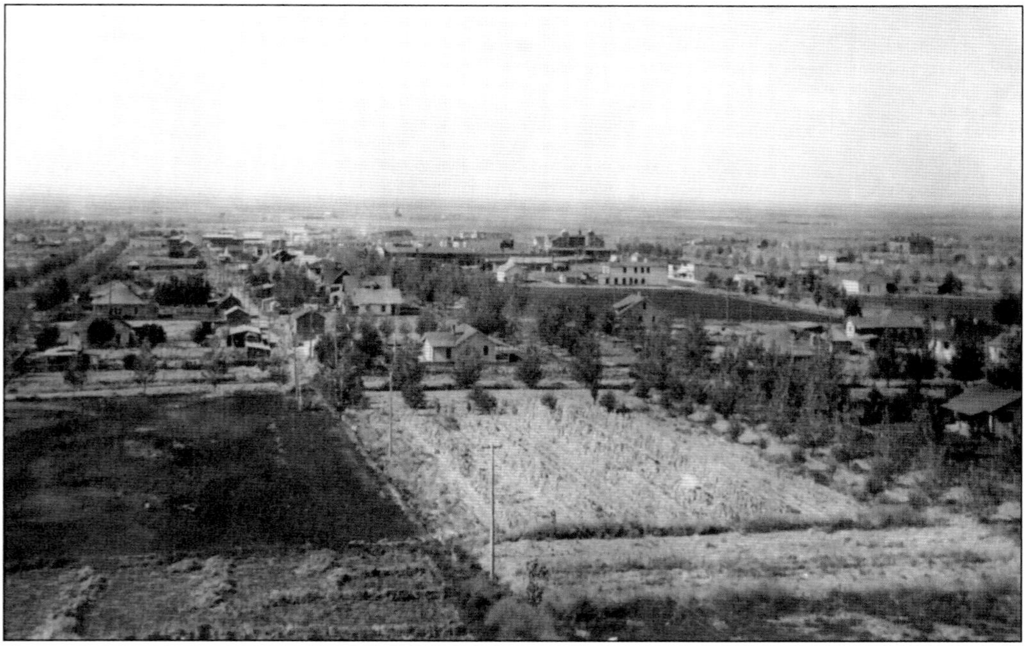

This bird's-eye view from the water tower looking west in 1918 shows the North Side Inn in the middle background and Lincoln School at far right. The open land in the middle of the far right is South Park and North Park, with Main Street running between them.

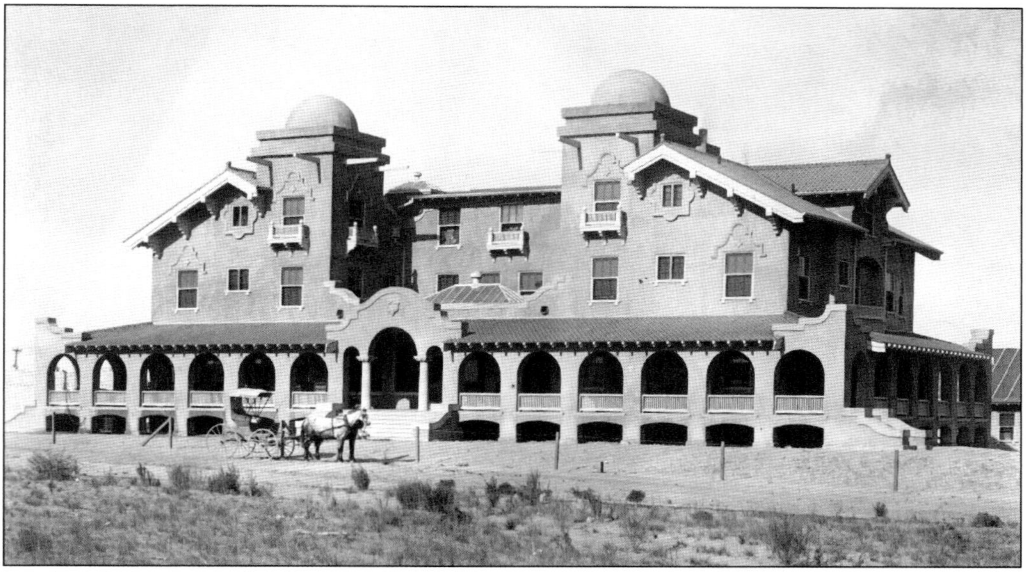

North Side Inn, initially christened the Idaho Hotel, began construction in October 1908 and enjoyed a grand opening on July 1, 1909. It included a basement and three stories for a cost of $40,000 and was built with lumber from Portland, Oregon. Travelers, teachers, businessmen, and others resided here. There was a large dining room in the south area. In 1935, the south veranda was removed, and a divided brick building for the Wood Café and the National Laundry was added. The Greyhound and Trailways bus depot was housed in the lobby, and a barbershop was located in the basement. Sadly, the North Side Inn was demolished in June 1967.

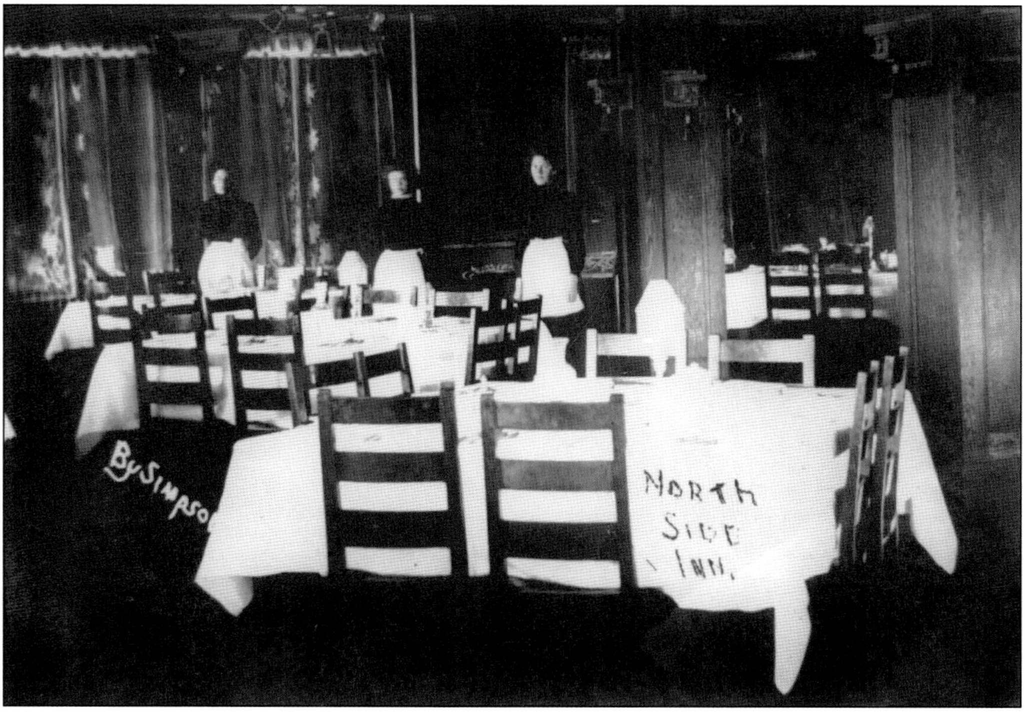

The waitresses wait to take dinner orders at the dining room in the North Side Inn in the early 1920s.

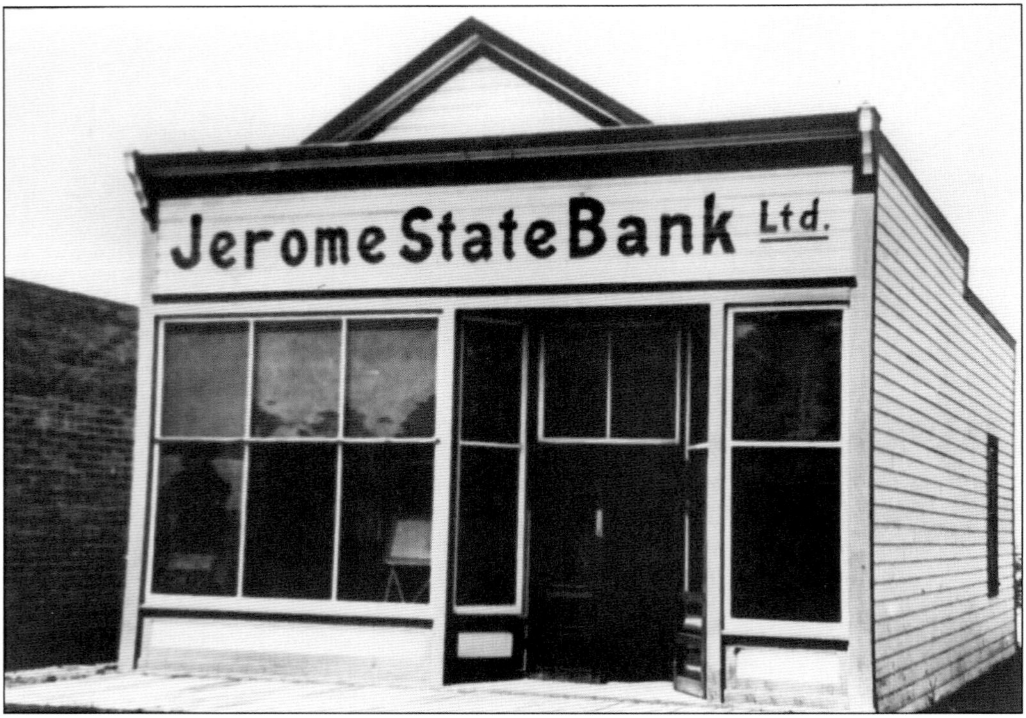

The first bank in Jerome was on the north side of East Main Street. Even though the 4,500-pound safe and 2,800-pound vault door were in place, the building was not ready for occupancy on the days of the land drawings on September 30 and October 1 in 1907, so the bank operated in a tent.

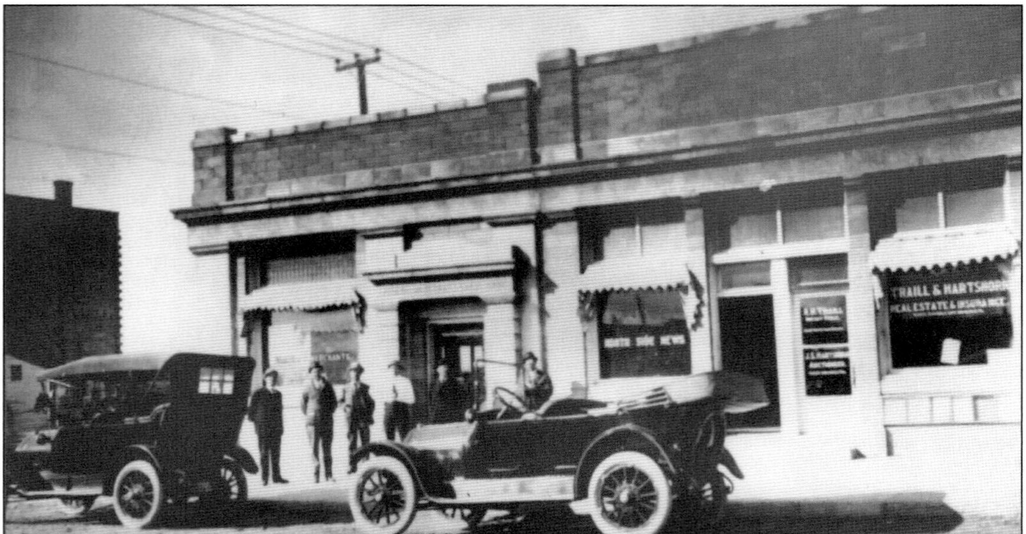

The second bank, Farmers and Merchants Bank, opened January 2, 1909, on the northwest corner of Main Street and Maple (Alder) Avenue. The fixtures came from the Commercial Bank in Hailey. Bank officers reported $15,000 in deposits on the first day of business. On that day, it was the largest bank in Lincoln County. (Jerome was part of Lincoln County until 1919.) To the right of the bank was the second home of the *North Side News* newspaper. The next building housed Traill & Hartshorn Real Estate & Insurance and the office of auctioneer J.S. Messersmith.

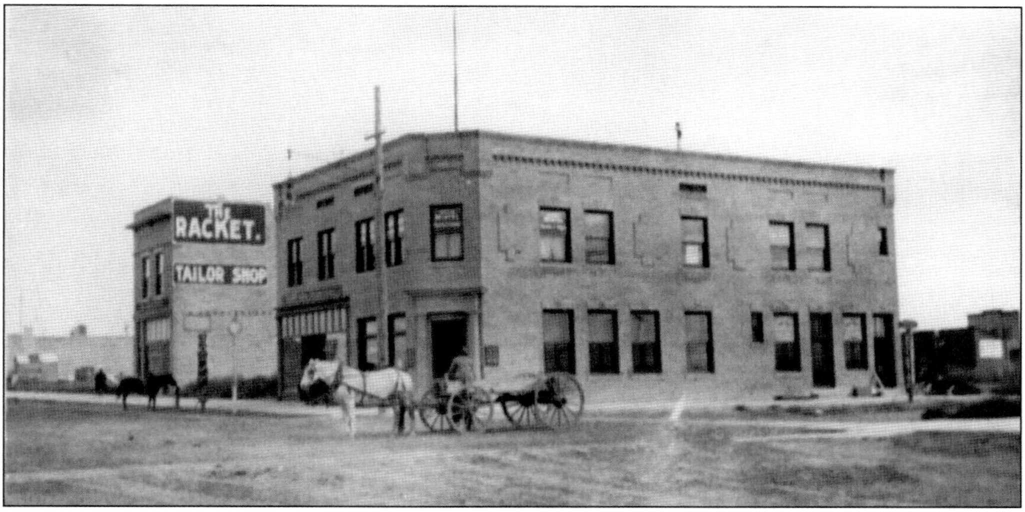

A third bank, First National Bank, occupied the W.A. Heiss building on the southeast corner of Main Street and Lincoln Avenue. In February 1909, it merged with Jerome State Bank. This building has continuously housed Prescott & Craig Insurance since 1908, and the bank vault is still in place. Many smaller businesses occupied space in this large building, including a hospital on the second floor during the 1918 flu epidemic.

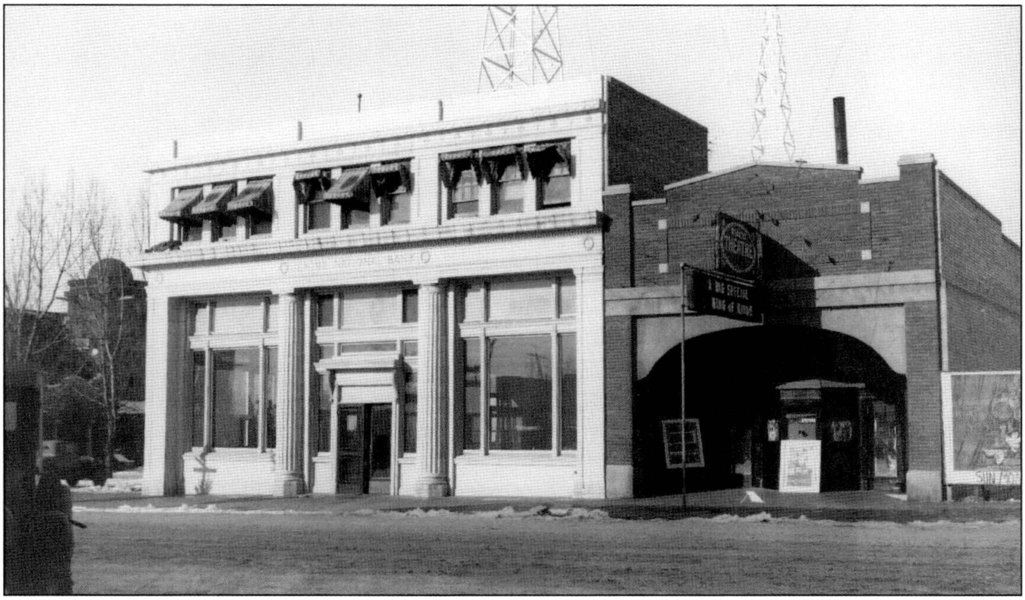

The Jerome National Bank building was constructed in 1920. The Farmers and Merchants Bank surrendered its charter as a state bank to become the Jerome National Bank. The banking area had 18-foot-high ceilings, which were lowered five feet after a fire in the basement and on the first floor. Apartments and business offices occupied the upper floor, and the KFXD radio station tower can be seen on the roof. The first radio station in the area was established in 1926 in the Rialto Theatre, but in 1930, KFXD moved to Nampa, Idaho. In 1933, First Security Bank opened in the Heiss building across the street. It purchased the Jerome National Bank building in 1942 and moved directly across the street. In 1975, the ceiling was moved back to 18 feet high. With the mergers, it was the only bank in Jerome until 1967. Rialto Theatre was in use from the 1920s to the 1940s.

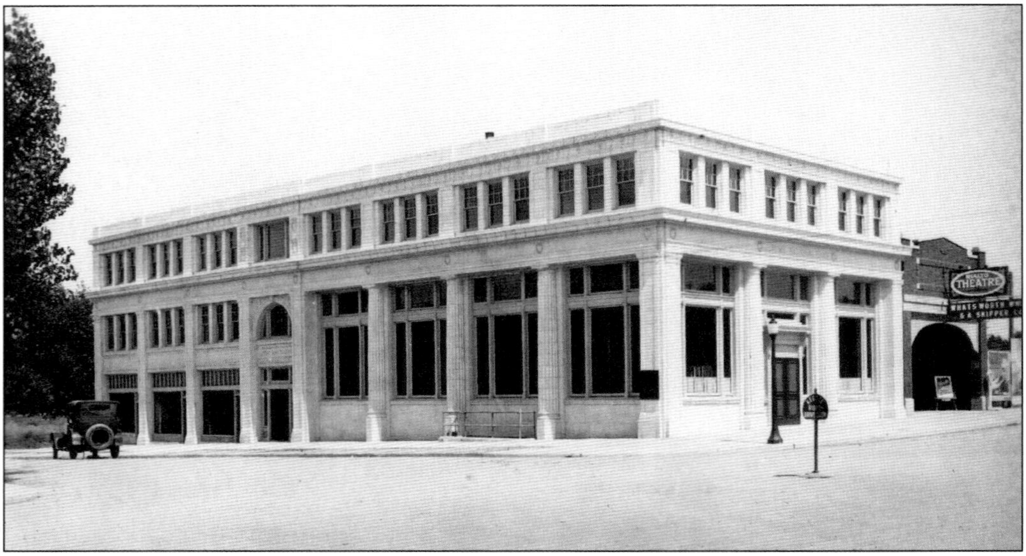

Pictured are the west side entrances in the First Security Bank building. The door with the arch above is for the Bank Club, an upscale lounge. The metal railing–covered steps lead down to Leyson Photography. From 1924 to 1939, the courtroom was in the back of the bank building on the main floor. The offices of the commissioner, auditor, and treasurer-auditor were on the second floor, and the offices of the sheriff and probate judge were on the third floor.

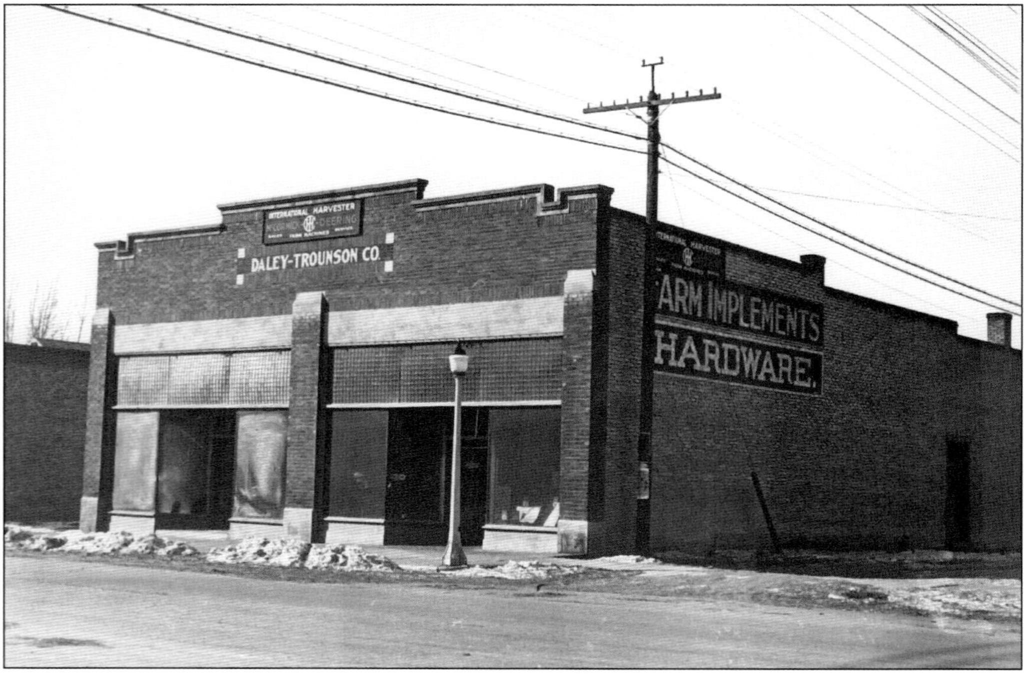

A fourth bank, the City National Bank, with $30,000 in capital, operated in the Daley-Trounson building in the south half of the first block of South Lincoln Avenue from November 1919 to February 1923. It moved from this building to an area in the Heiss building. On April 23, 1923, it failed to open for business and went into receivership. The Daley-Trounson Co. also sold farm implements. In the early 1950s, the building housed Earl Greenawalt's furniture store. At present it houses Buzz's Antique Mall.

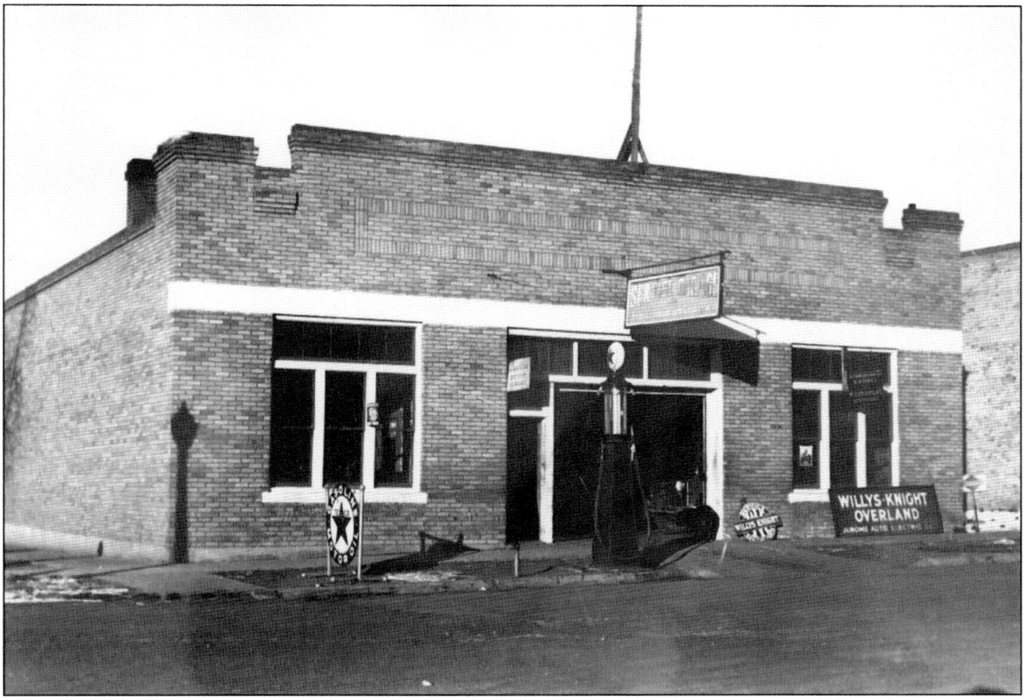

The Kelso-Newman Garage, located at 1916 South Lincoln Avenue by the corner of West Avenue A, was one of the early gasoline stations.

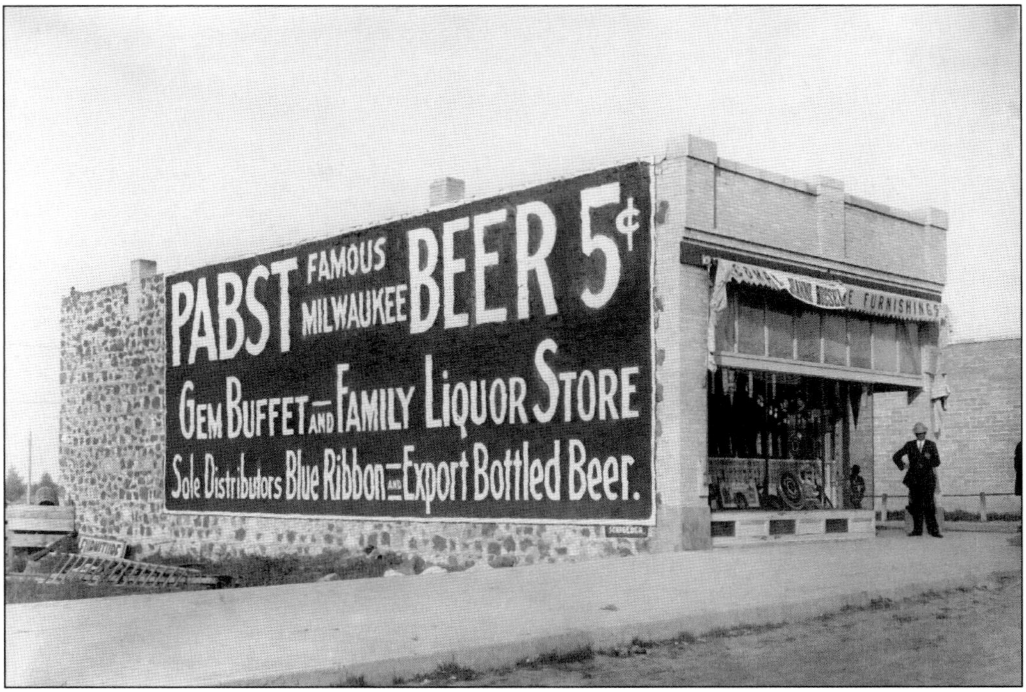

The Gem Buffet and Family Liquor Store sign was on the side of a home furnishings store on East Main Street.

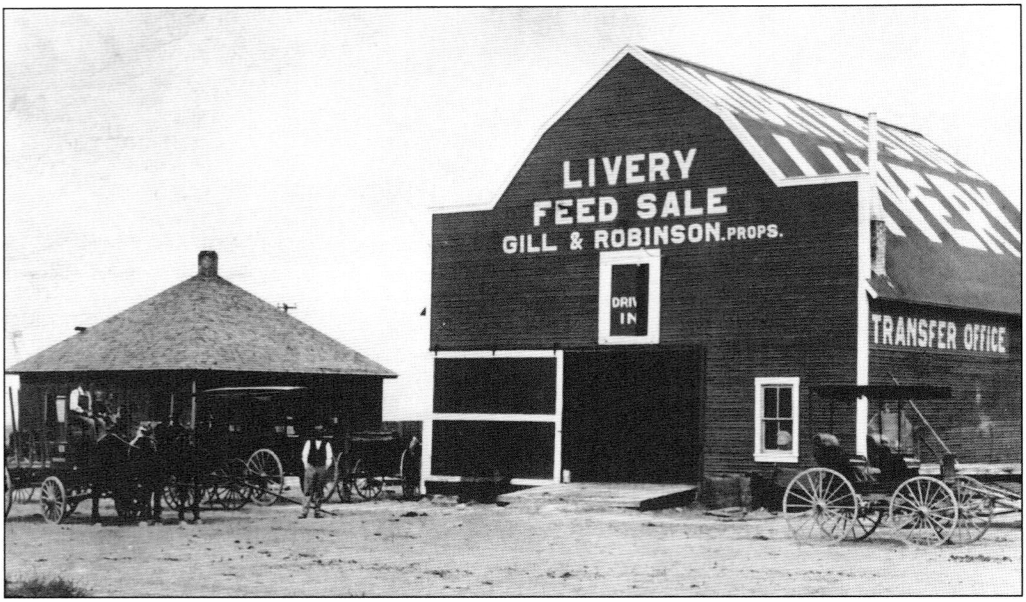

Ed Gill and Ed Robinson's Livery and Feed Sale, built in 1909, was located on the 200 block of West Avenue A. This picture was taken in 1912.

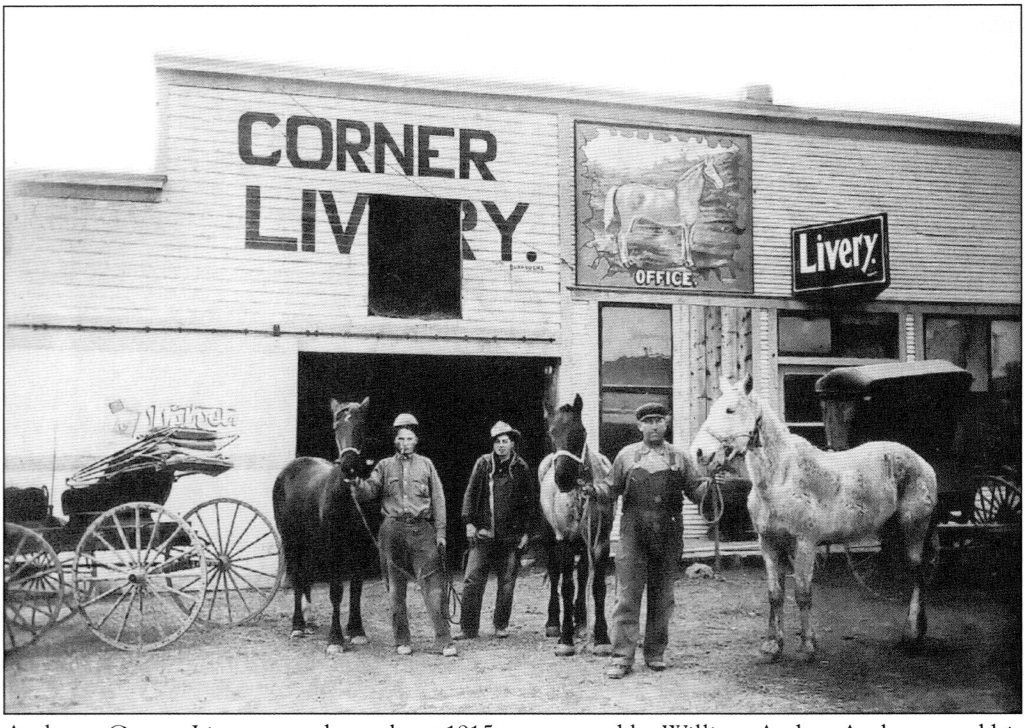

Ambrose Corner Livery, seen here about 1915, was owned by William Arthur Ambrose and his two sons and located one block west of South Lincoln Avenue on West Avenue A. Pictured from left to right in March 1914 are Rupert Ambrose, William Arthur Ambrose, and Henry Ambrose. The Ambrose brothers operated the portion of the Jerome–Twin Falls Stage Line that crossed the Snake River daily on the Shoshone Falls ferry. The company also advertised rigs for rental, as well as competent drivers, from its livery stable. (Courtesy Bobbi Ambrose.)

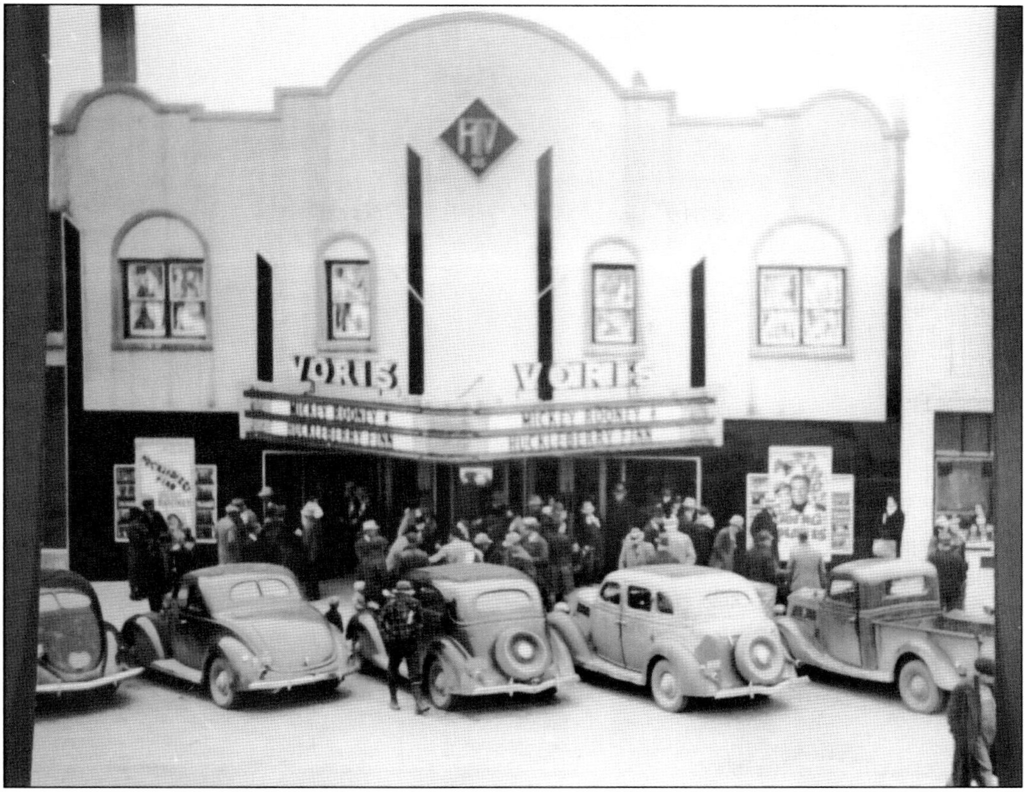

The Voris Theatre, situated in the middle of East Main Street, operated from 1935 to the mid-1960s. At one point, Mac McKinney ran the projectors. After that, the proprietor decided to run XXX-rated films, which brought national attention when CBS news reported it. Soon after, the theater closed, and the building was demolished.

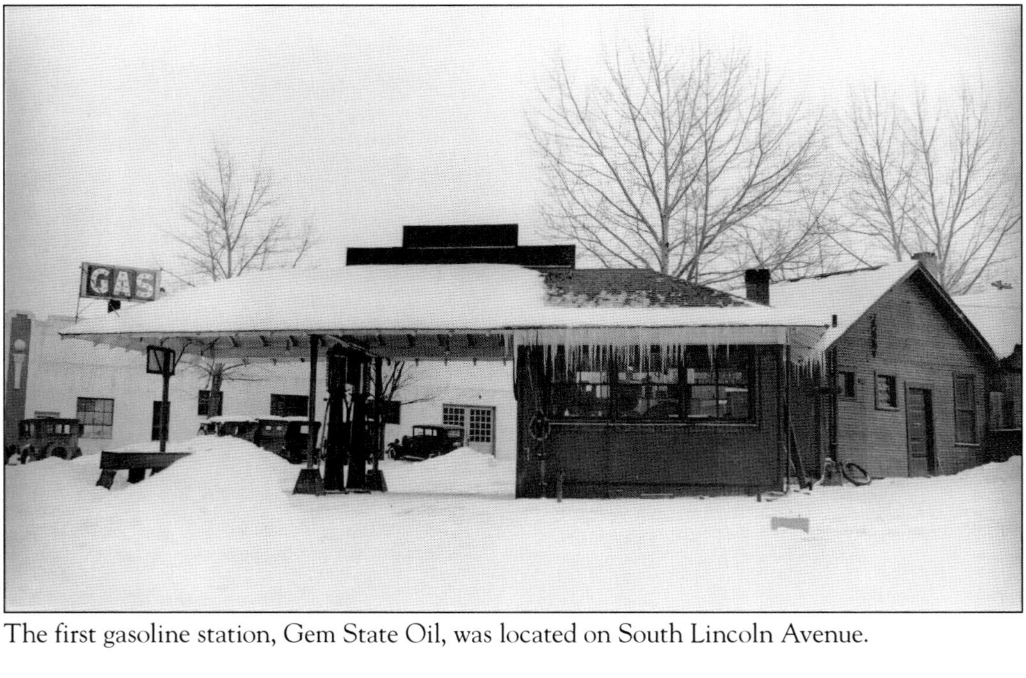

The first gasoline station, Gem State Oil, was located on South Lincoln Avenue.

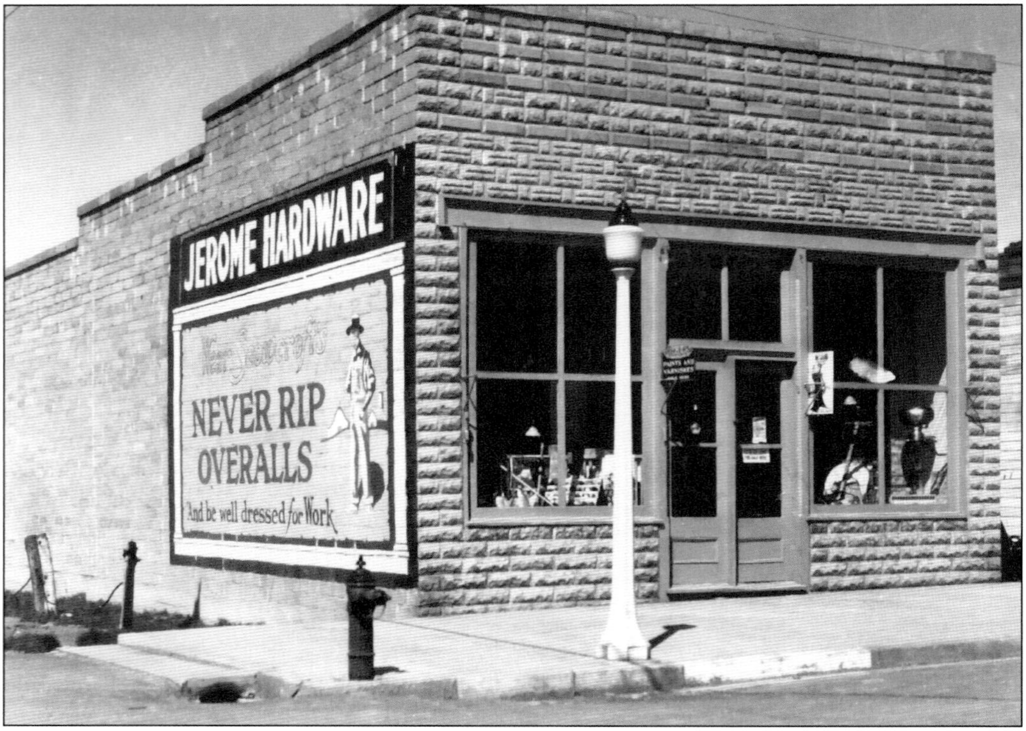

Jerome Hardware was in the Gerboth building on the corner of East Main and North Ash (Adams) Streets. Note the cream separator and nonelectric push lawnmower in the right-side window. The building now houses Elaine's Doll Shop.

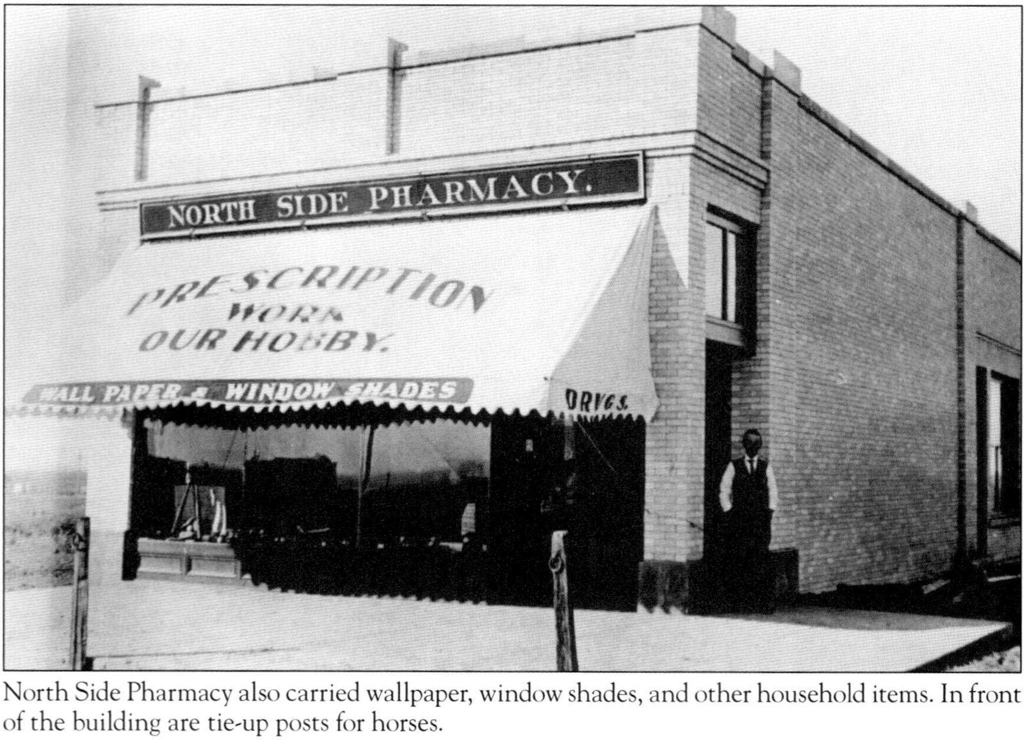

North Side Pharmacy also carried wallpaper, window shades, and other household items. In front of the building are tie-up posts for horses.

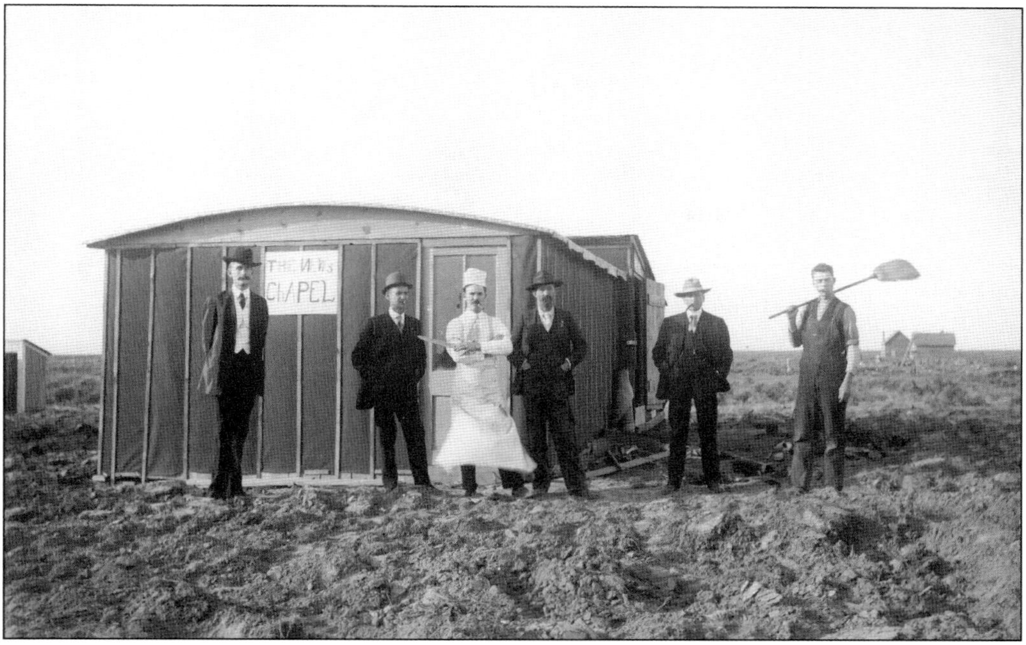

The first building for the *North Side News* newspaper is pictured here in November 1908. From left to right are unidentified, William Kennedy, Harry McPherson, Ralph Burroughs, editor John Nims, and Bill ?.

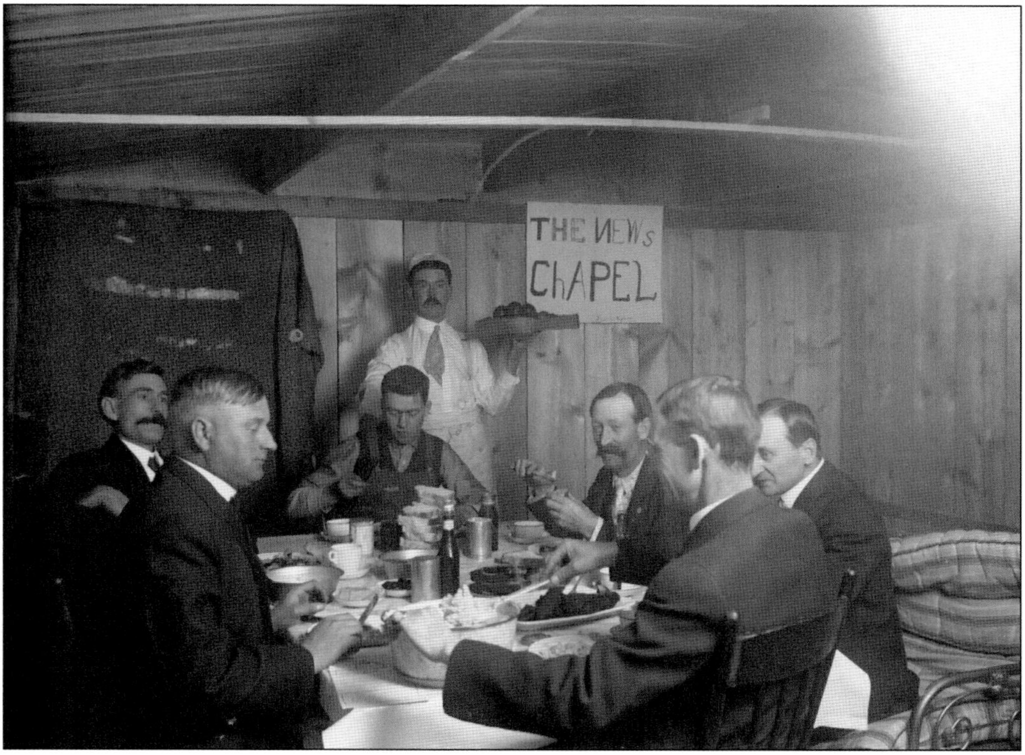

This image was captured during lunchtime at the news office, which also doubled as John Nims's home, as illustrated by the mattresses. Harry McPherson serves the food.

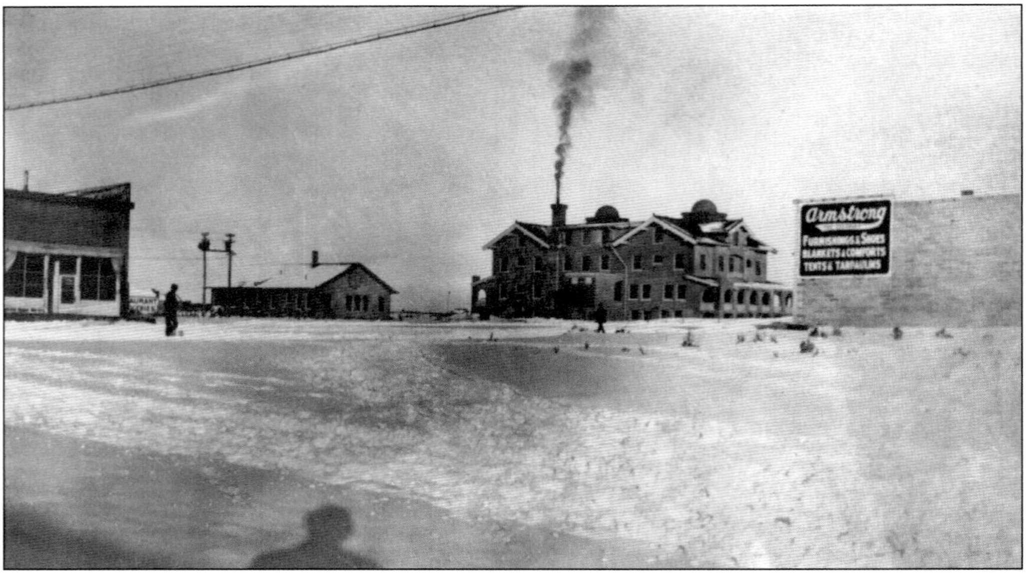

In December 1908, the coal furnace runs strong at the North Side Inn. The Armstrong building advertises the store and its tents, tarpaulins, blankets and comforters, furnishings, and shoes.

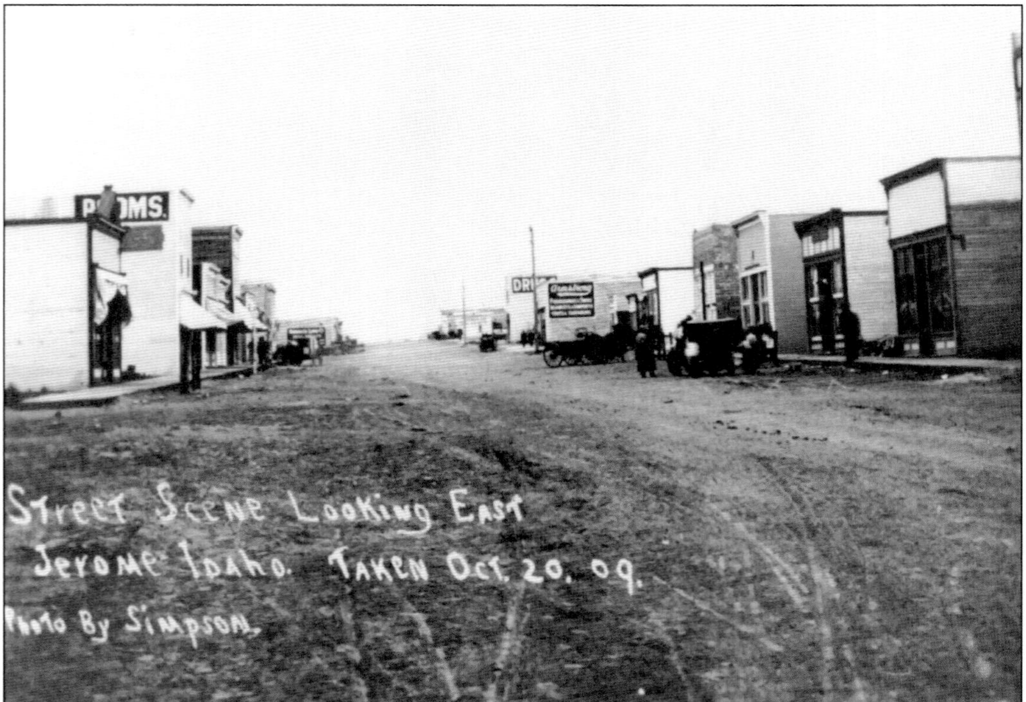

Pictured is the second block of West Main Street during the early days.

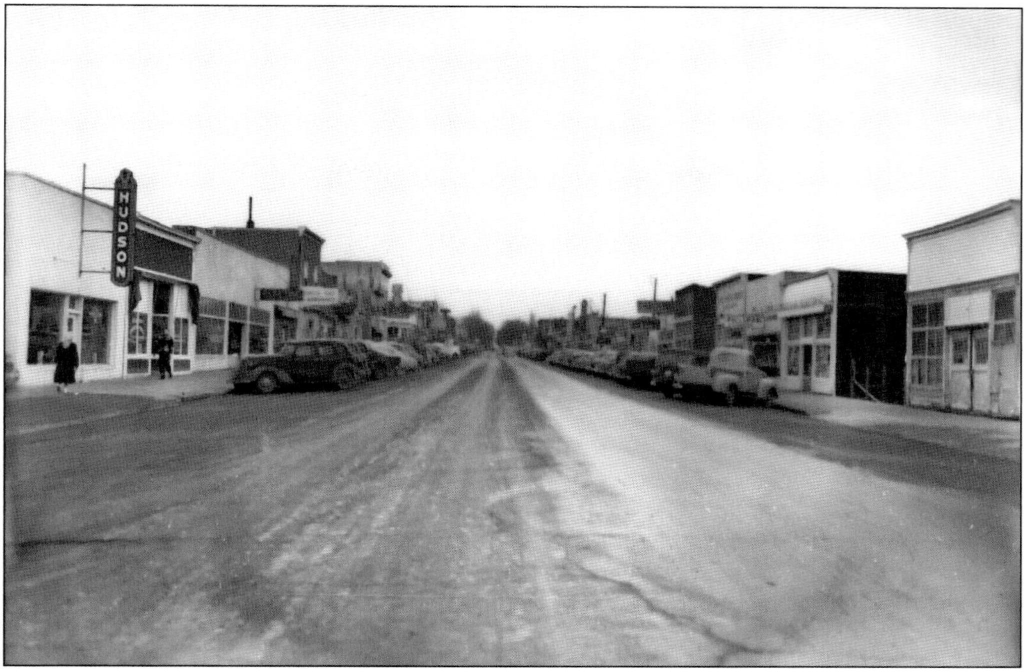

This 1940s view on West Main Street's second block looks east. The buildings on the left side of Main Street are still standing, but the last five on the right have been demolished, and the area is now a parking lot. None of these businesses presently exist.

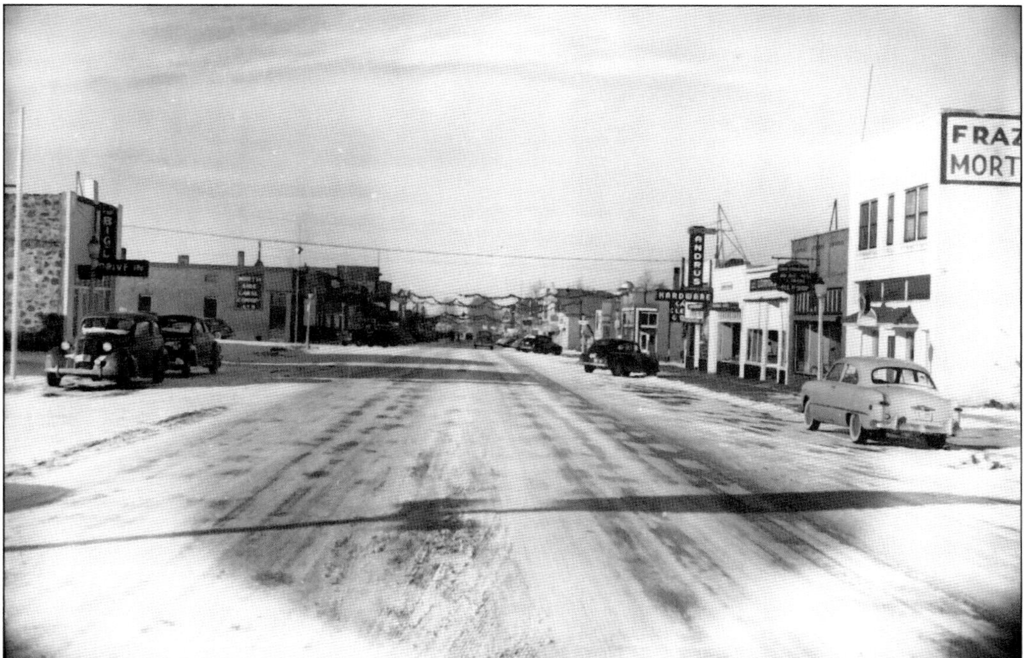

This 1950 photograph of East Main Street's second block facing west shows Connor's store on the right, where the first bank had been located. Note that even though side parking was the rule, several cars are parallel parked.

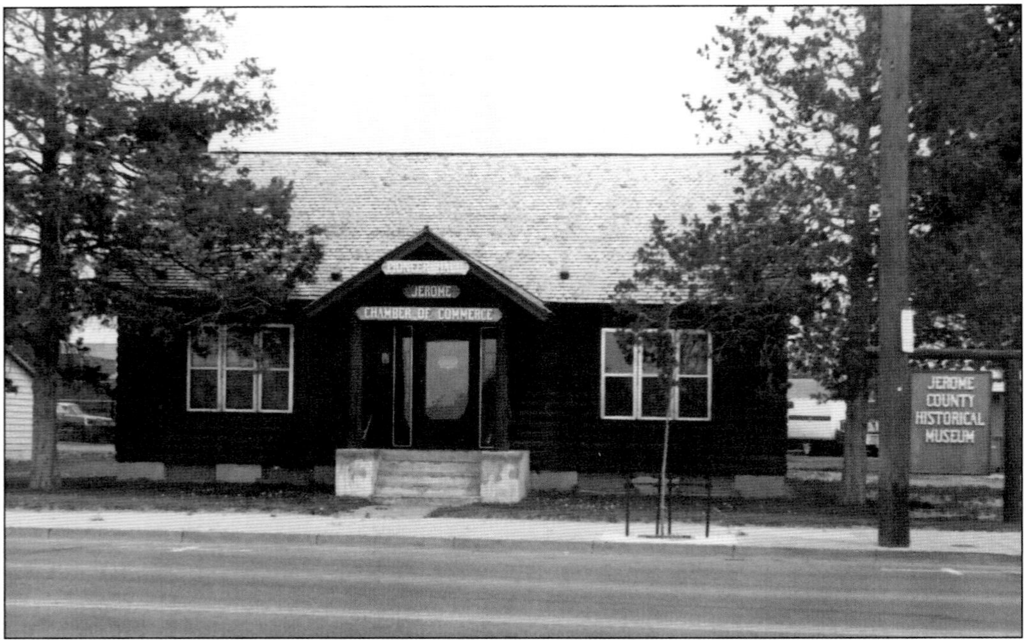

The Pioneer Hall was built in 1933 by the Works Progress Administration. It was first used as a Boy Scout hall. Over the years, it was also used by the Girl Scouts, for square dances, as a depository and distribution center for food commodities, and by the chamber of commerce. For almost 20 years, it was the home of the Jerome County Historical Society Museum, which was housed on both the main floor and in the basement. In 2011, the museum moved into the railroad depot, and this city-owned building is now waiting for a new project. The back door offers ramps to the main floor and basement.

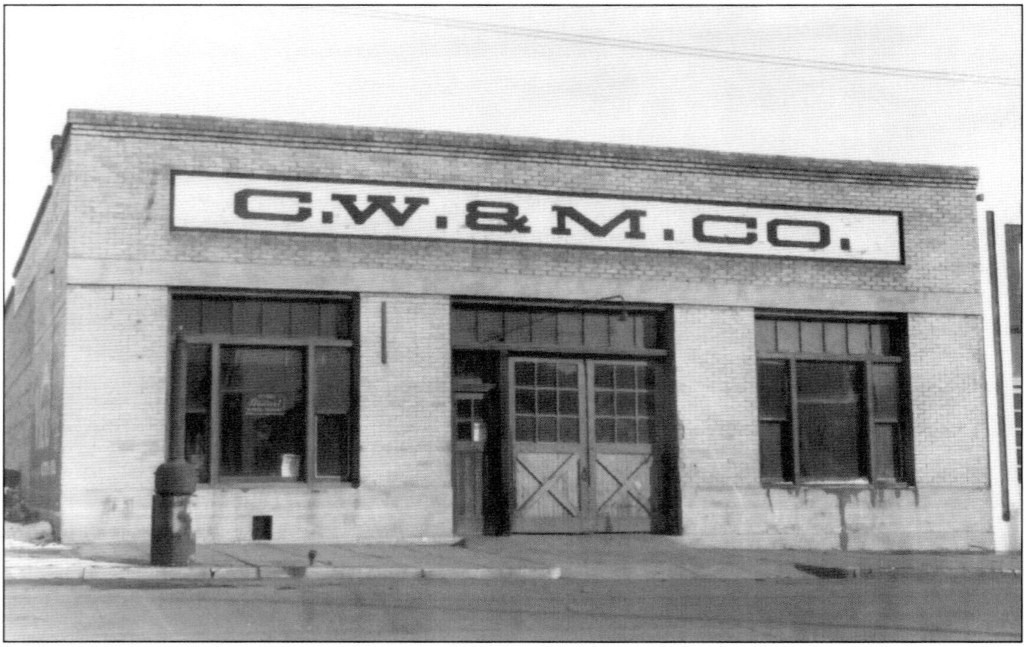

The C.W. & M. Company was built in 1916 on the west side of the second block of South Lincoln Avenue, but very little is known about this company.

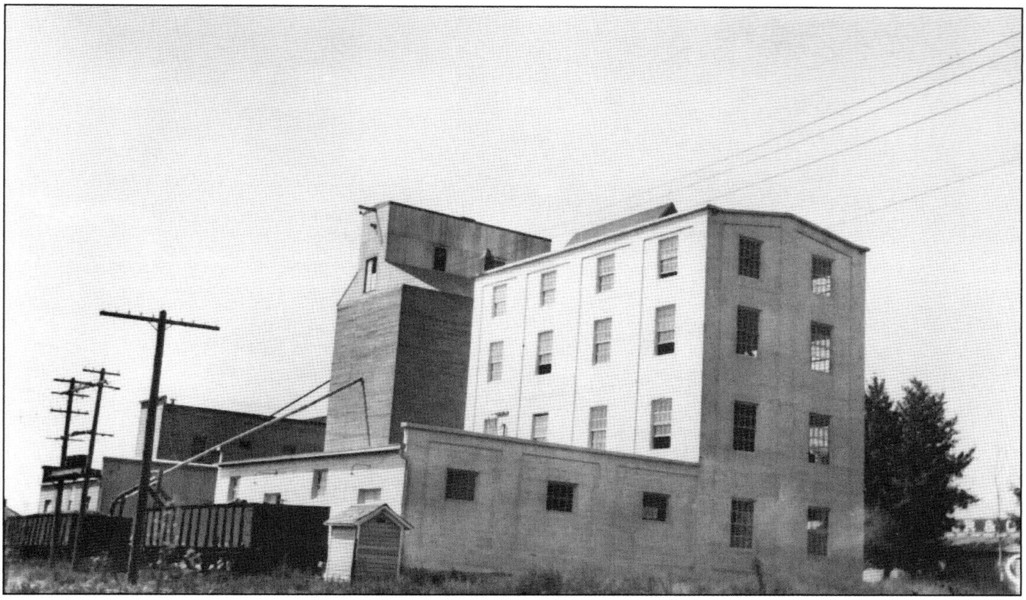

Wheat was grown in abundance in the area, and grain storage elevators were necessary. After the grain was brought to town, it was unloaded into the elevator for storage. If it was sold out of the area, the grain was loaded into railcars and shipped to a flour mill or to another storage area in another city.

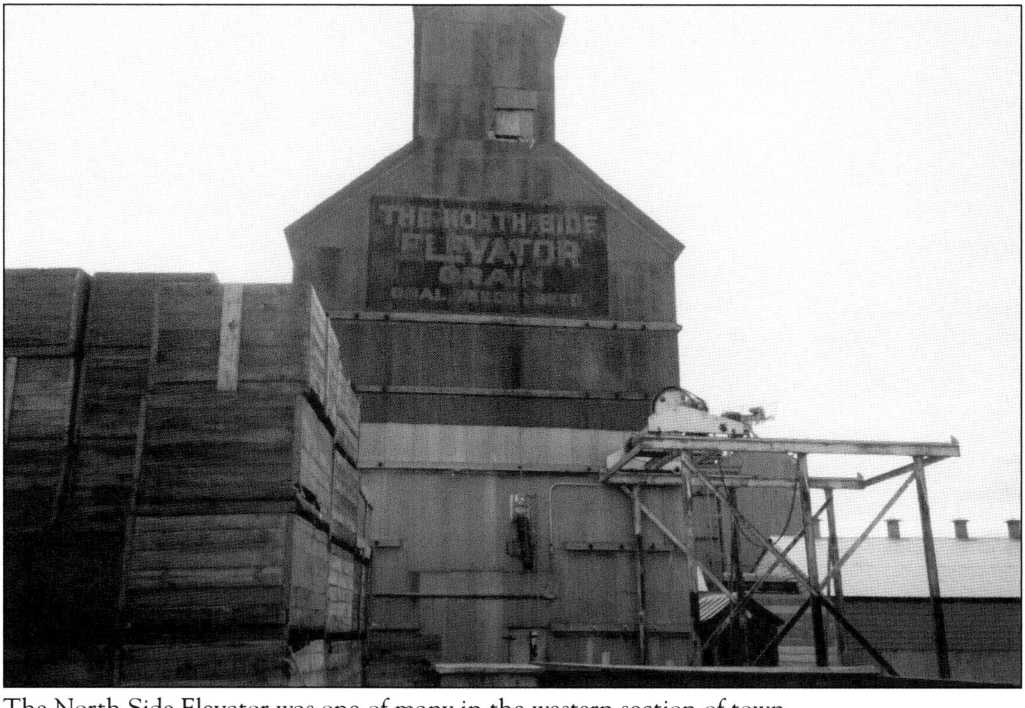

The North Side Elevator was one of many in the western section of town.

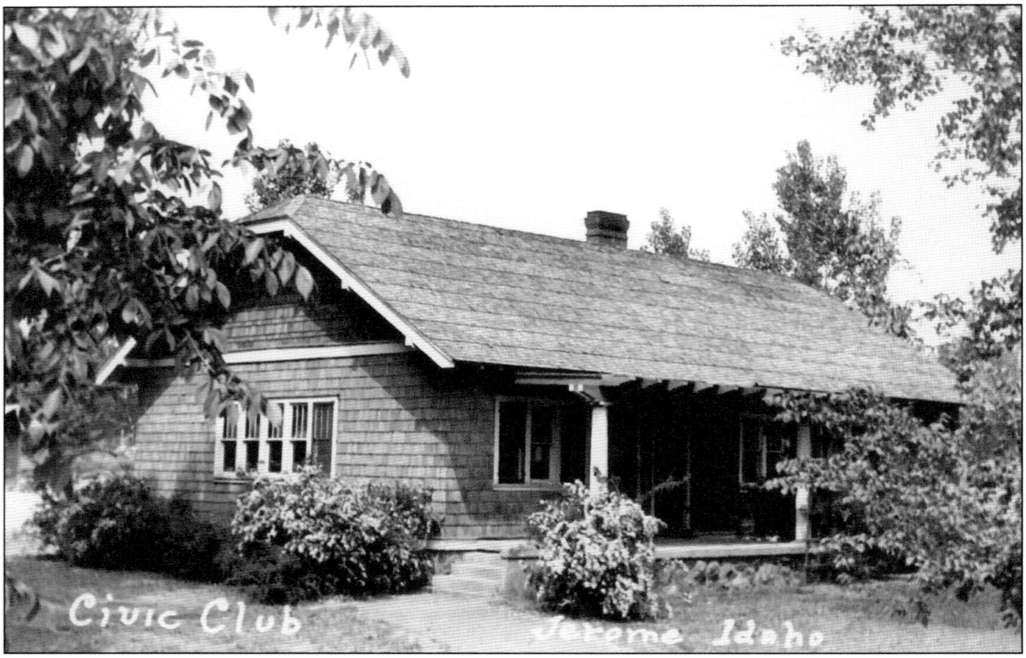

The Jerome Civic Club Library was formed in 1908. The Civic Club ladies hosted a community social with admission being a book to build Jerome's own library, instead of continuing with the Idaho Traveling Library. In 1919, a group of Chicago ladies also donated books. From monetary donations, club dues of $10 per year, and a small bank loan, the building was completed in 1923. Within five years, the loan was repaid, and in 1966, the library was outgrown. The Civic Club still meets at the library once per month and charges $10 yearly dues.

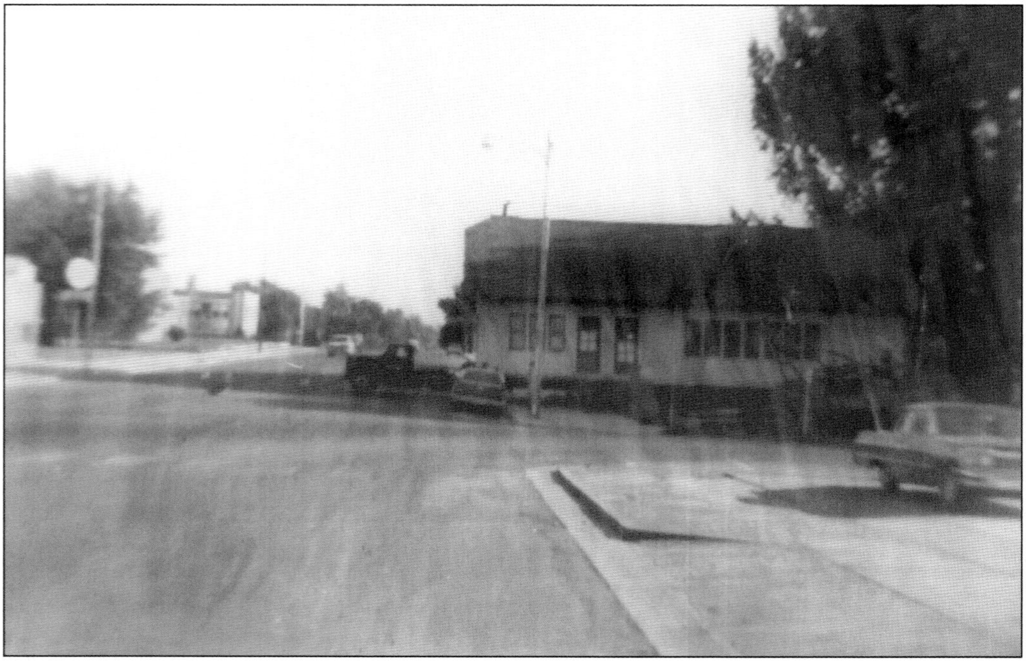

In 1966, the old Civic Club Library building was moved three miles north of town and became a private residence. A new brick library building was erected on the same lot.

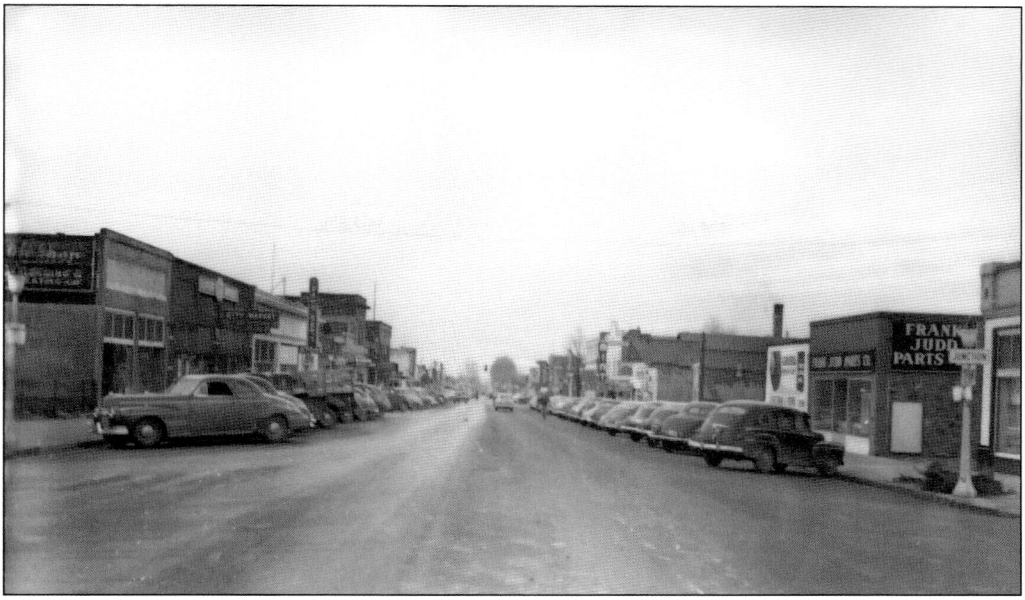

Occasionally, the businesses just moved from one building to another. Idaho Power moved from East Main Street's south side to West Main Street's north side, and Fisher's Furniture relocated north across Main Street to a building just west of Frank and Judd's Parts store after this photograph was taken.

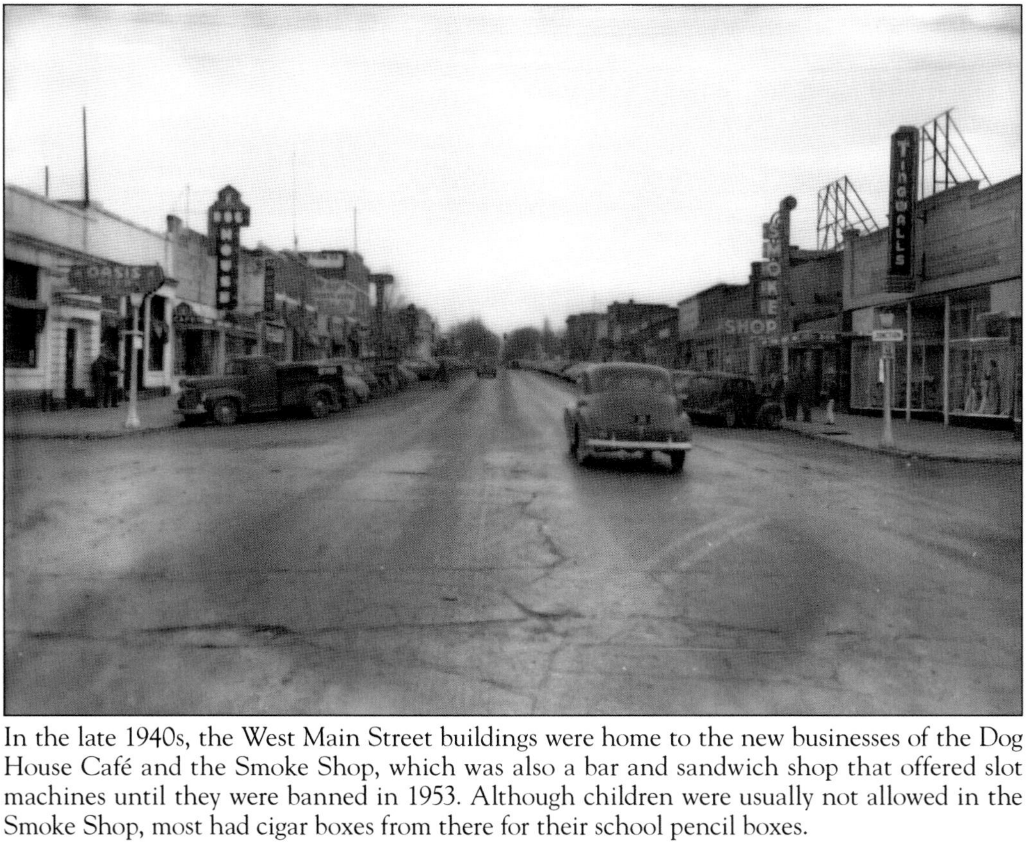

In the late 1940s, the West Main Street buildings were home to the new businesses of the Dog House Café and the Smoke Shop, which was also a bar and sandwich shop that offered slot machines until they were banned in 1953. Although children were usually not allowed in the Smoke Shop, most had cigar boxes from there for their school pencil boxes.

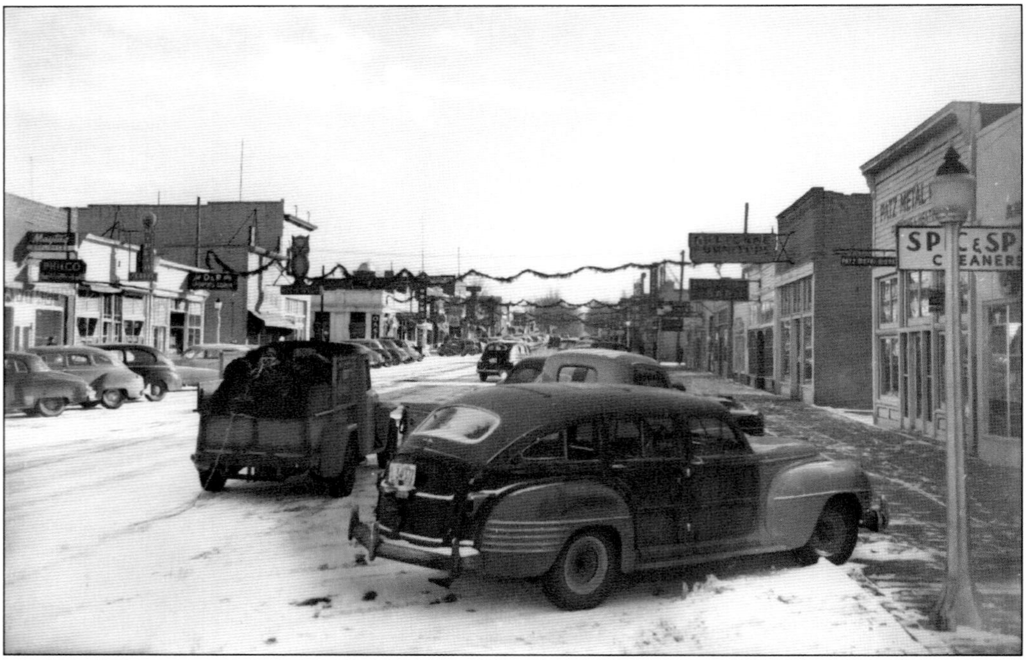

Snowy roads did not keep residents from downtown Christmas shopping about 1950. Some businesses on the second block of West Main Street included D&R Sporting Goods, State Café, Buttcane Furniture, Knotty Pine Bar, Patz Metal Works and Plumbing, and Spic and Span Cleaners. Note the over-the-street Christmas decorations on wires strung between building roofs.

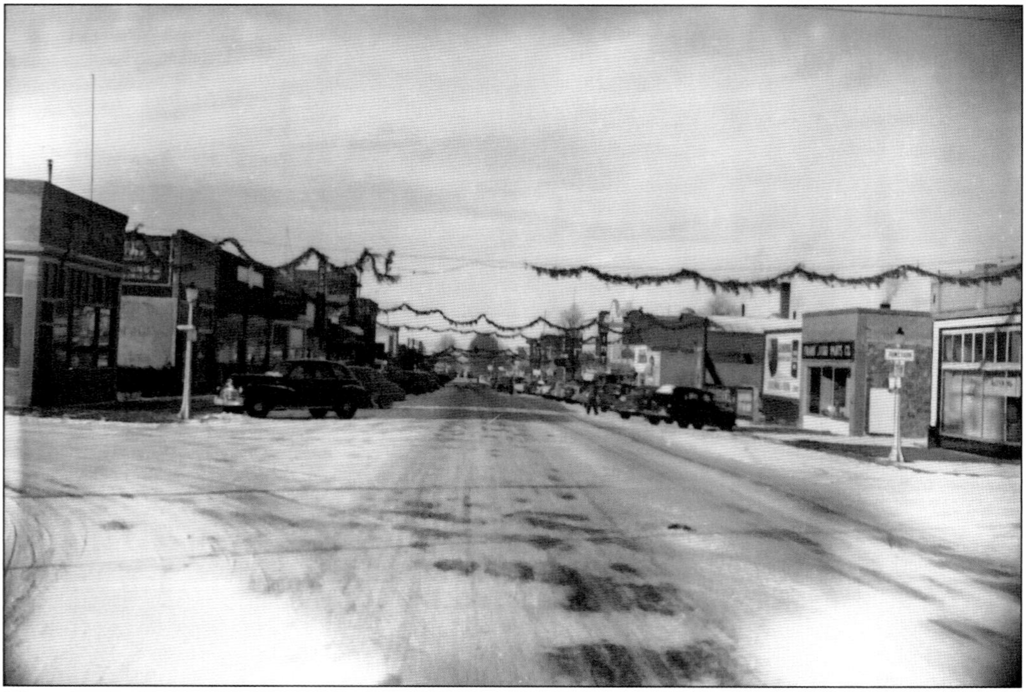

This view of east Main Street businesses was also taken during Christmas time. Perhaps some residents are watching a movie at the Voris Theatre before stopping at the City Market as they head home.

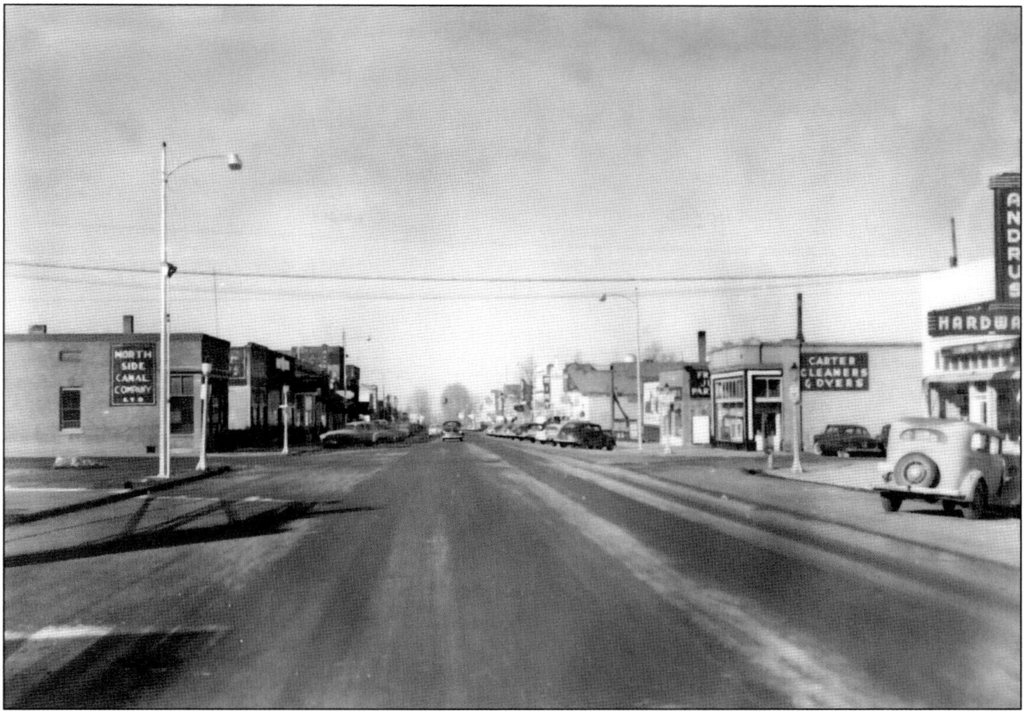

North Side Canal Company (left) takes care of the canal water rights of Jerome County in regard to the irrigation canal traveling through the north side of town from east to west. Carter's Cleaners and Dyers (right) was a dry-cleaning business. At one point, family-type movies were shown in Carter's basement when the Voris was showing XXX-rated movies.

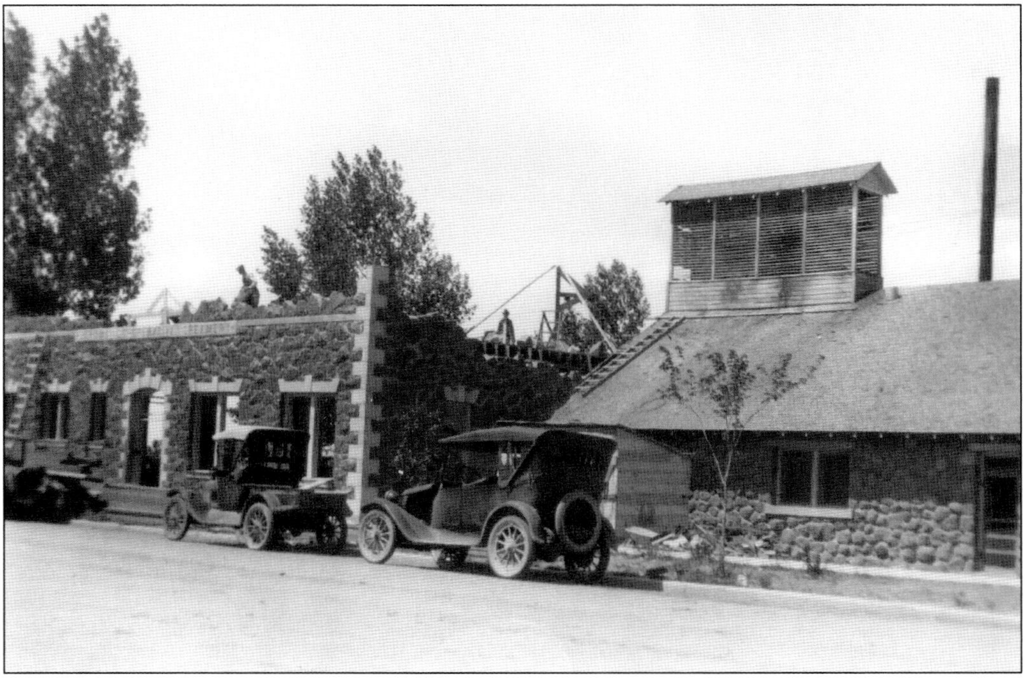

In this photograph, men finish the roof of the new Jerome Cooperative Creamery in 1924.

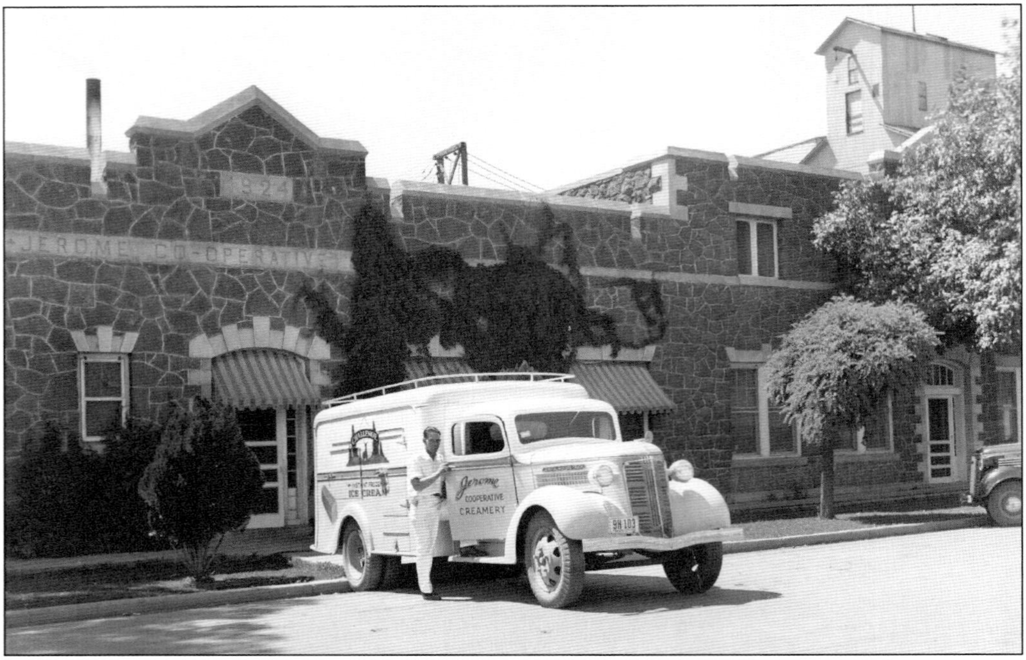

The Jerome Cooperative Creamery was built in 1924 from basalt rock on the west side of South Locust (Birch) Street between West Avenue A and West Avenue B. This picture was taken in 1937. Many schoolchildren and Boy Scout and Girl Scout troops, as well as other groups, were given tours and samples of ice cream sealed in small paper cups to be eaten with tiny wooden spoons.

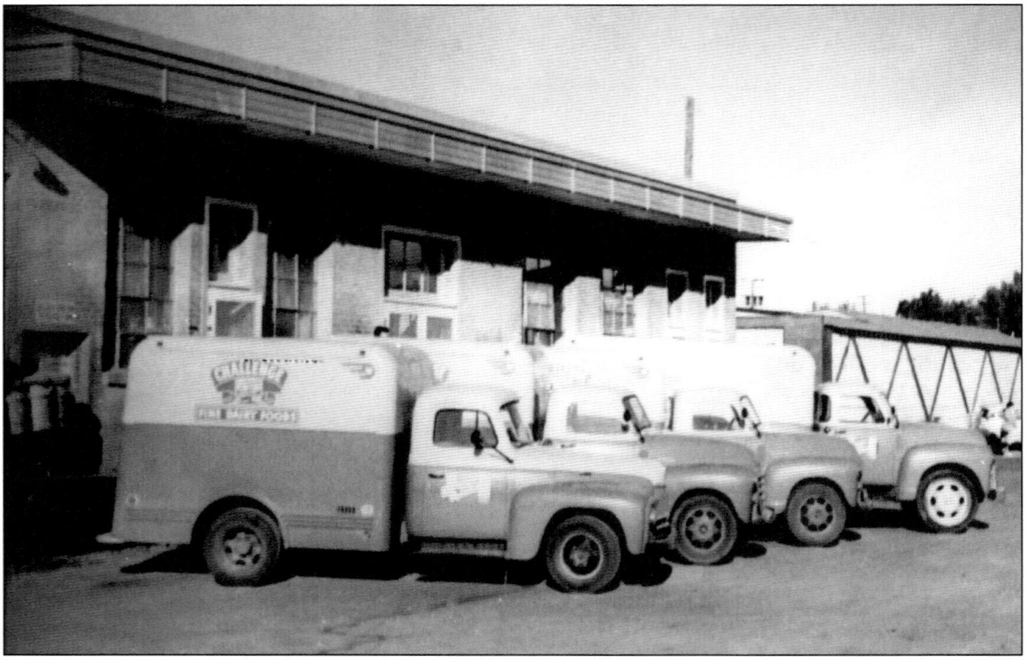

Challenge milk trucks went to the dairy farms each morning to pick up five-gallon cans of fresh milk, about four or five cans per dairy, depending on the amount of cows each dairy milked. The cans were hefted onto the two-tier racks in the trucks. They were then delivered to and unloaded at the creamery.

Wayne Johnson, a milk hauler for the creamery, lifts a full milk can onto his truck at the Herbert Helms ranch and dairy in the 1950s. (Author's collection.)

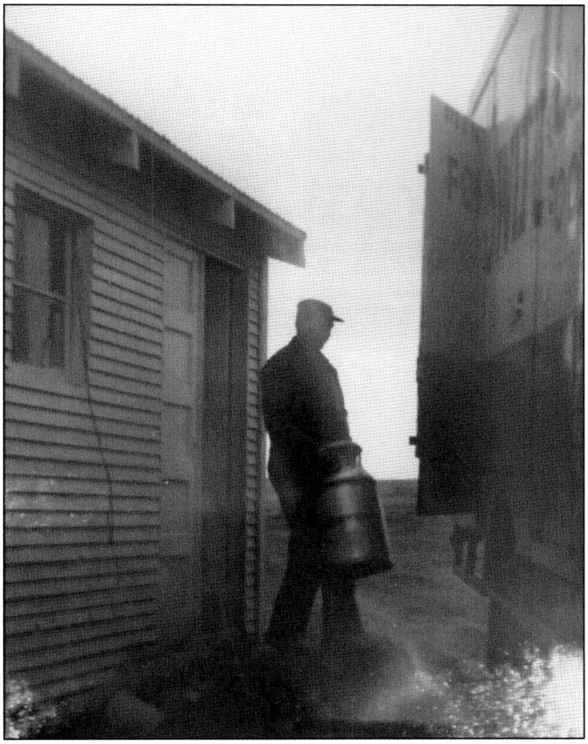

This display at the Jerome County Fair shows the Challenge products produced from Jerome County dairies, such as butter, ice cream, cottage cheese, and brick cheese.

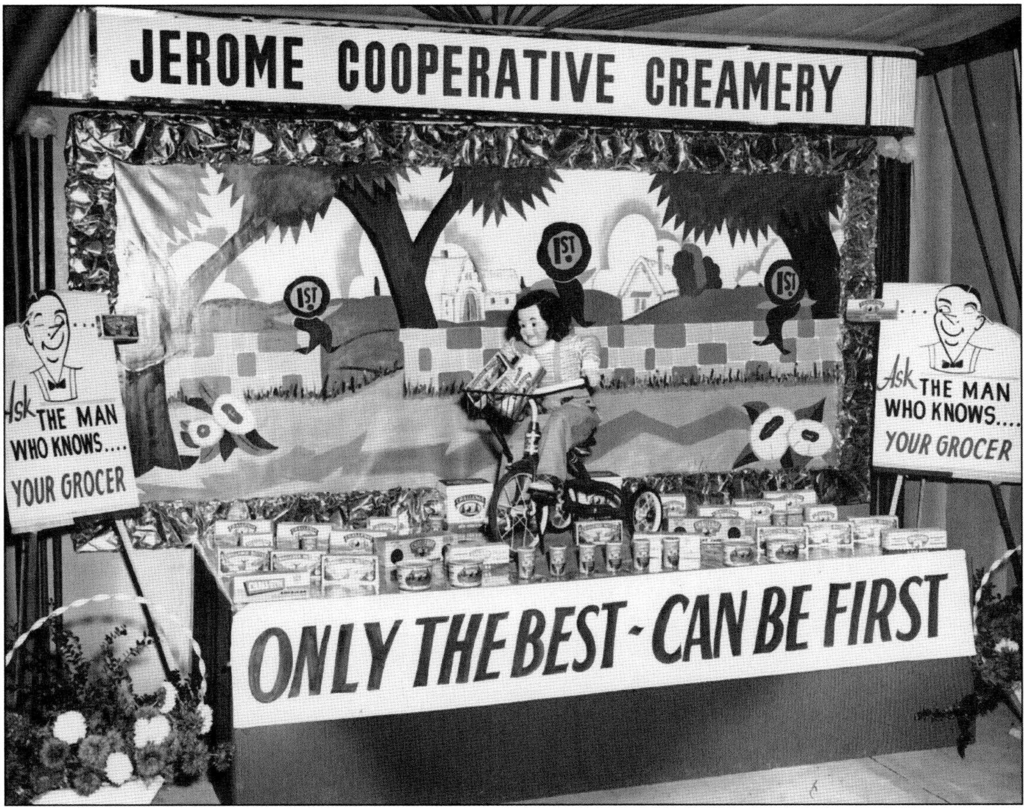

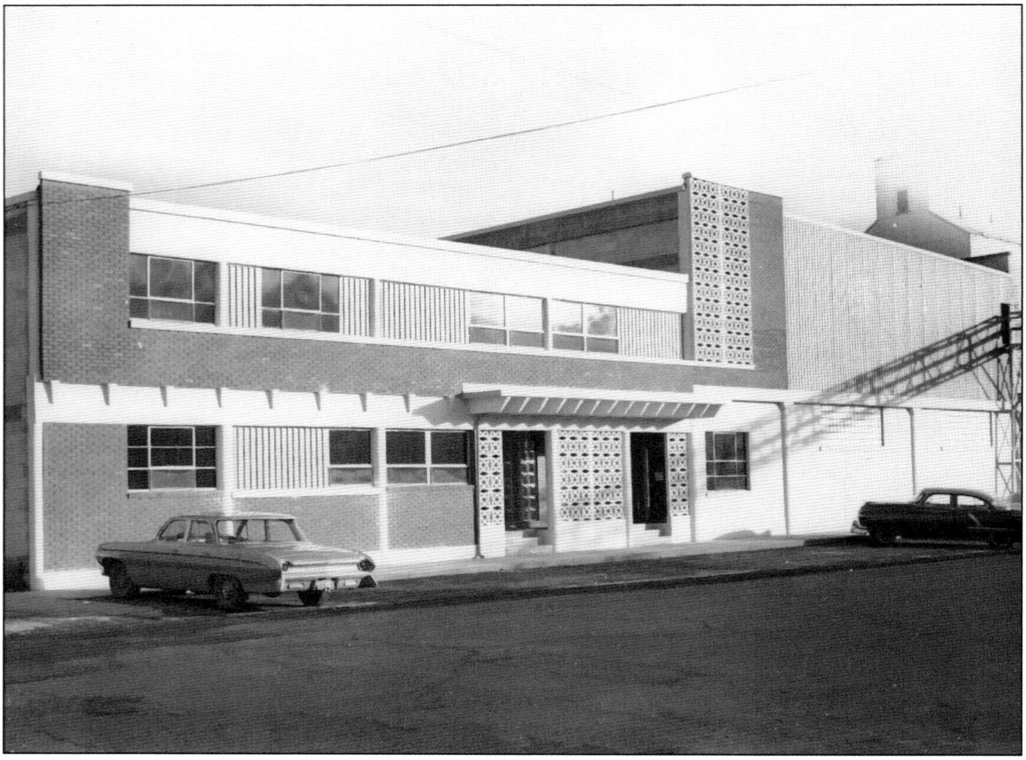

In the 1970s, an addition was built to the creamery across Birch Street, and a walkway was constructed above the street to connect the two buildings.

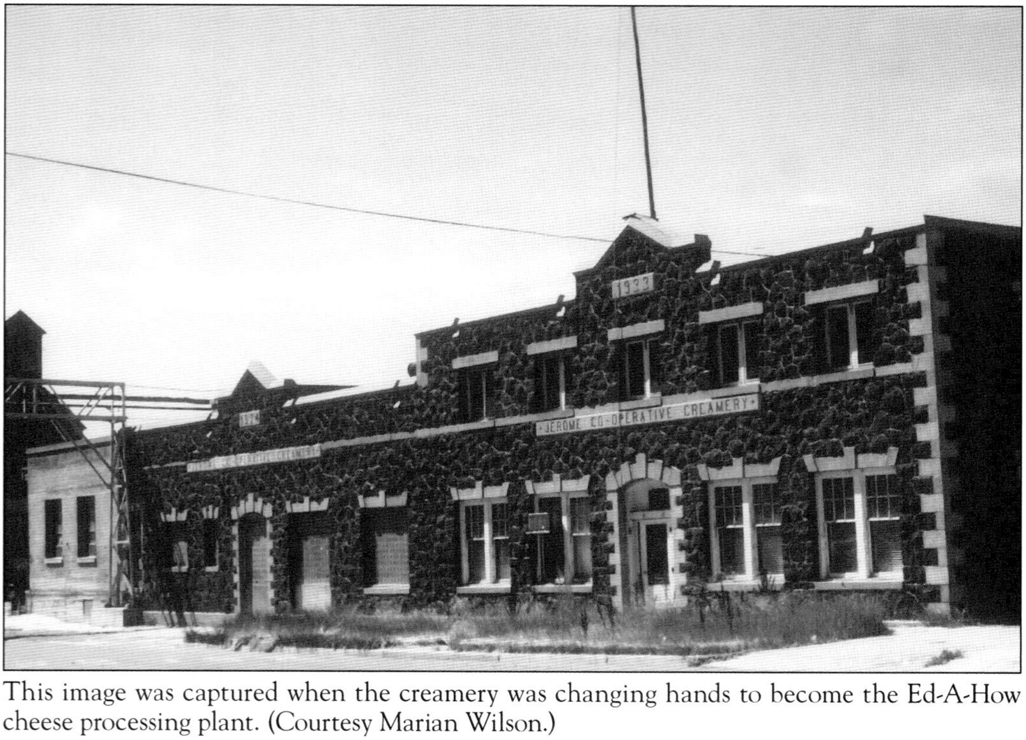

This image was captured when the creamery was changing hands to become the Ed-A-How cheese processing plant. (Courtesy Marian Wilson.)

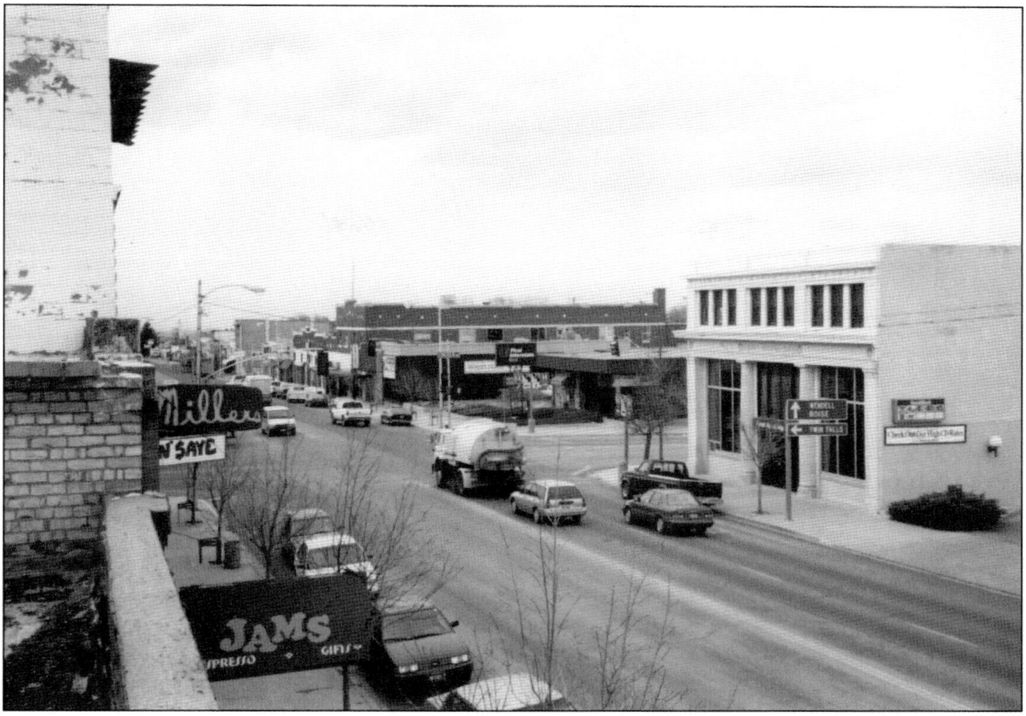

Businesses often changed, as this 1970s photograph demonstrates with the First Interstate Bank in the south part of the space once graced by the North Side Inn.

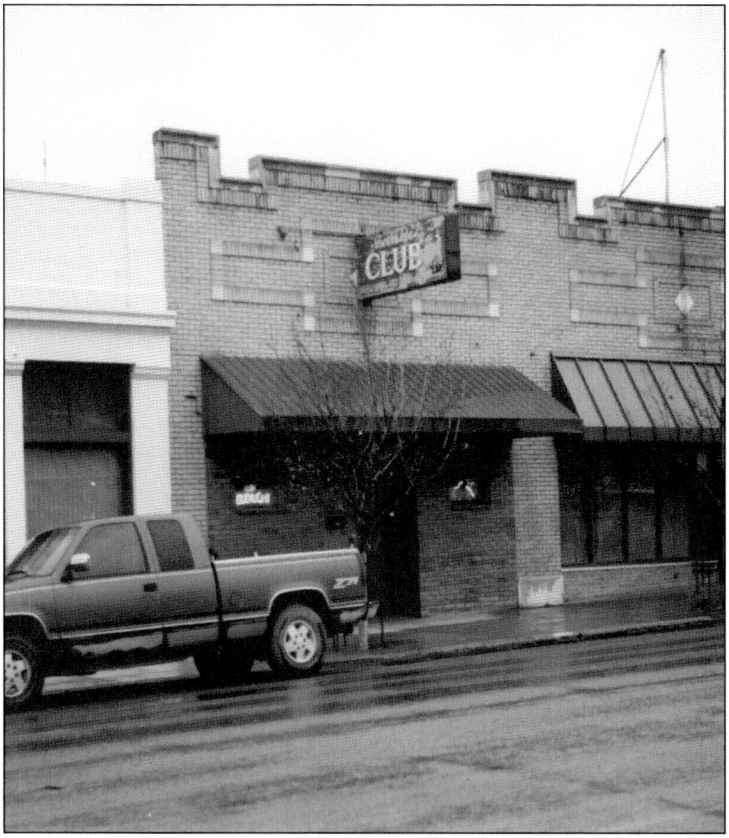

Pictured here is the exterior of a favorite place for locals looking to take a break on a rainy afternoon for a beer or soda or a game of table shuffleboard until the 1970s. Frances Robinson ran the Northside Club in the 1970s.

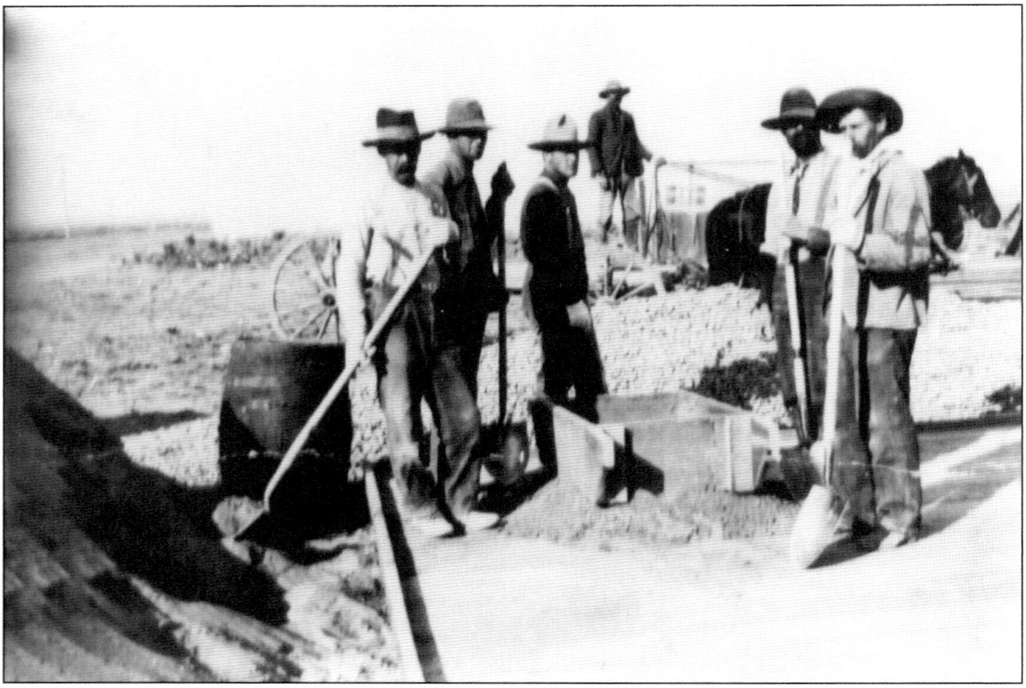

The Tillman brothers (the first two men on the left) and their employees dig the town well in 1907.

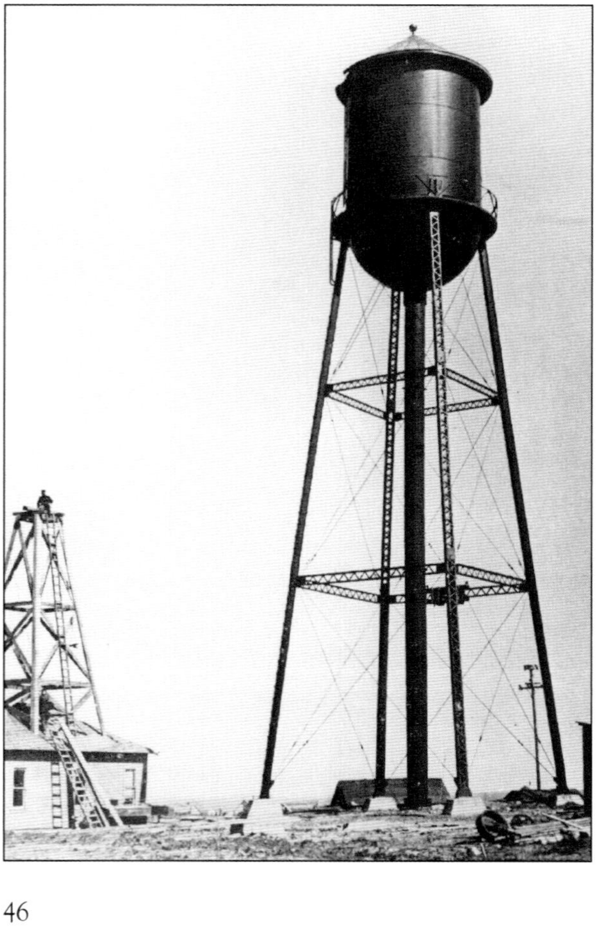

Workers began drilling a well on July 5, 1907, and water was struck on August 9, 1907, at 347 feet. A water tower from the Des Moines Bridge & Iron Company was placed over the well on October 9, 1908. It was 95 feet high with a capacity of 50,000 gallons. It was built next to the William A. Peters home. He was the water master.

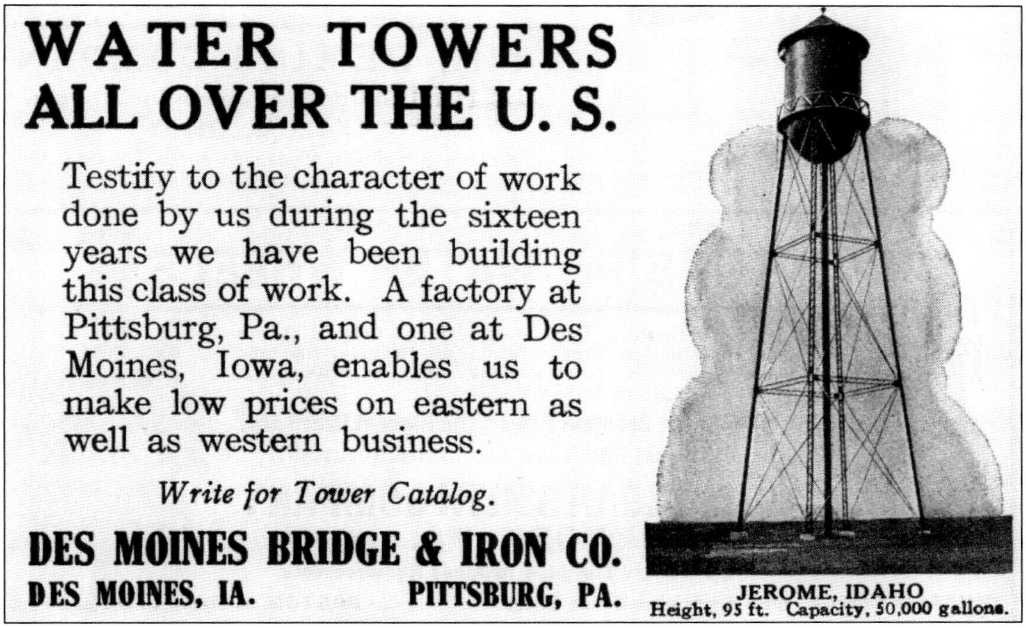

This ad for Des Moines Bridge & Iron Company water towers, featuring the Jerome tower, was found in a 1909 national magazine. (Author's collection.)

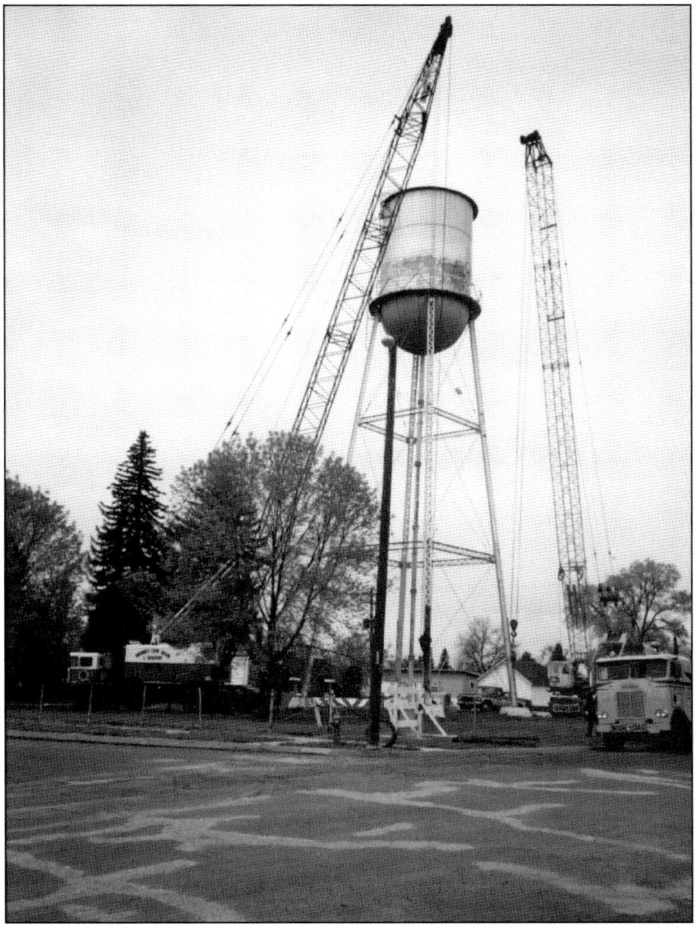

In June 1989, the water tower was abandoned when a new ground-level water container was built. Even though it was discouraged, many schoolchildren climbed the tower legs and painted their class years on the tower's container.

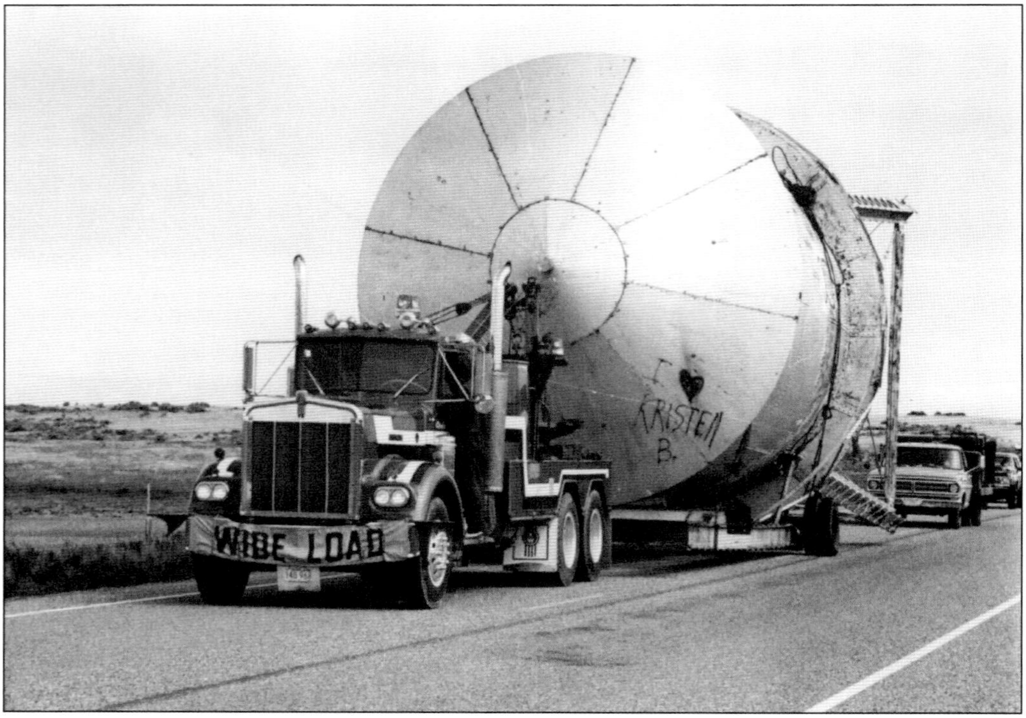

The water tower was dismantled and moved to the Petro (now Flying J) gasoline station at the crossroads of Interstate 84 and US Highway 93 situated six miles east of Jerome.

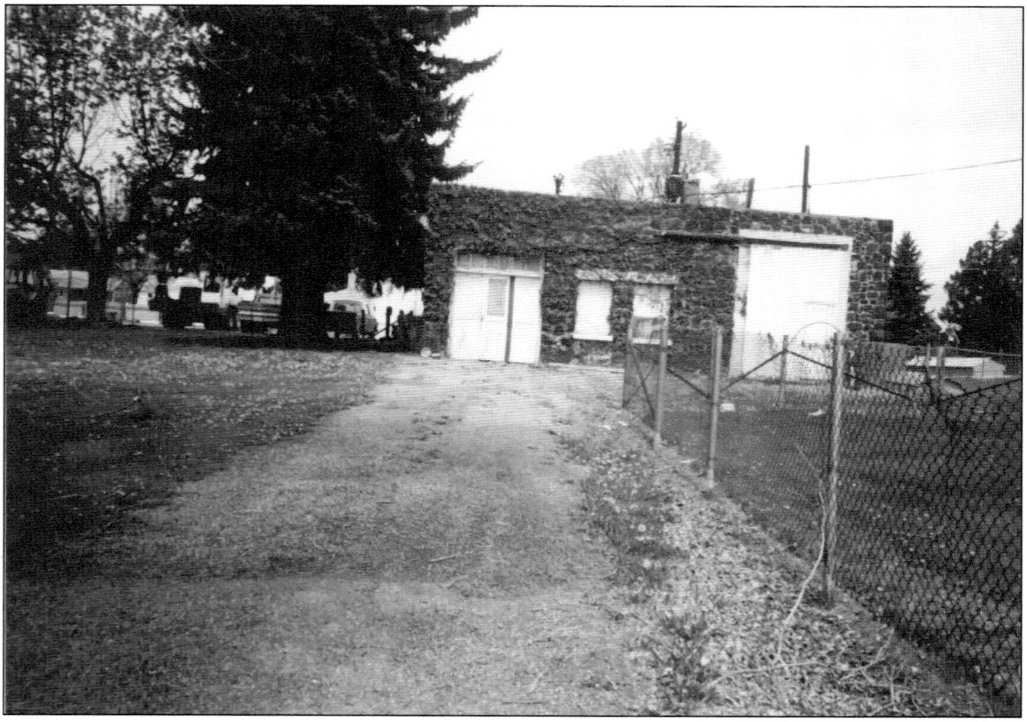

This is the well house still in use for the new ground-level storage container, located on the Peters property on East Avenue A.

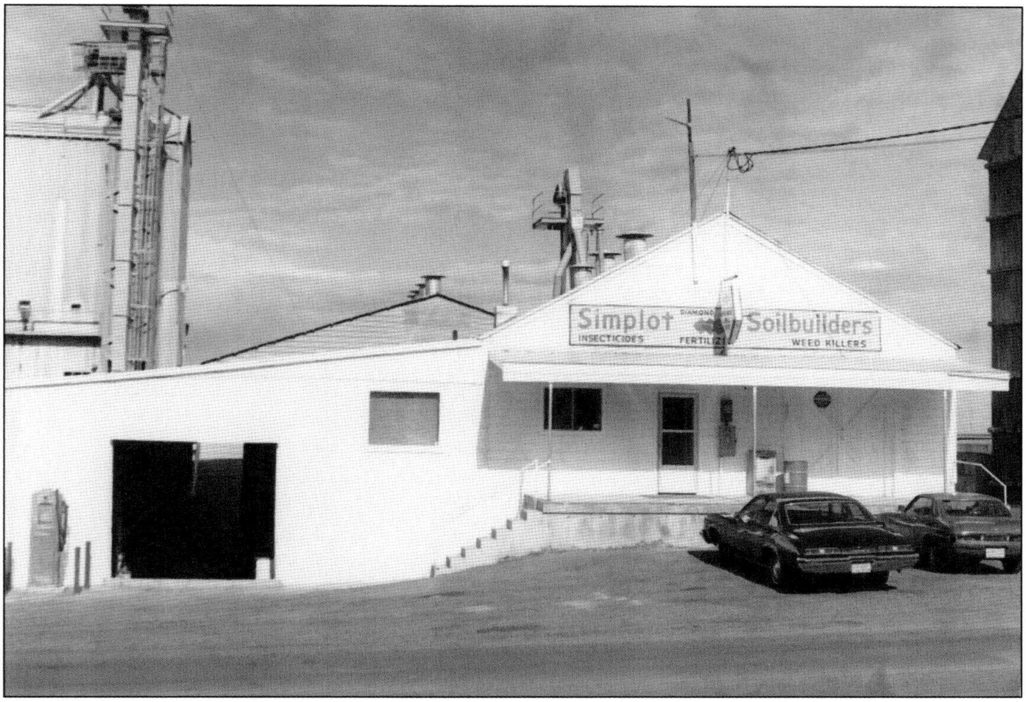

Simplot Soilbuilders on South Birch Street provided the local farmers with chemicals to improve the crops, such as insecticides, fertilizers, and weed killers.

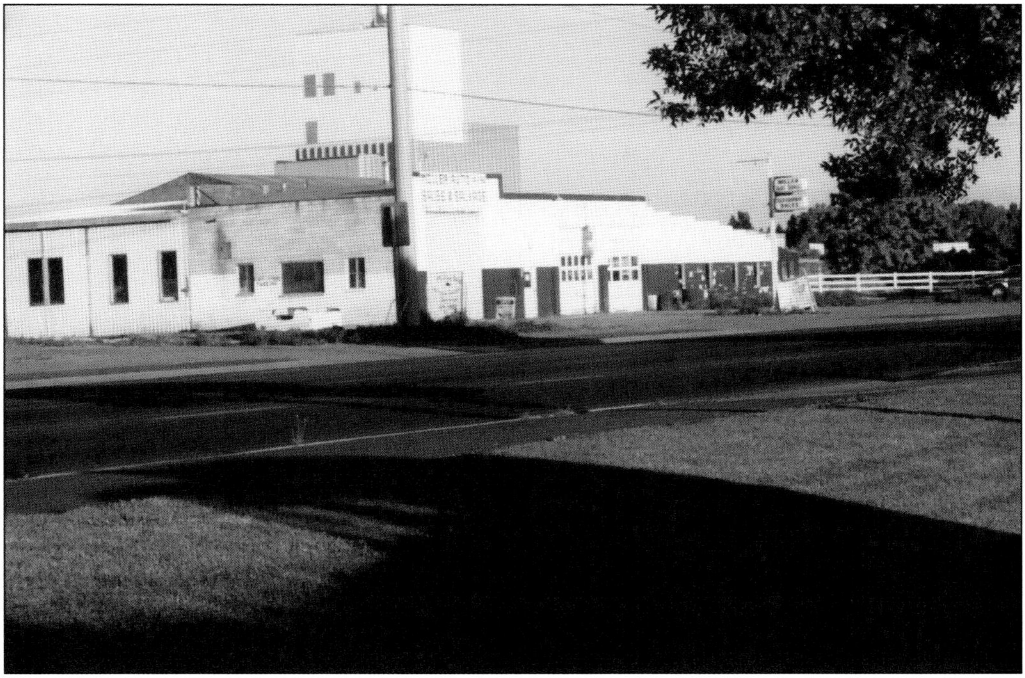

"Buzz" Miller owned a used car sales, repair, and salvage business from the 1950s through the 1980s at the southeast corner of South Lincoln Avenue, almost to the One-Mile South Road. The high square tower in the background is not part of his business but is a component of the milk processing plant across the road. (Author's collection.)

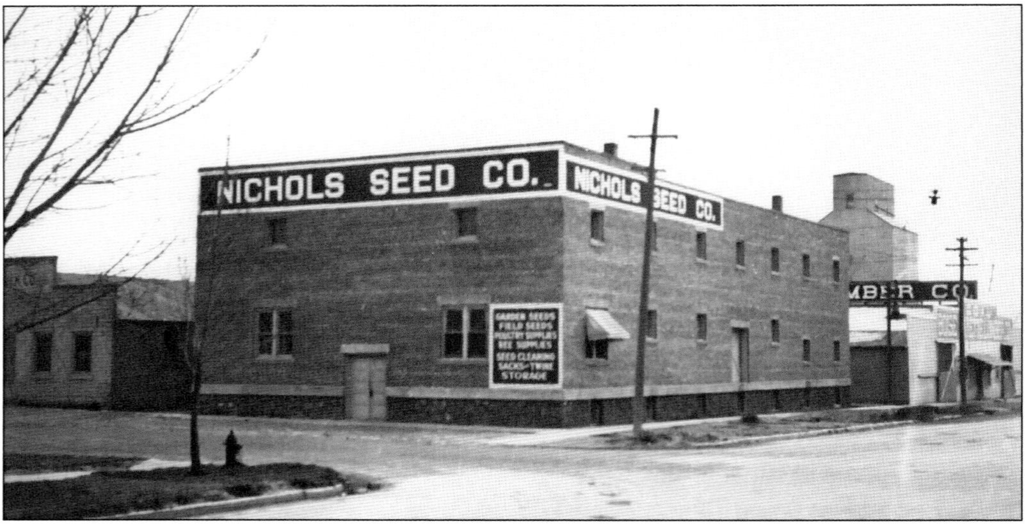

The Nichols Seed Company provided seeds for farm and city dwellers. Besides seeds, it also carried items for raising poultry, and both chickens and turkeys were commercially bred here. The company also offered beekeeping supplies. It was located on West Avenue B and South Locust (Birch) Street.

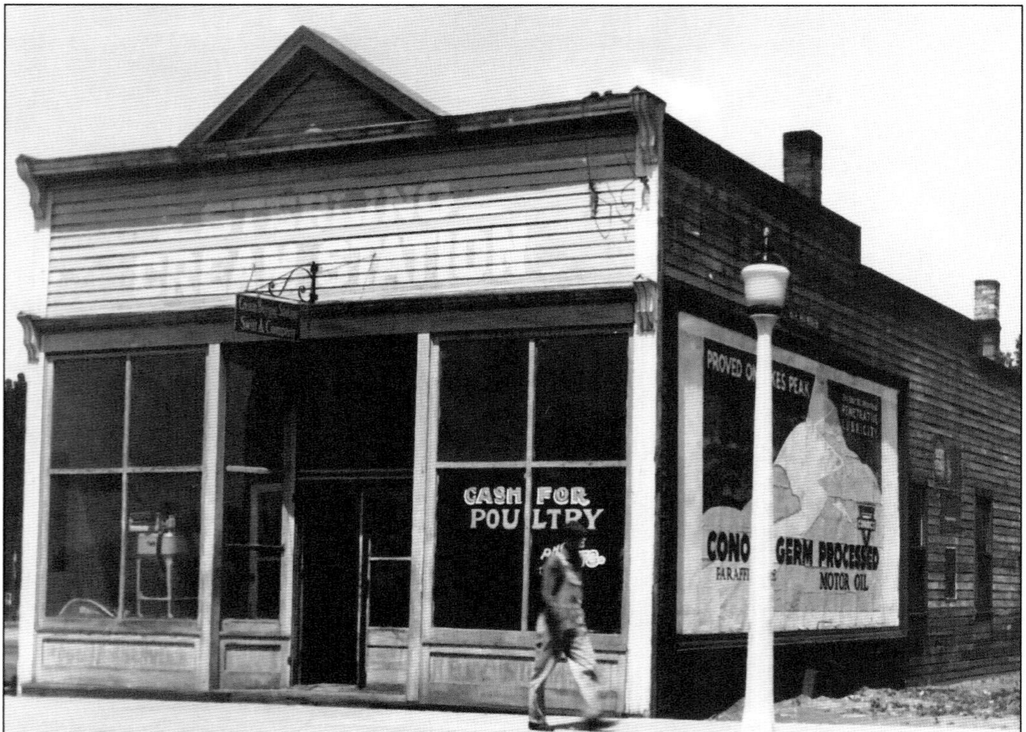

The Sterling Cream Buying Station for the Swift Company was competition for the Jerome Cooperative Creamery. But even in the 1920s, Sterling needed to diversify, so it procured poultry, advertised Conoco motor oil, and offered a gas-fired Maytag wringer washer for purchase, as seen in the left window.

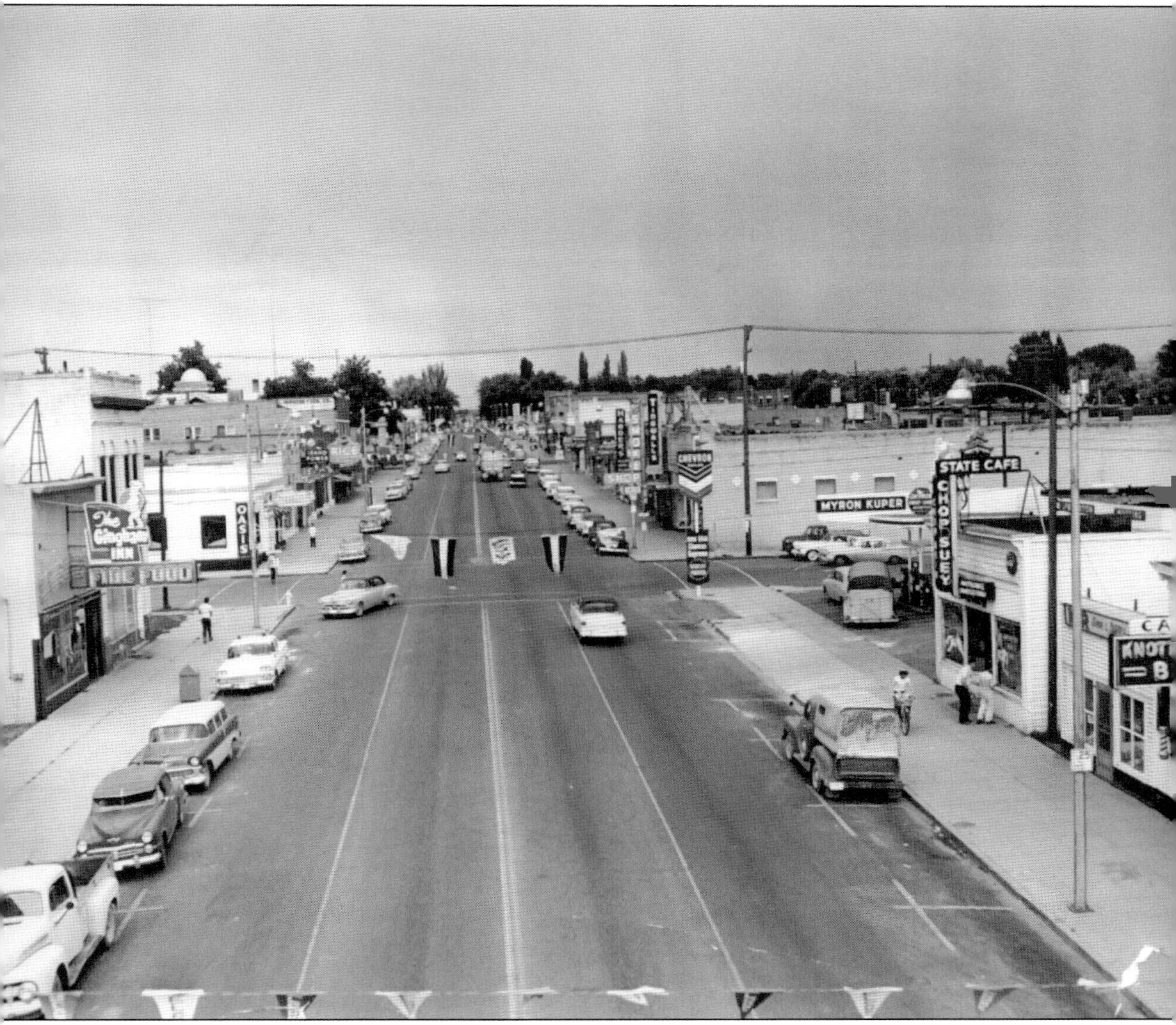

This view of Main Street looks east about 1960. The building between M&R Shoe and Saddle Shop and the Knotty Pine Bar & Café was Fullmer's Barber Shop, where the barber pole is seen. The shops on the lower right side of this block were demolished a few years later. The State Café was rebuilt in the back of this block and renamed China Village, and a large Safeway grocery store took up the rest of the block with a parking lot stretching to Main Street. The banners hanging across the street advertise the county fair and rodeo.

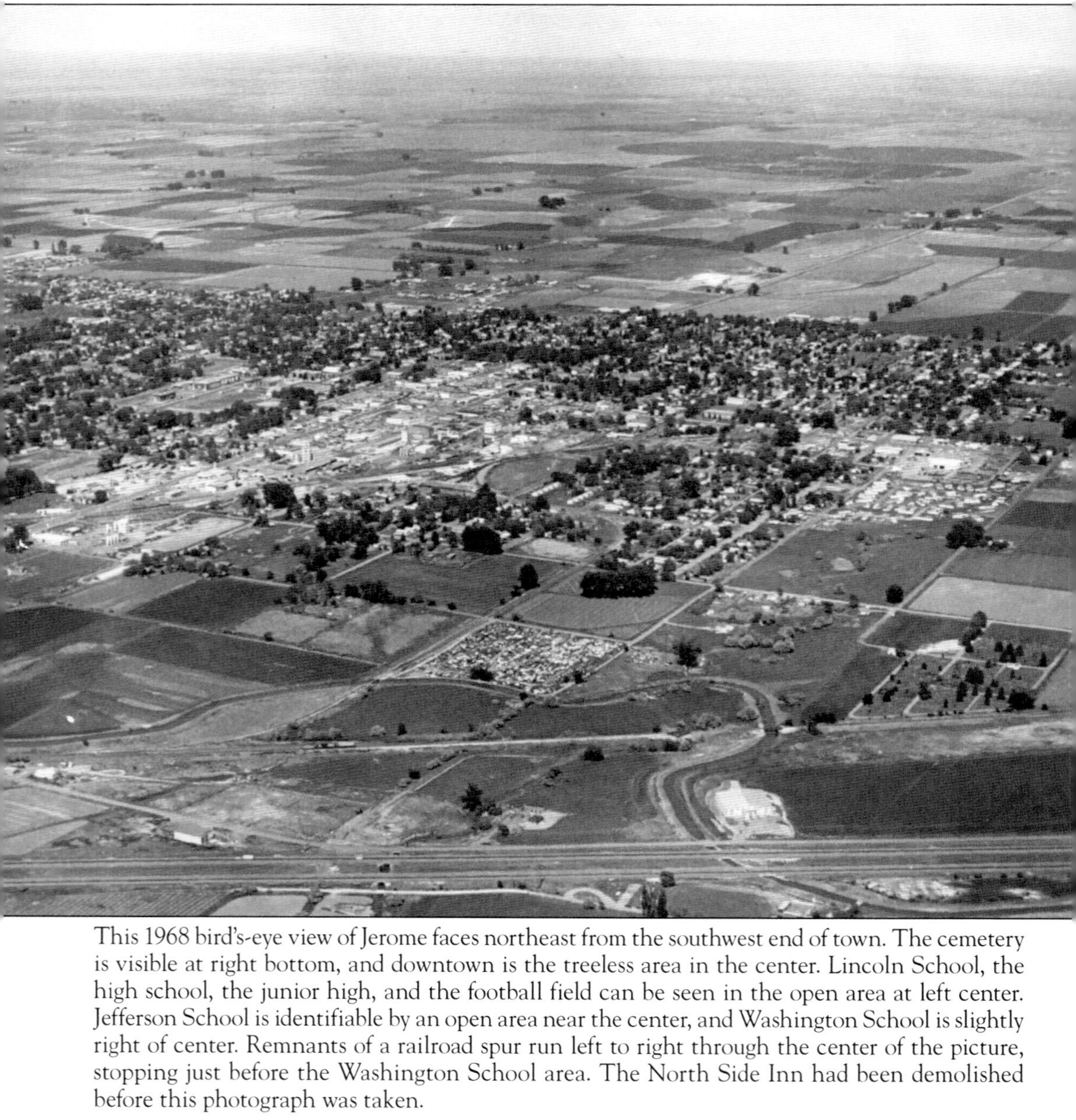

This 1968 bird's-eye view of Jerome faces northeast from the southwest end of town. The cemetery is visible at right bottom, and downtown is the treeless area in the center. Lincoln School, the high school, the junior high, and the football field can be seen in the open area at left center. Jefferson School is identifiable by an open area near the center, and Washington School is slightly right of center. Remnants of a railroad spur run left to right through the center of the picture, stopping just before the Washington School area. The North Side Inn had been demolished before this photograph was taken.

Two

The Early Schools

One of the most important needs of a new community is a school for the children, so the Jerome School District was created in 1908. The Twin Falls North Side Land and Water Company advanced the money for lumber for the first school buildings. Many country elementary schools were established in the county outside the four-mile boundary of the center of Jerome. The schools were named Pleasant Plains, Appleton, Canyonside, Lucerne, Auger Falls, Barrymore, Grandview, Falls City, Butte, Sugar Loaf, and East Perrine. The high school students then commuted to Jerome. Most of the country schools closed in the 1960s, and most were remodeled to be private homes; however, some were demolished over the years.

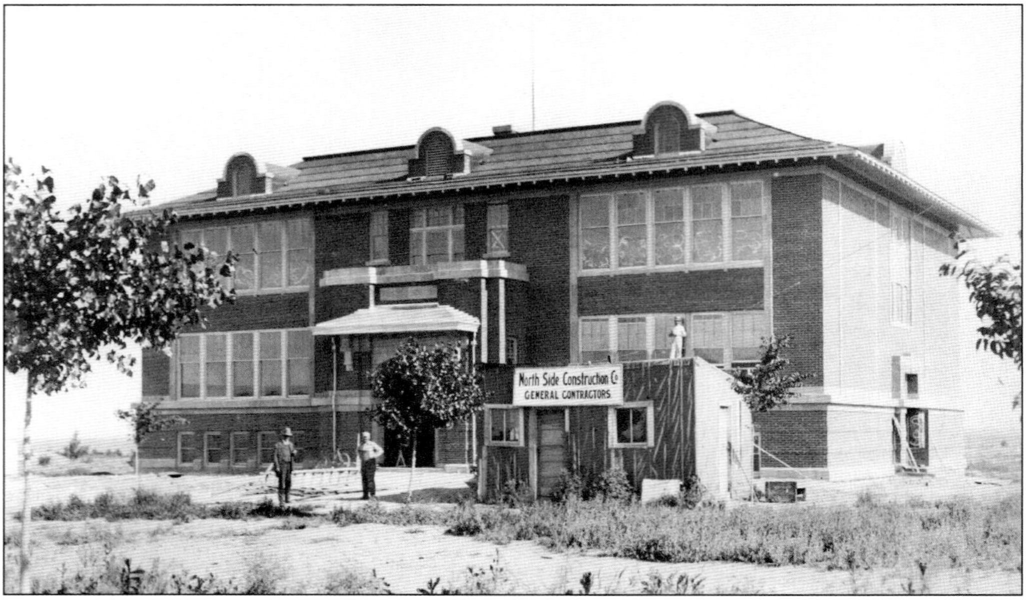

The North Side Construction Company employees, working from their small construction building in the foreground, stand in front of the new Lincoln School in 1910.

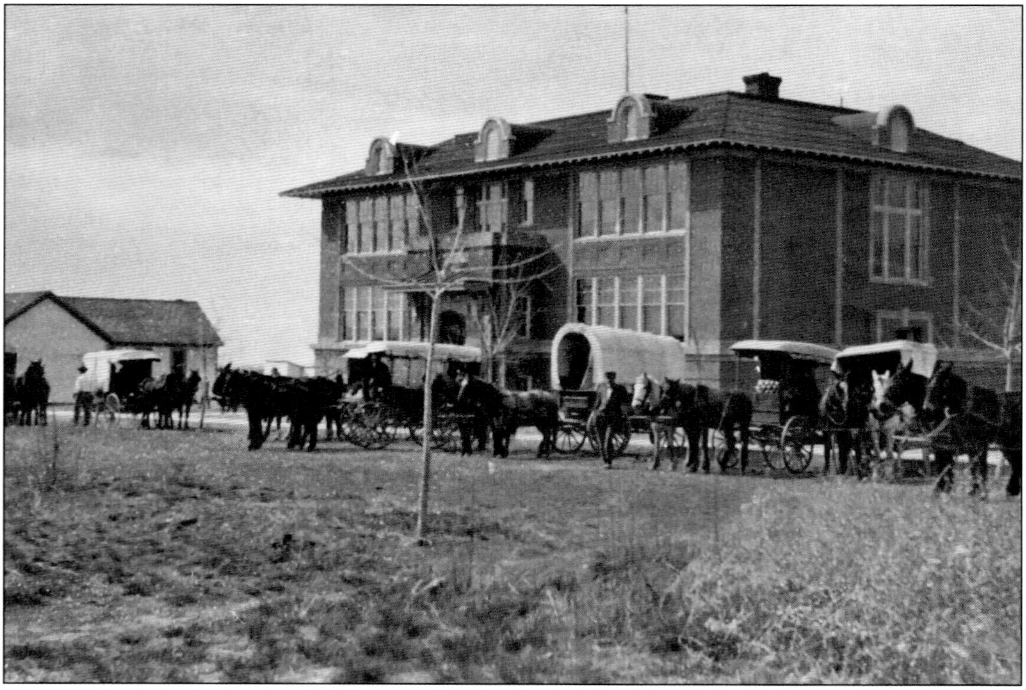

The North Side Construction Company built a small wood-frame schoolhouse on the corner of North Locust (Birch) Street and Third Avenue West. In 1910, a successful $40,000 bond election provided the money for construction of the brick Lincoln School situated east of the small school on the same block. It was three stories with eight classrooms and a full basement for restrooms, as well as a play area for all 12 grades, until the high school was built in 1920. Any first grade student who could spell *leaf* was promoted to the second grade. Lincoln School was demolished in 1978.

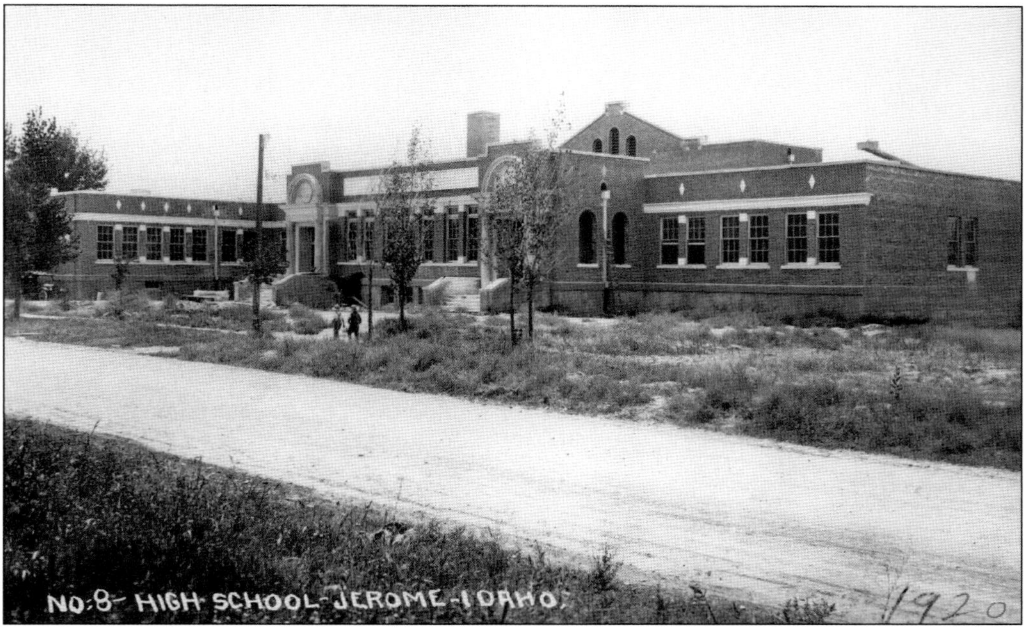

With the school overcrowding, a $150,000 bond election passed to build the high school on North Lincoln a half block south of West Third Avenue. In 1920, the new, larger brick building was enjoyed by 122 students. In 1949, another new high school was constructed, and the building pictured here became the junior high until 1976, when another new high school was erected east of town, and this structure became Central Elementary. Sadly, this building was demolished in 2009.

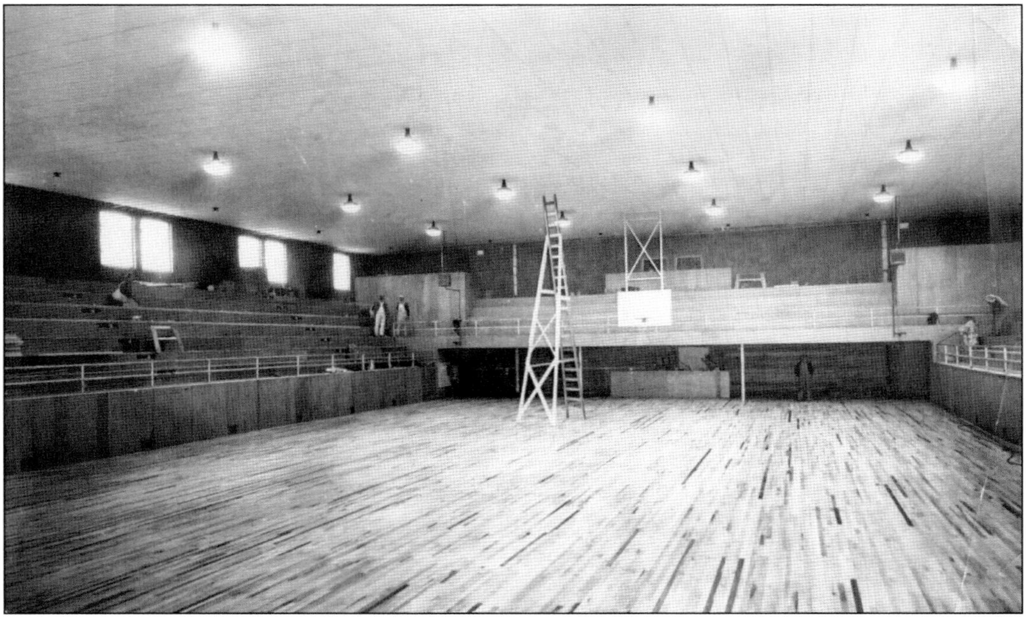

The Jerome High School gymnasium was built in 1949 before the new high school was finished in 1950. The first basketball game was held December 17, 1949, with the Jerome Tigers beating the Boise Braves 41–21. In May 1950, the senior class was happy to have its graduation ceremony in the new high school's gym instead of at the Voris Theatre, as many of the classes did before them.

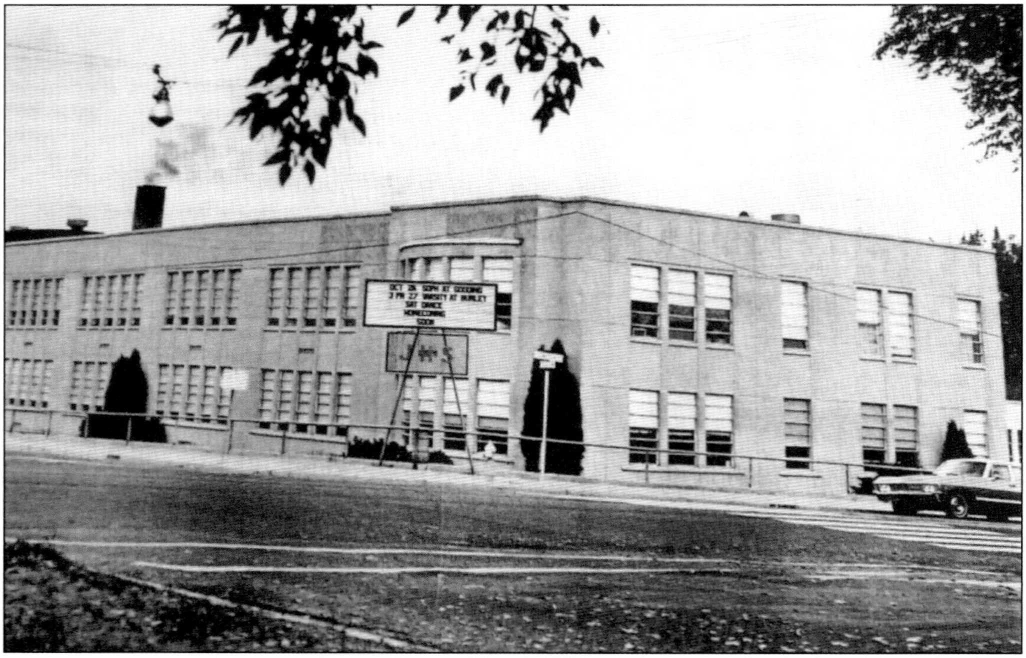

Built in 1950 at the northeast corner of North Lincoln Avenue and Third Avenue West, this was the high school until 1975, when a newer high school was built east of town, and this building became the new junior high. The gymnasium was situated on the west end of this building, farther to the left, just out of frame. Part of the annex is seen on the right behind the car.

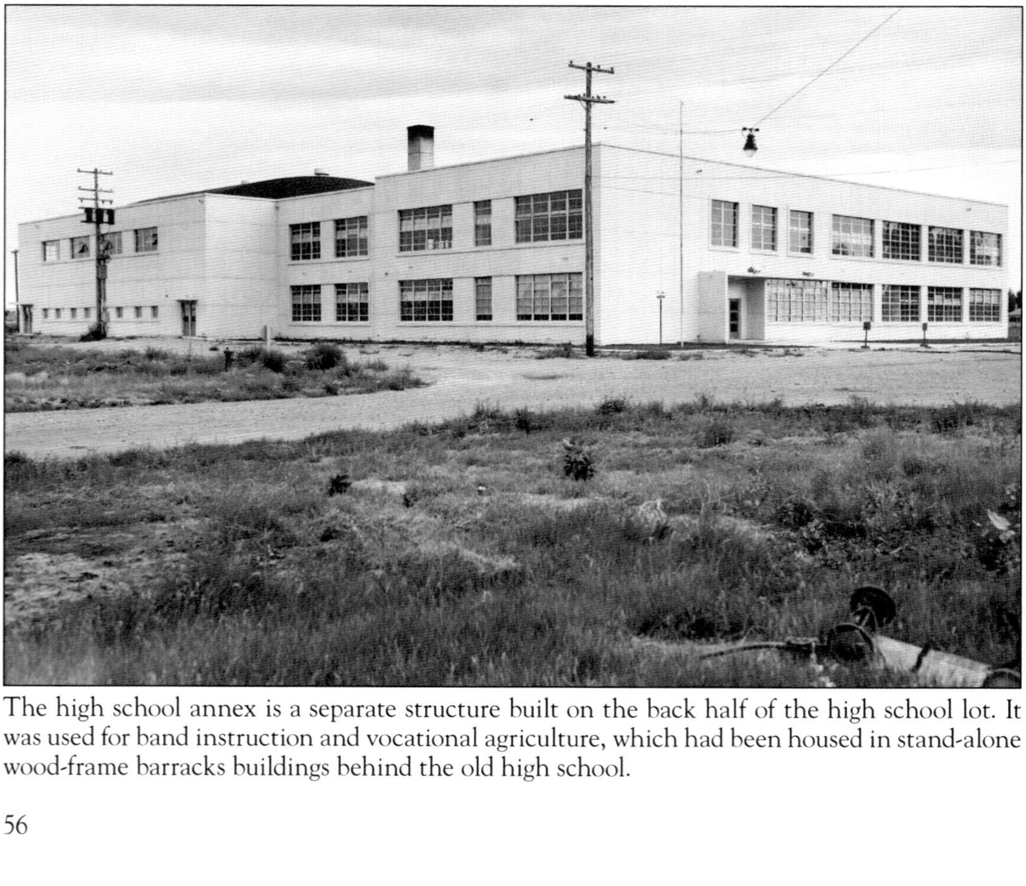

The high school annex is a separate structure built on the back half of the high school lot. It was used for band instruction and vocational agriculture, which had been housed in stand-alone wood-frame barracks buildings behind the old high school.

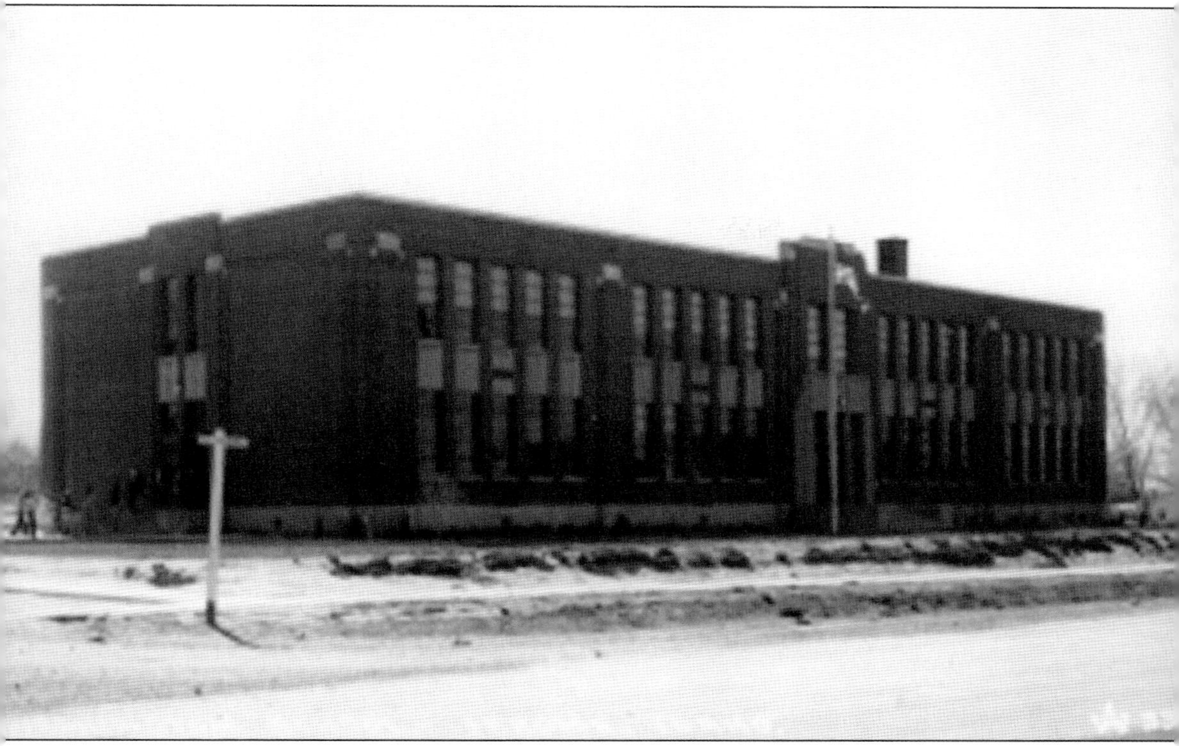

One grade school was not enough, so Washington School was built in 1937 on South Lincoln Avenue between East Avenue D and East Avenue E. The rest of the block behind the school and to the east was the playground. With two elementary schools in town, all students living south of Main Street attended Washington, while all students living north of Main Street attended Lincoln. Some country students were bused to town and divided between the two schools. In the 1990s, the building was determined unusable, but a Christian group purchased and remodeled it before offering classes again. In 2011, it became a charter school.

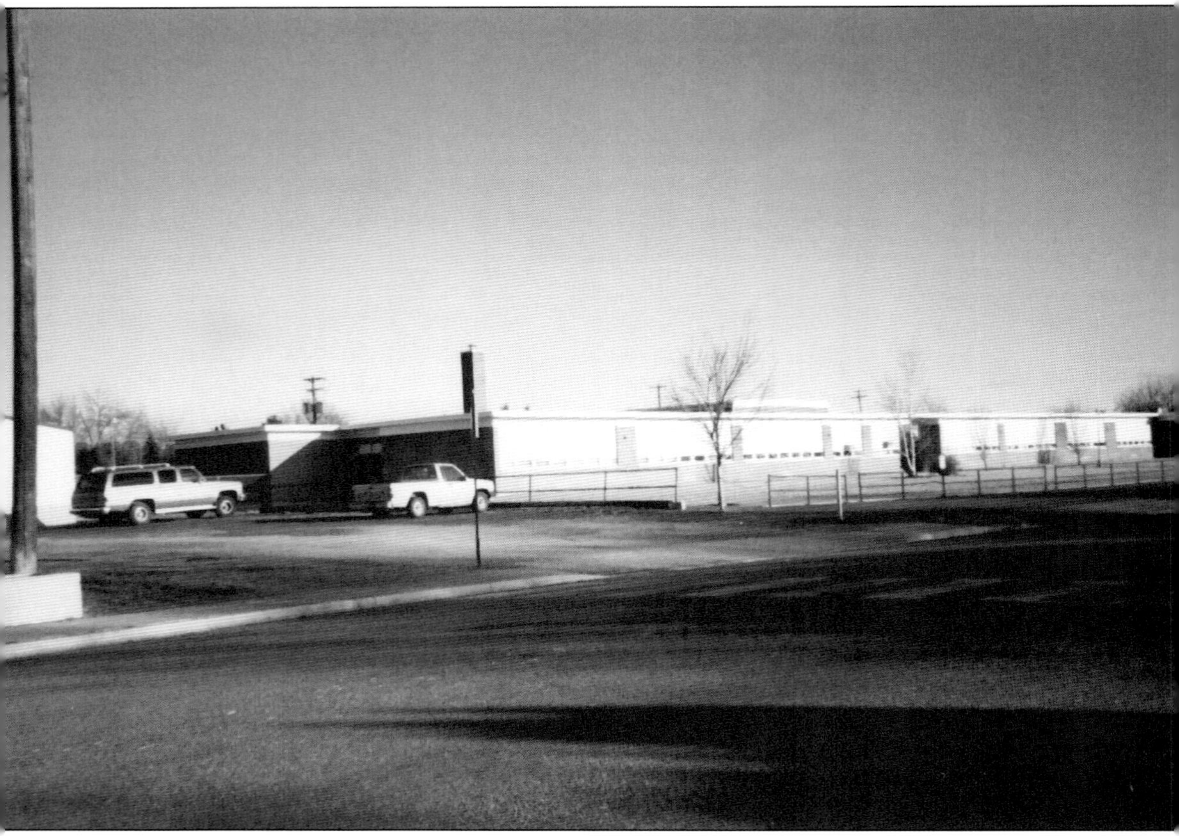

Jefferson Elementary School was erected in 1956 on North Fillmore Street between East Fourth and Fifth Avenues. Some schoolchildren from Lincoln and Washington Schools residing in the eastern part of town, north and south of Main Street, were switched to Jefferson, as well as some country children. In the beginning, there were two classrooms for each grade to seventh, as well as a principal's office and nurse's room. The T-shaped building has a large cafeteria with a stage situated in the leg. The restrooms had doors opening to the playground and the inside halls. (Author's collection.)

Three

The Early Religious Community

From the beginning of Jerome, religion was important to the residents, as demonstrated by services first held in homes and a board-sided tent. Several city lots were donated for churches in the beginning, which accounts for the placement of seven early churches near the park area, consisting of Episcopal, Presbyterian, Methodist, First Christian, First Baptist, Catholic, and Bible Baptist congregations. Many other early religions purchased lots within the city limits, including Seventh Day Adventist, Nazarene, Assembly of God, Church of Christ, Latter Day Saints (Mormon), Free Will Baptist, Church of God, Lutheran, and the Christian Science Society. Many other religions eventually founded churches in Jerome as well.

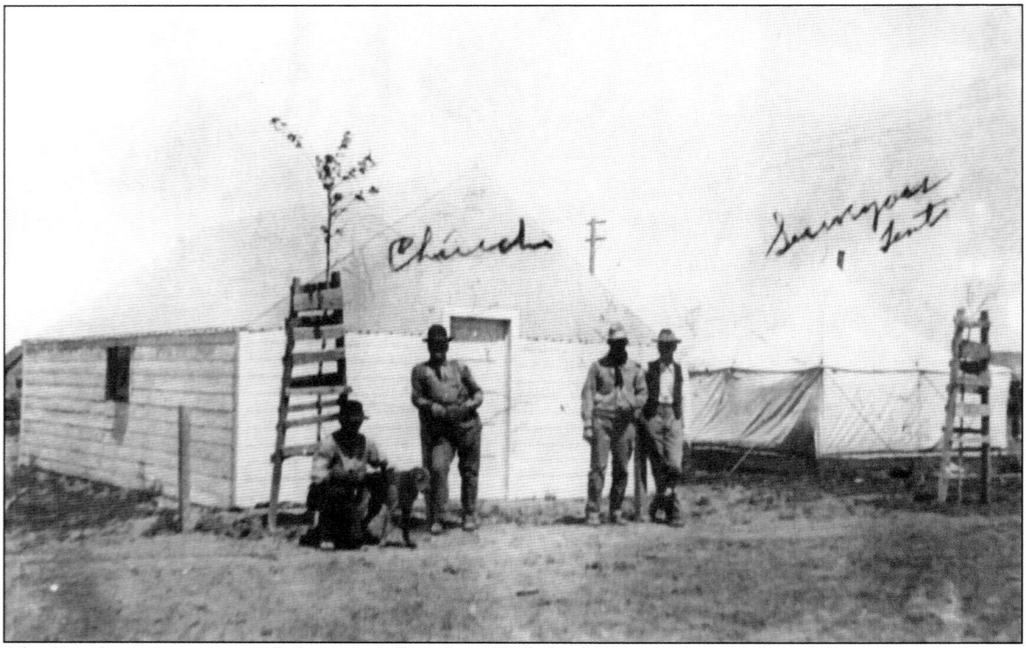

The Presbyterians erected this tent church called the Tabernacle in July 1908 in the northwest corner of the North Park. Other congregations used the tent for services until their own churches were built.

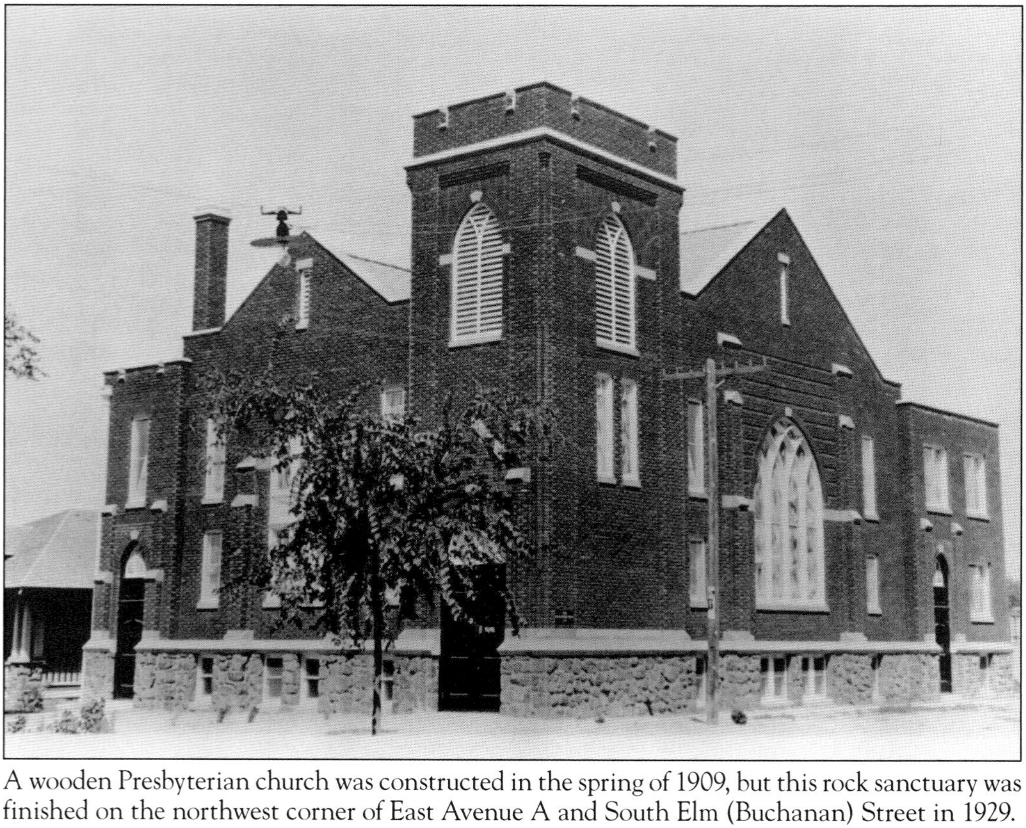

A wooden Presbyterian church was constructed in the spring of 1909, but this rock sanctuary was finished on the northwest corner of East Avenue A and South Elm (Buchanan) Street in 1929.

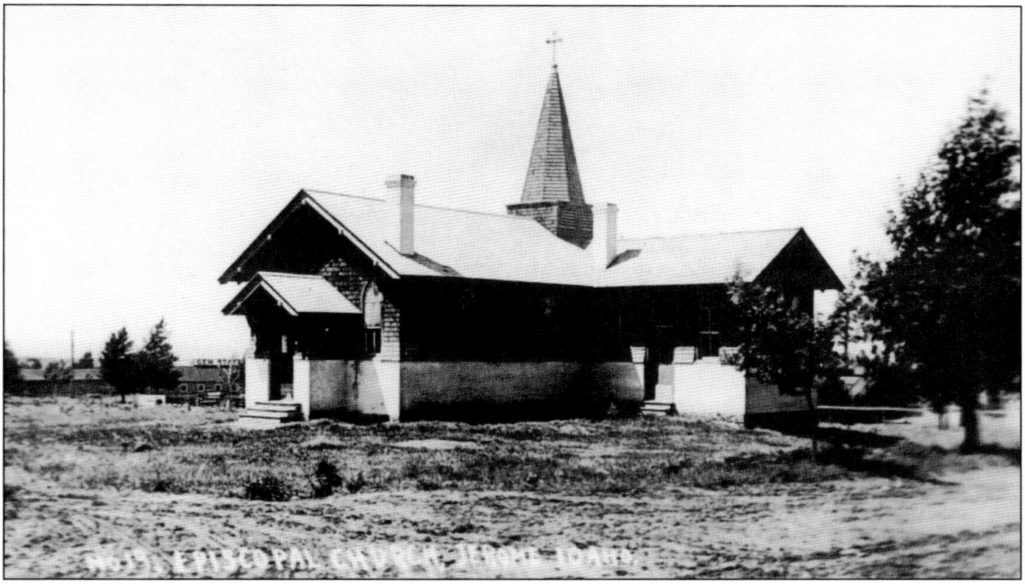

The Calvary Episcopal Church was actually the first house of worship built in Jerome. Constructed in 1909, it was situated on the southwest corner of East Avenue A and South Ash (Adams) Street. The church rented out the building for a few years to other religious bodies until they were able to build their own churches. This structure has a separate building added for use as a kitchen and dining room.

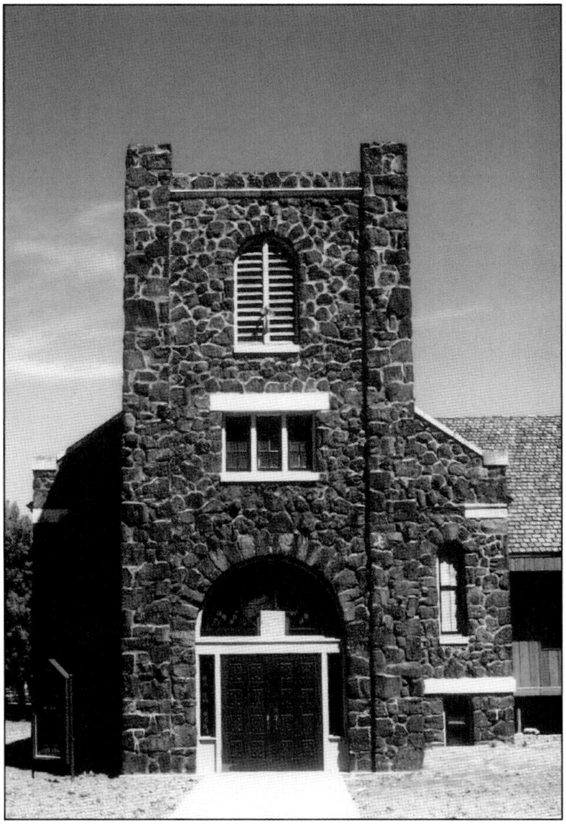

In 1909, the First Baptist congregation was sharing the Tabernacle tent. The American Baptist Home Mission Society brought in a chapel car, a railway coach outfitted to be a chapel. The townsite company gave the church a lot on the northeast corner of North Ash (Adams) Street and Second Avenue East. The sagebrush was cleared, and a small frame building was erected. In 1910, the Baptist congregation was asked to exchange this lot for one on the northeast corner of North Elm (Buchanan) Street and First Avenue East, and the first lot was used for the Catholic Church. This lava rock building was completed in 1931 by Welsh master mason Howell Trevor Pugh, who also built many other lava rock buildings in and near Jerome. (Courtesy Marian Wilson.)

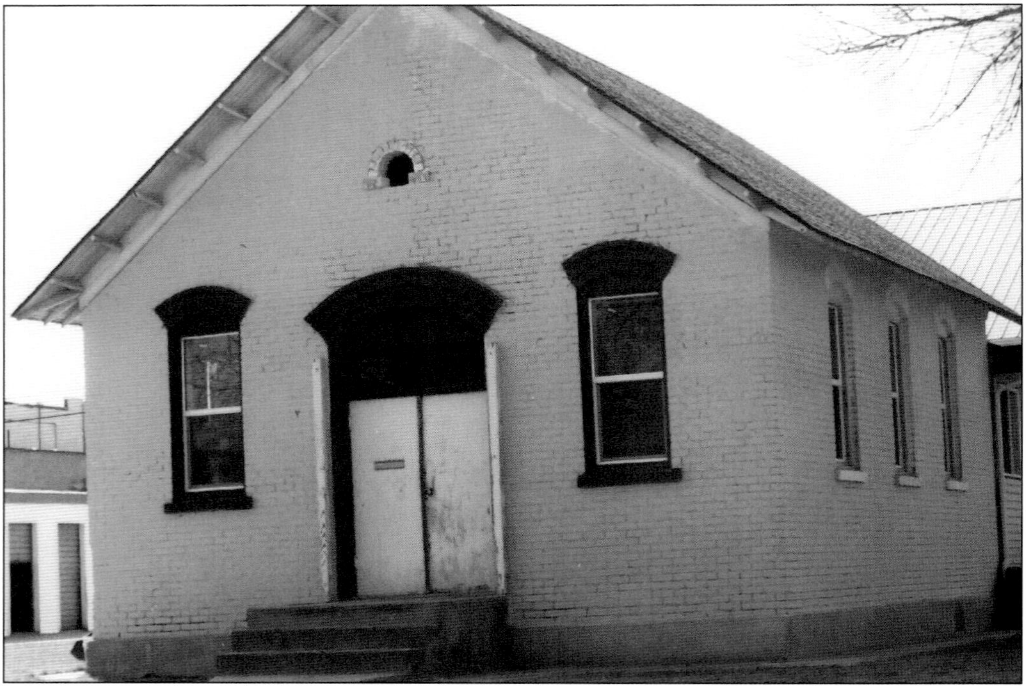

In 1909, four Mormon families met in homes for their religious services. In 1914, the Church of Jesus Christ of Latter Day Saints erected a small brick building on the southeast corner of First Avenue West and North Locust (Birch) Street.

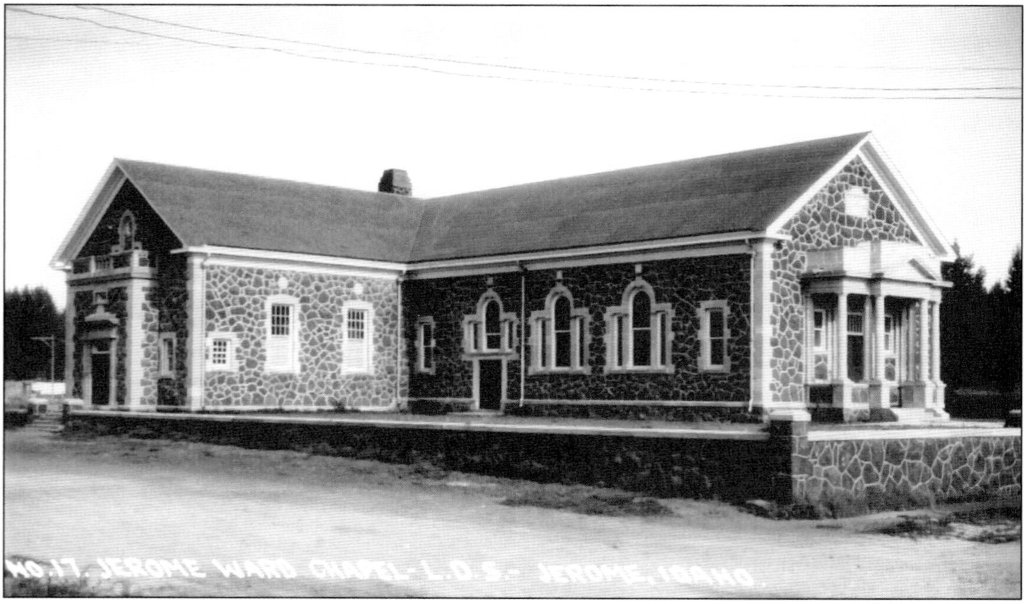

By 1922, over 200 Mormons had purchased a block of land on North Lincoln Avenue between Fourth Avenue East and Fifth Avenue East. This land was on a basalt rock pile, and it took almost seven years for a volunteer group to blast and move the rock to build the church. Also, a rock wall produced with the leftover rock acted as a barrier to Lincoln Avenue. In 2003, this church was determined inadequate, and it was demolished after three other Mormon church buildings had been erected in different areas of town. The rock wall has remained.

Four

FAMILY LIFE AND SOCIALIZATION

Life in Jerome was not all work. Organizations and clubs formed, and recreational activities abounded, such as playing basketball and swimming. Much like today, residents participated in parades, watched movies at the theater, gathered for lunch at the many fine restaurants, joined the art guild, read books at the library, picnicked, visited with neighbors, and took part in other activities.

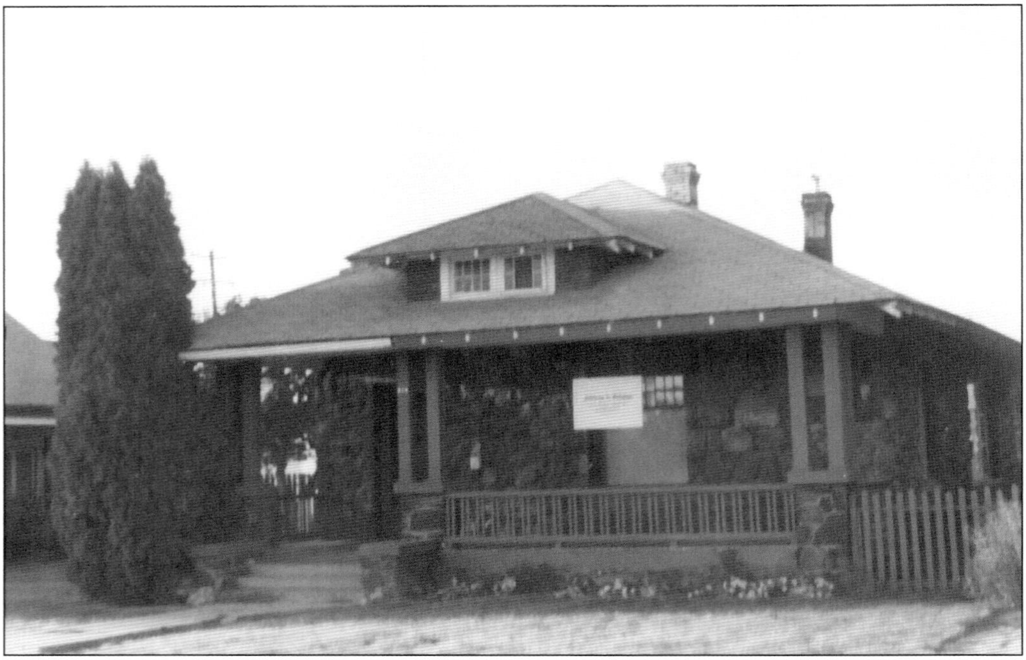

The first lava rock building constructed with the city limits was the Schmerschall House on East Avenue A (next to the Presbyterian church). It was constructed by master rock mason H.T. Pugh in 1917 for Dr. John F. Schmerschall, one of the first physicians in Jerome. The structure was once used as J.R. Wiley's funeral home.

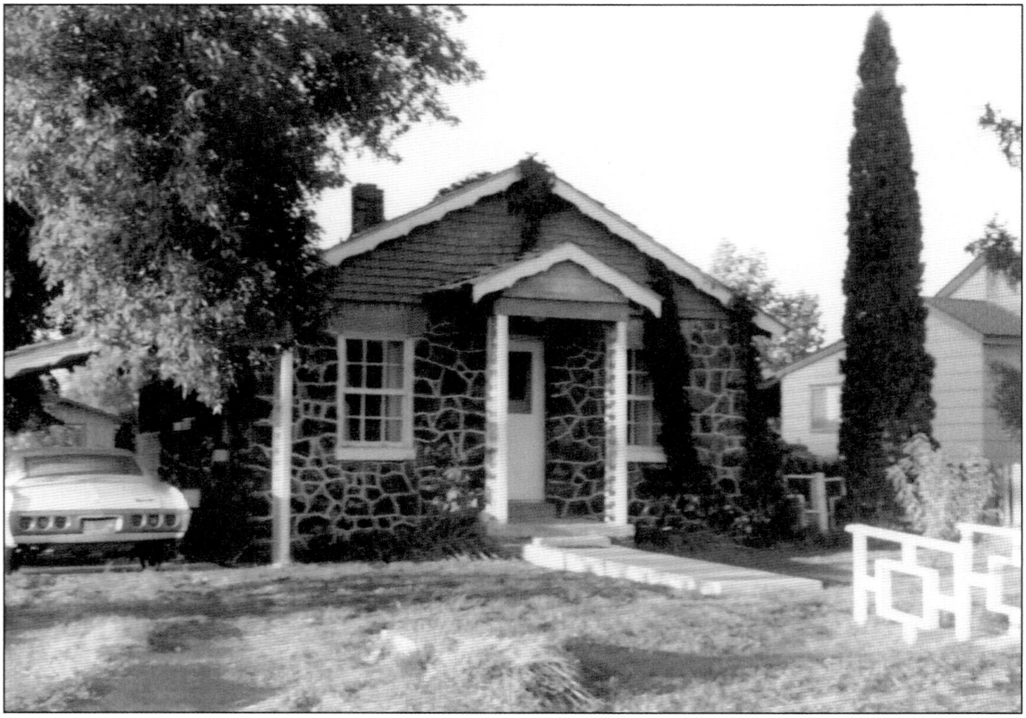

This lava rock home, known as the Tillman Home, was also built by H.T. Pugh in the 1930s and is located on the site of an early apple orchard in the 200 block of Seventh Avenue West.

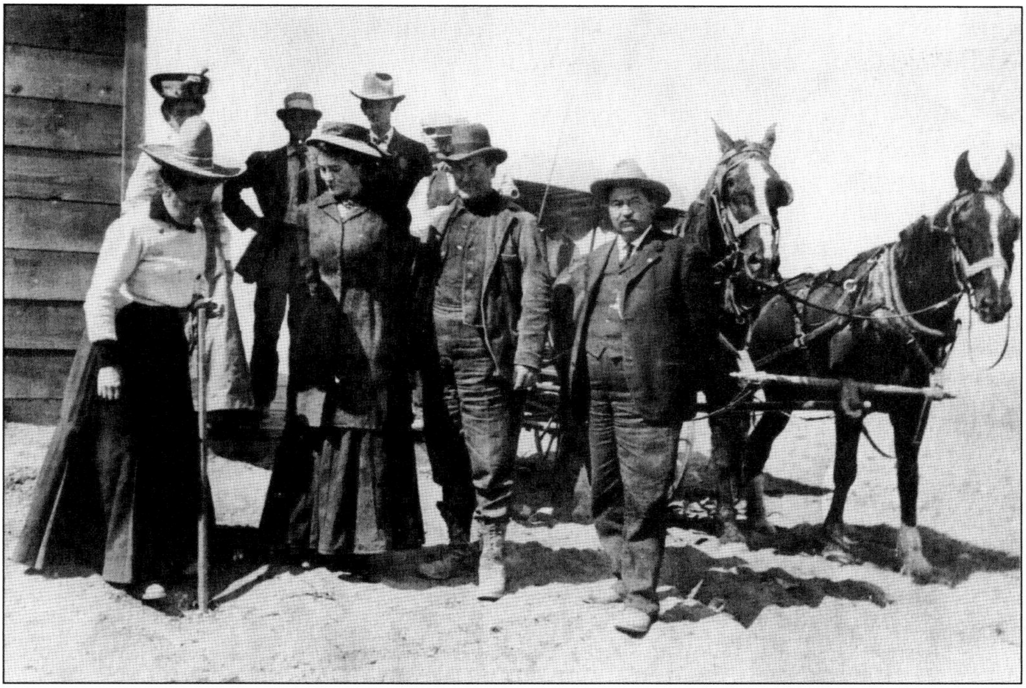

A frequent visitor to young Jerome was the 1908 Democratic nominee for US president and later secretary of state to President Wilson, William Jennings Bryan. He purchased 40 acres in the southwest area of Jerome in 1909. Part of his land includes the Jerome Cemetery. From left to right are (first row) William's daughter Ruth Bryan, wife Mary Bryan, William Jennings Bryan, and Bob McCollum; (second row) Hortense Perrine (wife of Ira B. Perrine) and three unidentified. This photograph was taken in front of the Jerome Lodging House in September 1912.

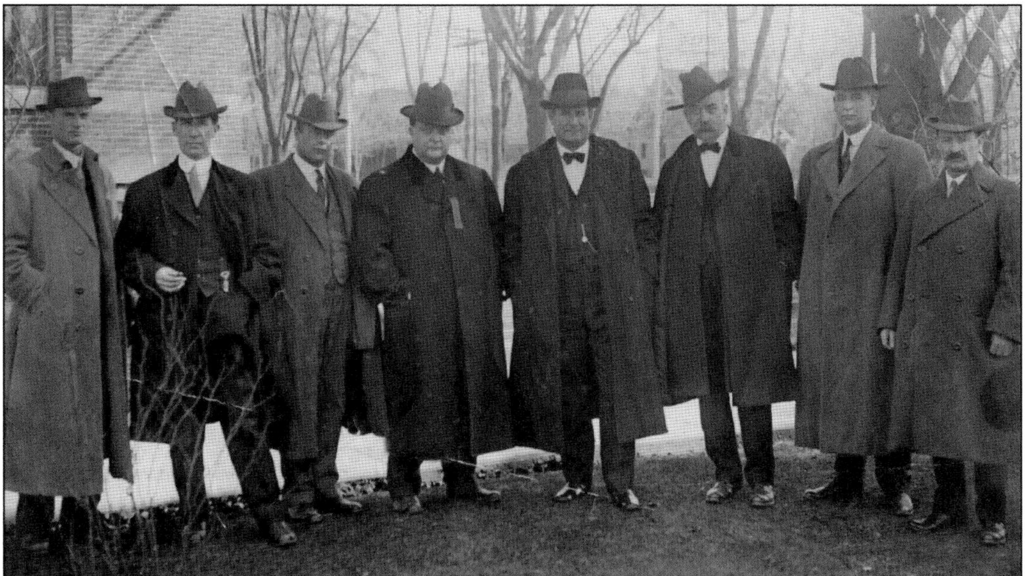

Besides William Jennings Bryan (fifth from left), another frequent visitor to the area was James H. Hawley (sixth from left), who was governor of Idaho from 1911 to 1913. Ira B. Perrine is on the far right; the other men are not identified.

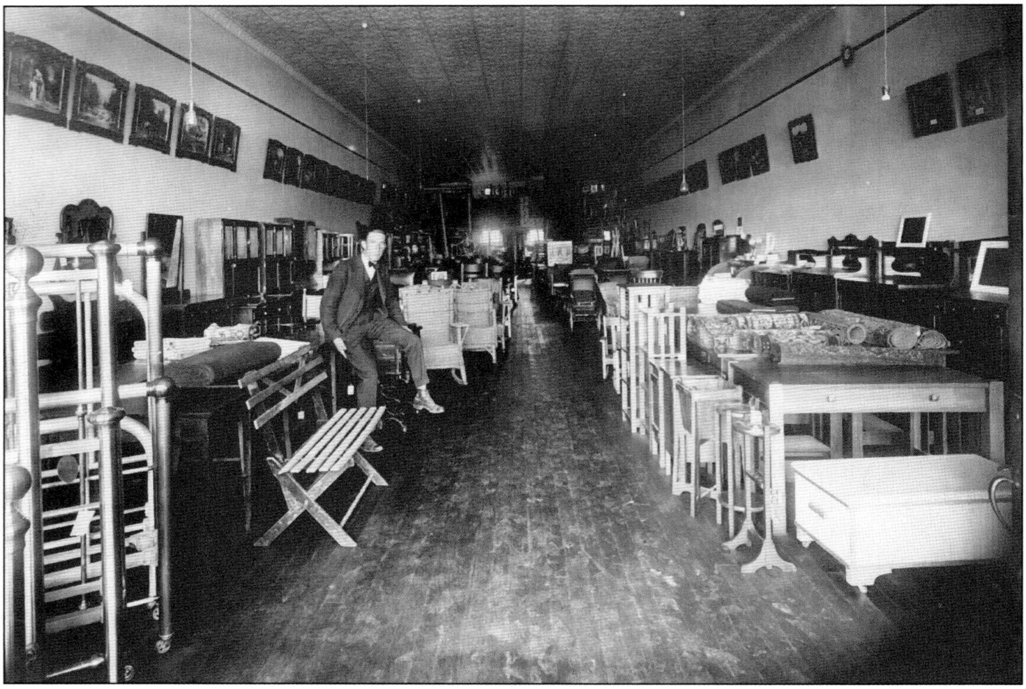

David L'Herisson's furniture store offered the best products a modern home would need when it opened in early 1908. Sam L'Herisson is pictured in this 1915 image. L'Herisson's Fine Furniture remained in business until the mid-1980s.

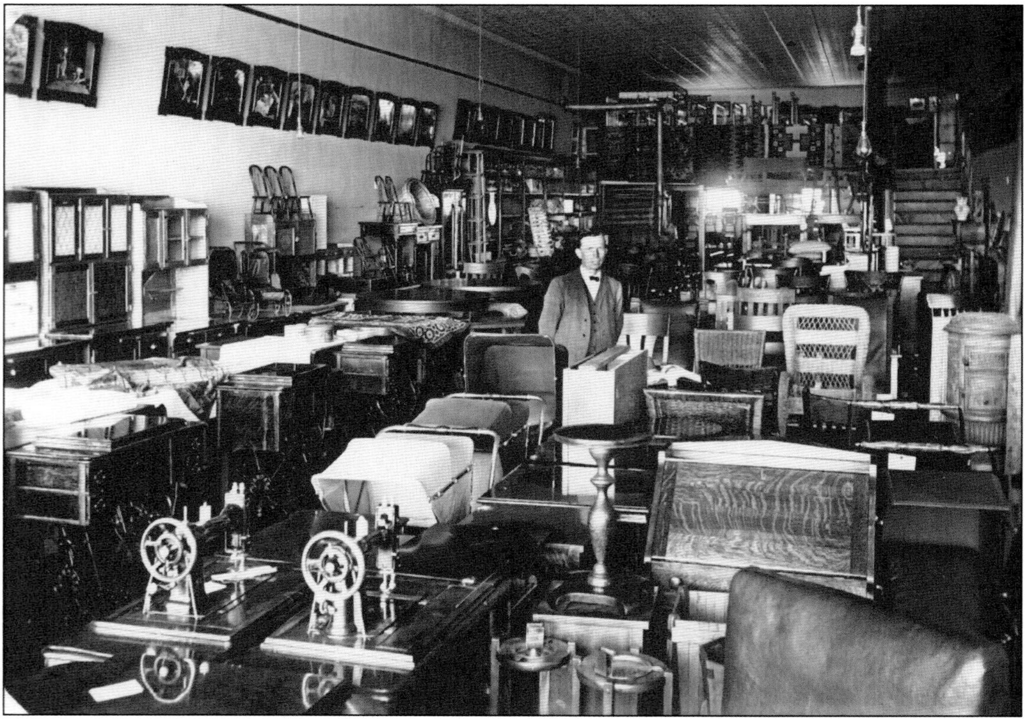

L'Herisson's Furniture added more products for sale. This photograph was taken in 1920. The salesman's name is unknown.

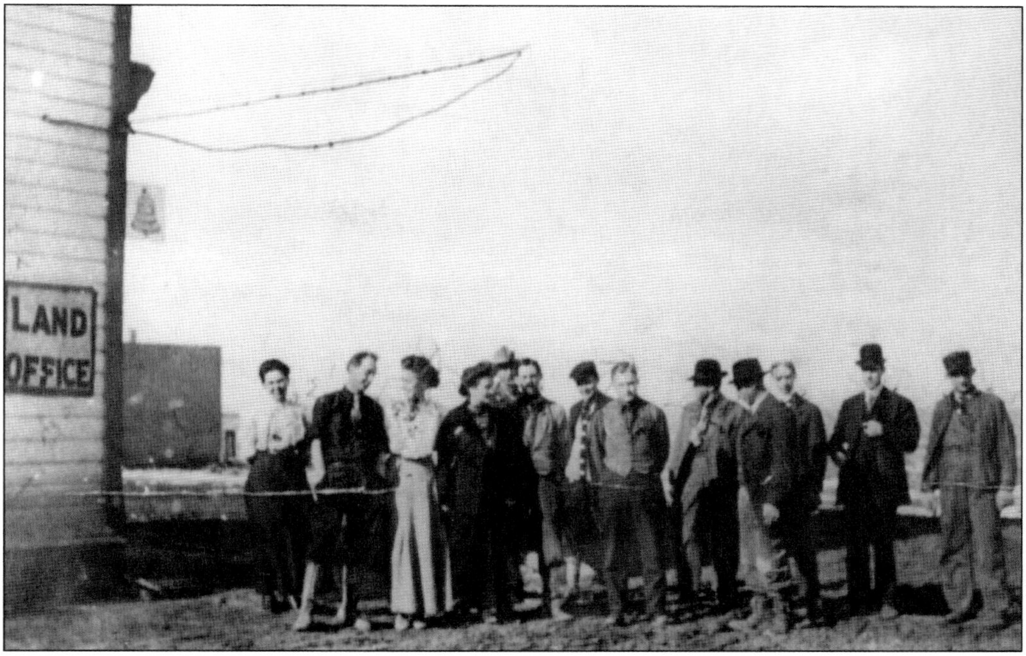

The land office crew is pictured here in 1908. The land office was on the southeast corner of Main and Ash (Adams) Streets. They are identified from left to right as Bill Wilson, Joe Bouton, Evelyn Covell, Louise Knuckey, ? McCormick, C.T. Carter, Wilson Bridges, Roy Sweitzer, Rex Hammond, ? Hovey, Harvey Hurlebaus, E.M. Churchman, and Joe Krivanek.

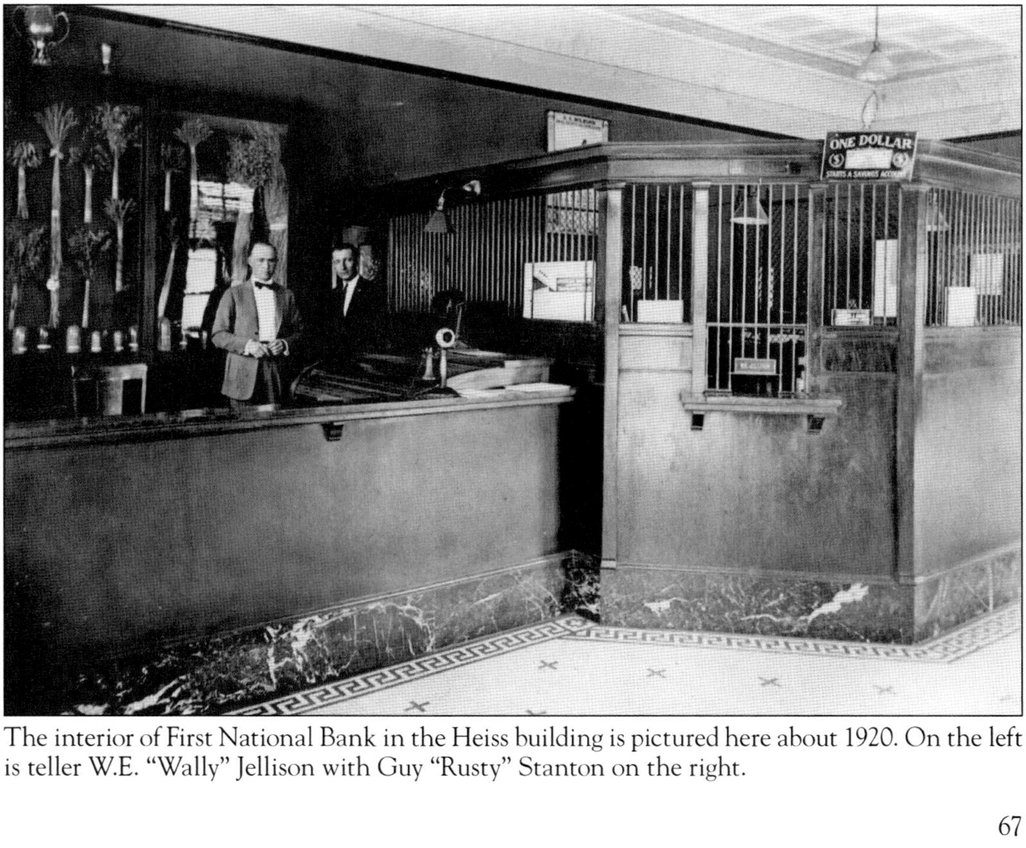

The interior of First National Bank in the Heiss building is pictured here about 1920. On the left is teller W.E. "Wally" Jellison with Guy "Rusty" Stanton on the right.

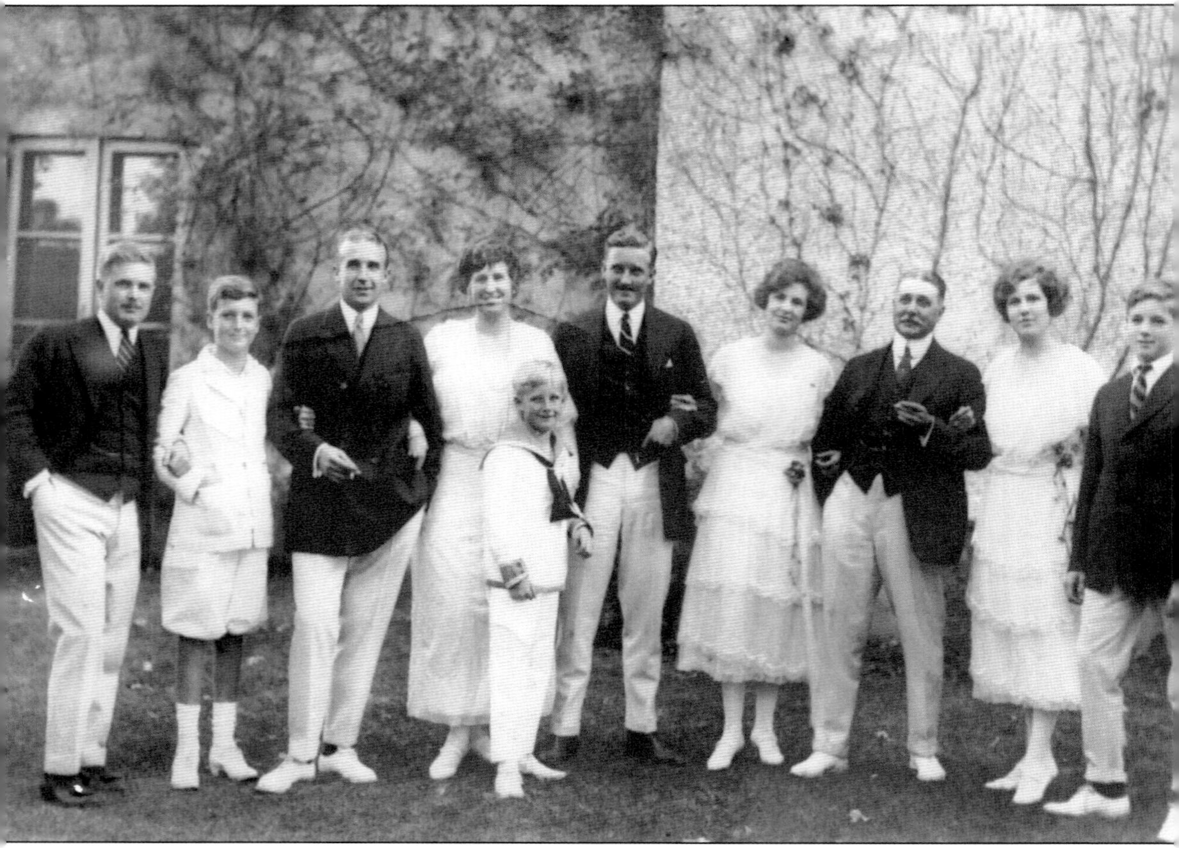

This photograph of the William S. Kuhn family was taken in 1921. From left to right are Jerome Hill Kuhn, Fentress Hill Kuhn, Wendel Speer Kuhn, Kate Hill Kuhn, John Lucien Kuhn, James Speer Kuhn, Mary "Dolly" Speer Kuhn, William Speer Kuhn, Katherine Hill Kuhn, and William Speer Kuhn Jr.

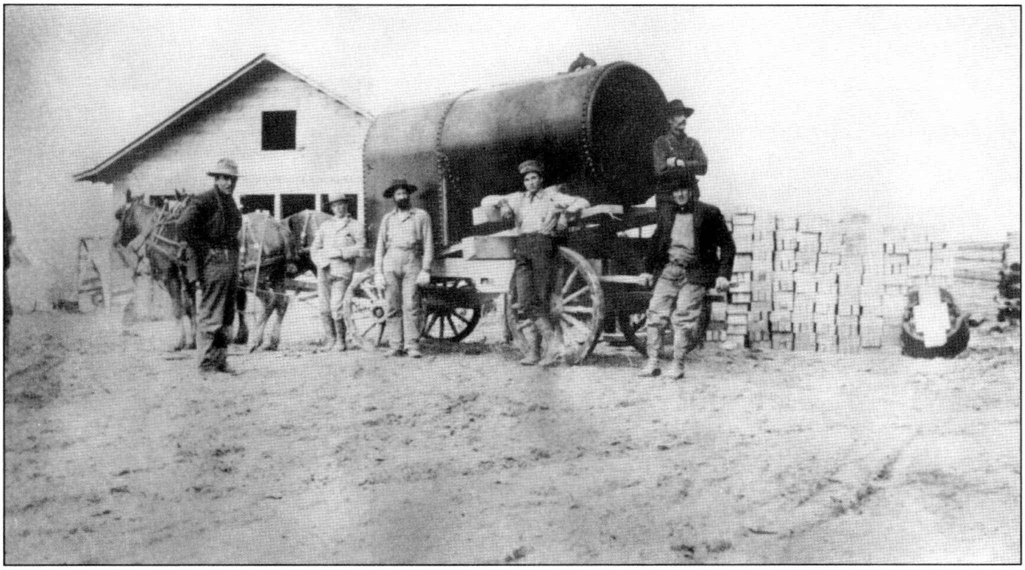

These unidentified men prepare to install North Side Inn's boiler.

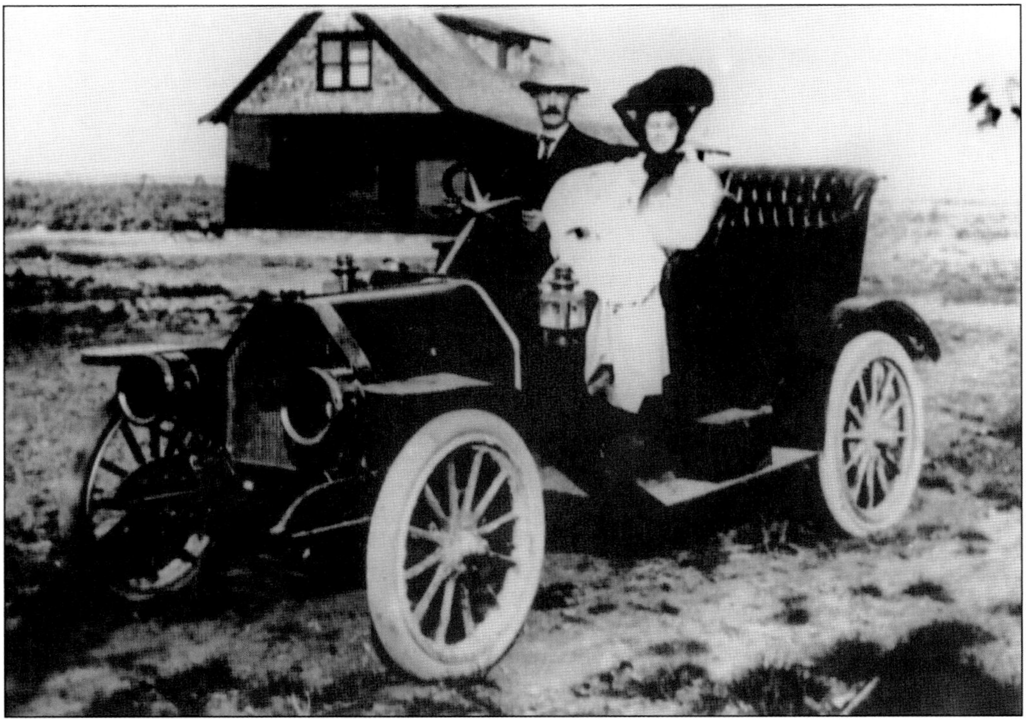

Pictured here in front of their home, Paul and Jane Kartzke sit in one of the first cars in town.

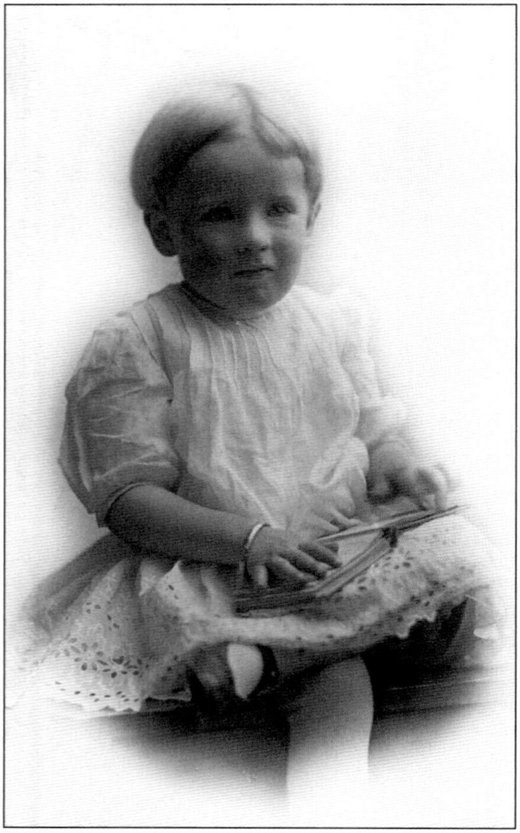

This little girl is Virginia Kartzke, the daughter of Paul and Jane Kartzke.

A crowd in front of Jerome Mercantile Company waits for the stagecoach to bring the mail in 1907.

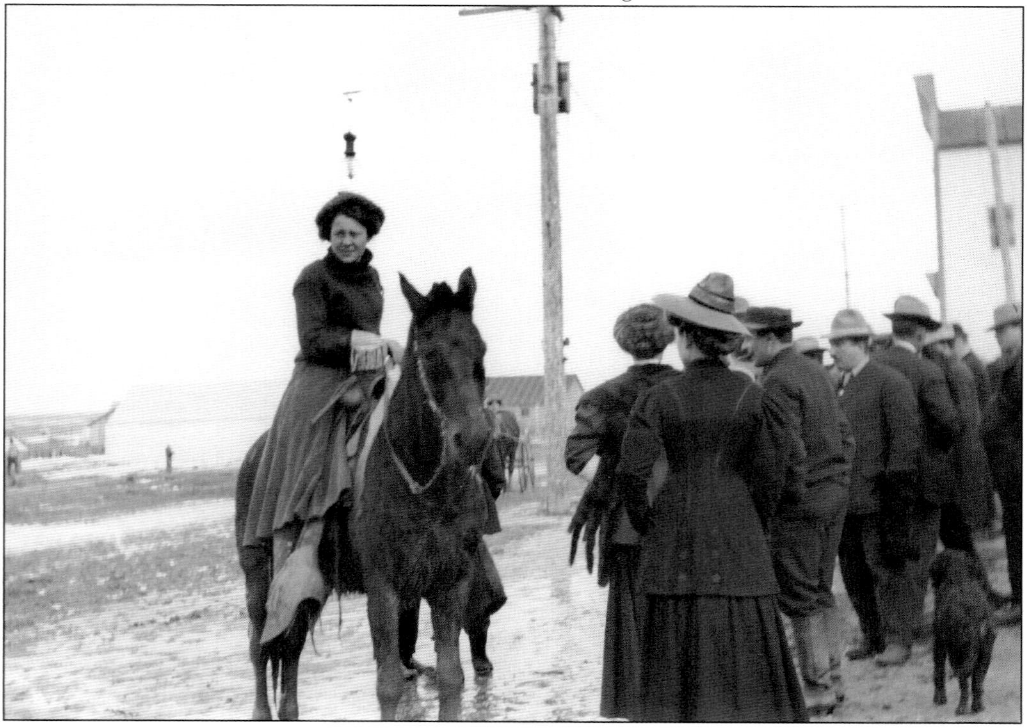

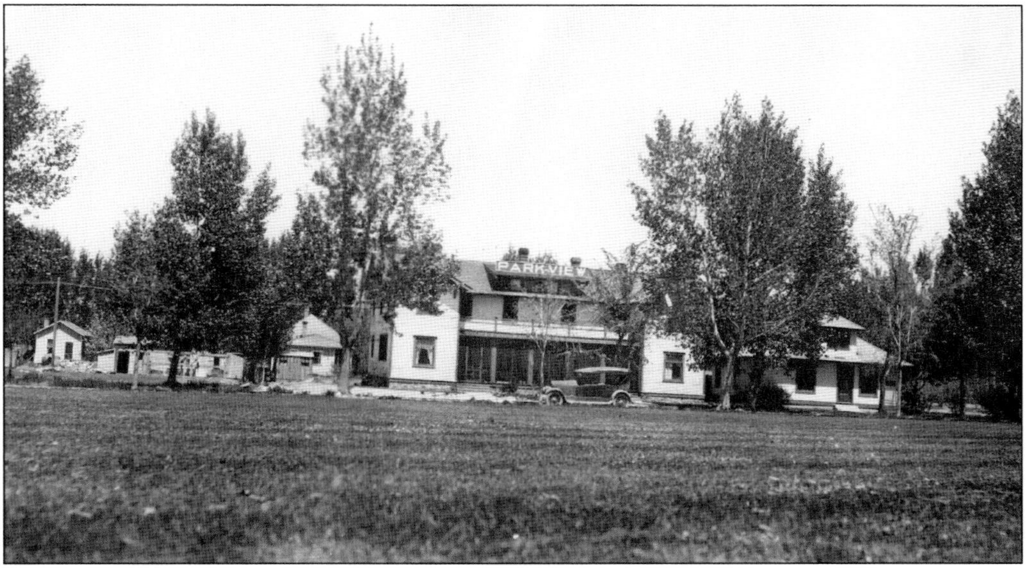

The Parkview Apartments on First Avenue East are appropriately named, as they face North Park.

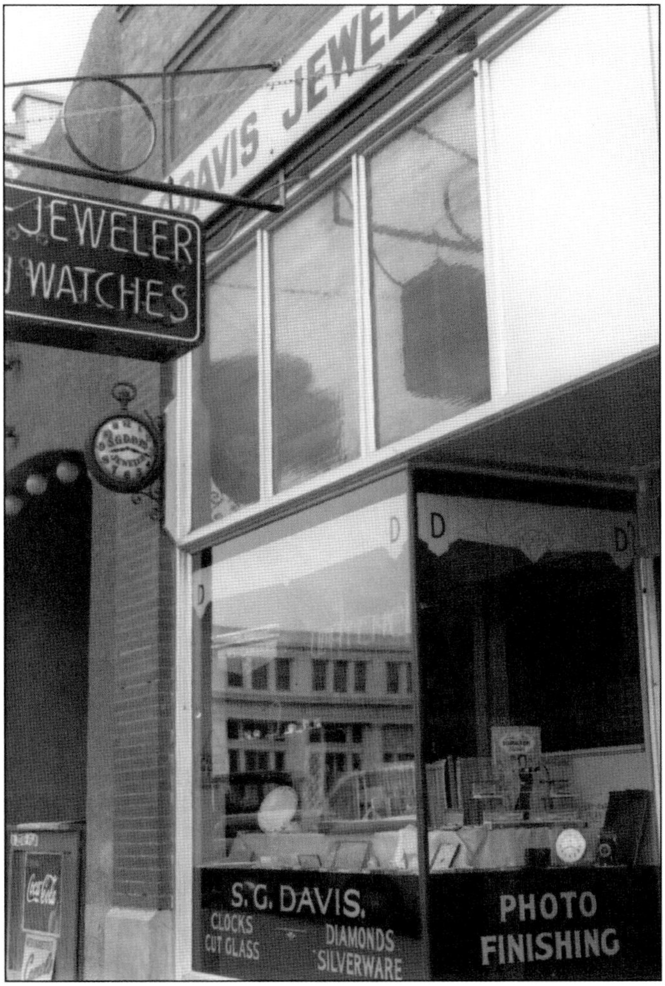

S.G. Davis opened Davis Jewelry in 1923 in the middle of the south side of Main Street, west of Lincoln Avenue and just east of Maple (Alder) Street. Davis's son Rex eventually took over the business, which ran for over 60 years.

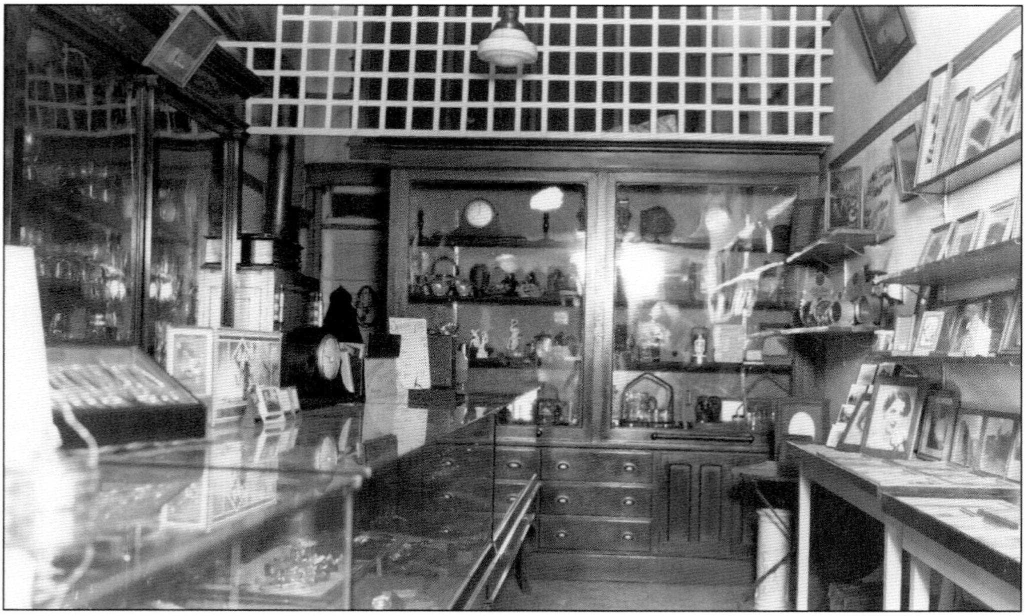

The inside of Davis Jewelry included fine items such as jewelry, clocks, china, and glassware. Many high school seniors purchased their class rings and class keys, a pendant with a Jerome medallion, here.

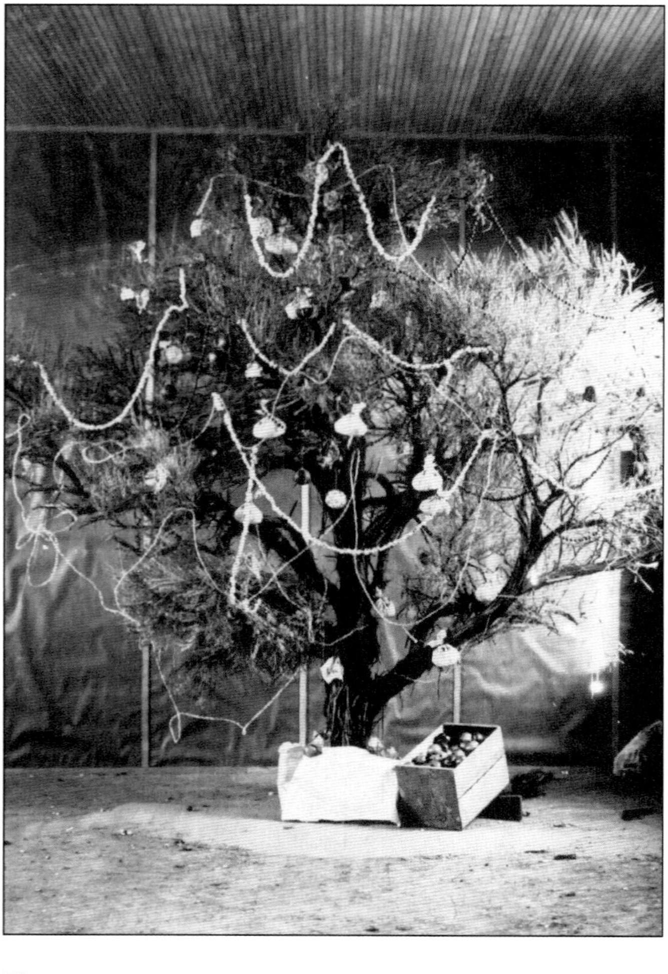

Since there were no trees in this section of the desert, many Jerome residents used sagebrush as a Christmas tree, decorating it with popcorn and dried cranberries on strings, cloth bags filled with nuts, oranges or apples, and homemade candies or some type of trinkets. Sagebrush plants grew to five feet in some areas, but most were around three feet high.

The area's first high school girls' basketball team in 1911 featured, from left to right, (first row) Dorothia Martin, Alta Graham, and Helen Robb; (second row) Griselda Martin, Coach Hughell, and Grace Lind.

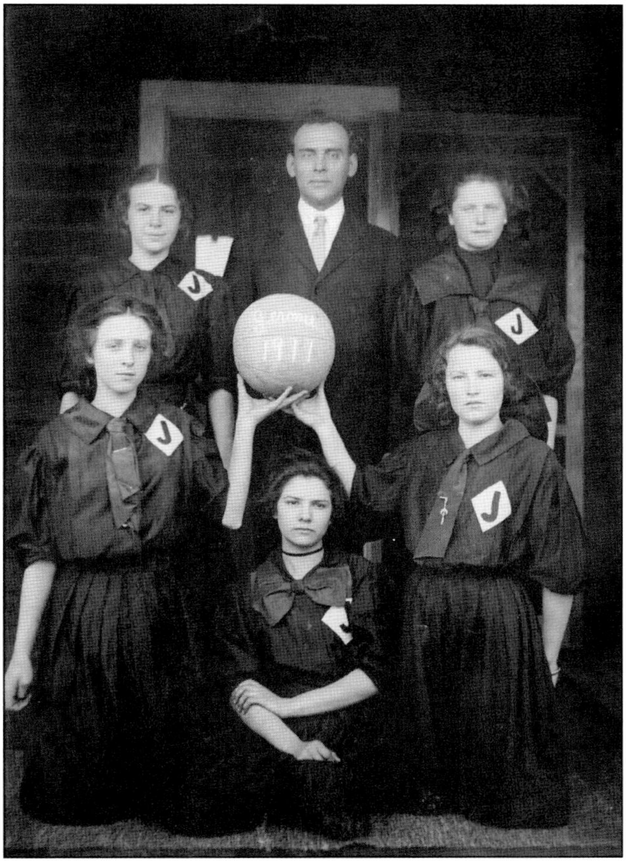

This sophomore class enjoys a picnic on the Snake River north rim above Shoshone Falls at the site of Charles S. Walgamott's Hotel in 1913.

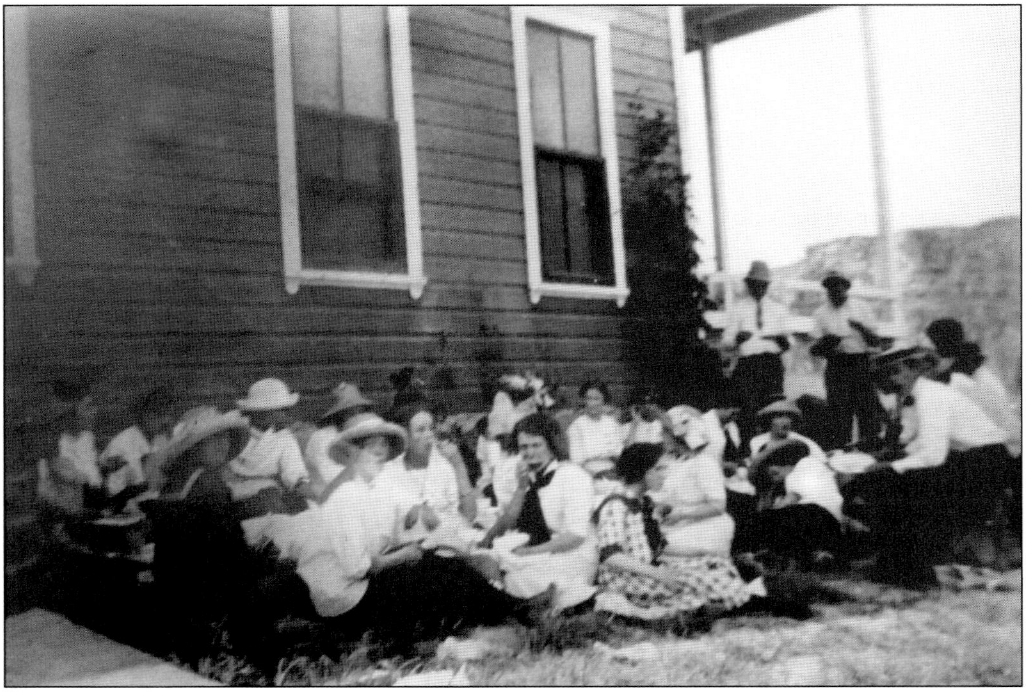

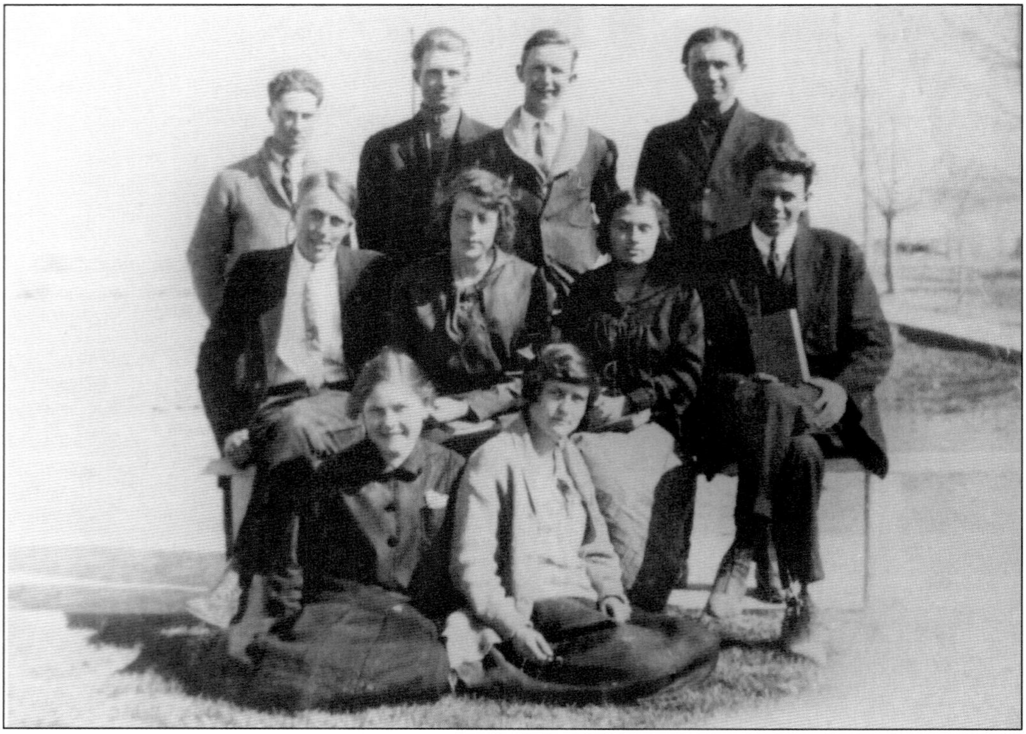

This 1917 high school senior class consisted of, from left to right, (first row, on ground) Johanna Arps and Alma Walker; (second row, seated) Carl Kleinau, Ruth Jordan, Alice Pifer, and Homer Robertson; (third row, standing) Addison McCorkle, Dale Atwood, Bryan Henry, and Buena Roberts.

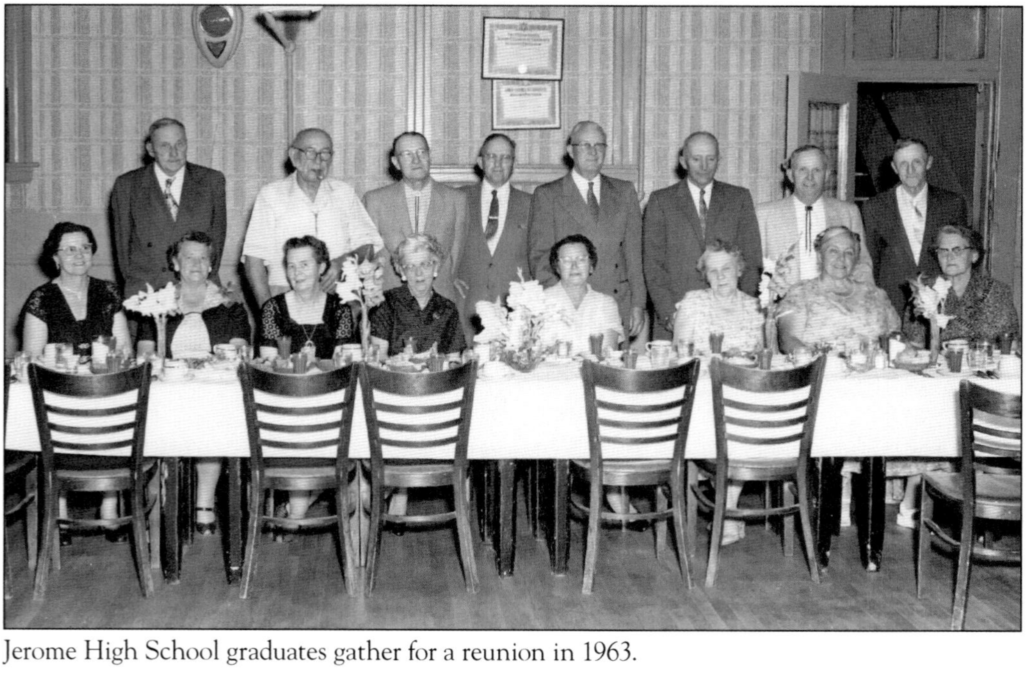

Jerome High School graduates gather for a reunion in 1963.

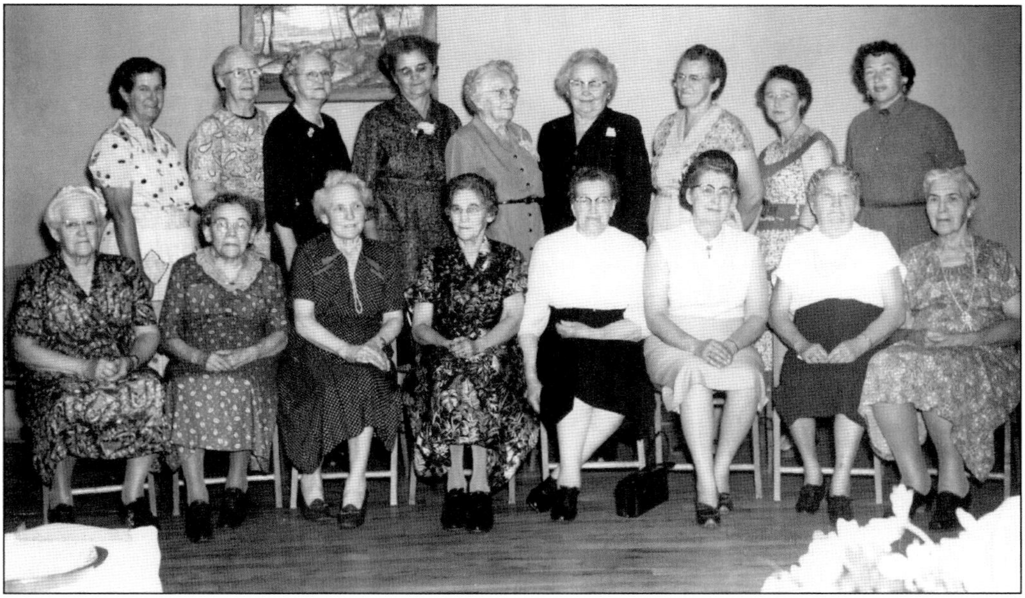

The first ladies of Jerome are pictured here in 1957. The Pioneer Ladies Group was established in 1912; to be a member, a lady had to be "a resident before the water was turned into the canals," also known as April 1, 1909. Fifty-seven ladies attended the first meeting, but thirty-eight more eligible ladies were unable to attend. Member Lula Graves pulled names out of an old milk churn on September 30, 1907, for the drawing for town lots. The only person named in this 1957 photograph is Mary Speakman (first row, second from left).

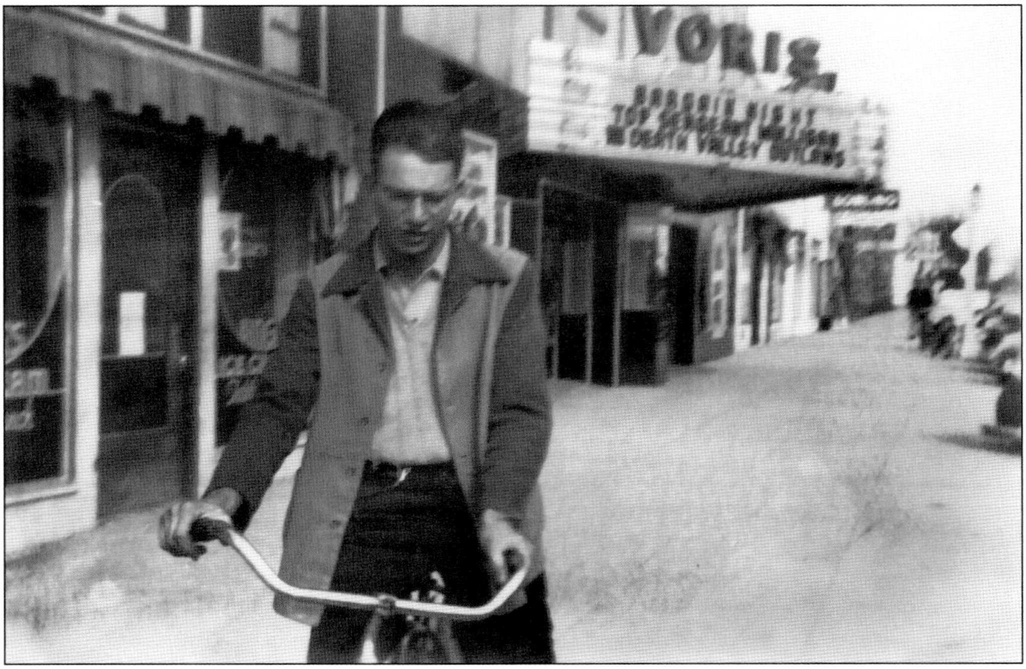

Mr. Atwater rides his bicycle in 1941, perhaps after seeing a movie at the Voris Theatre.

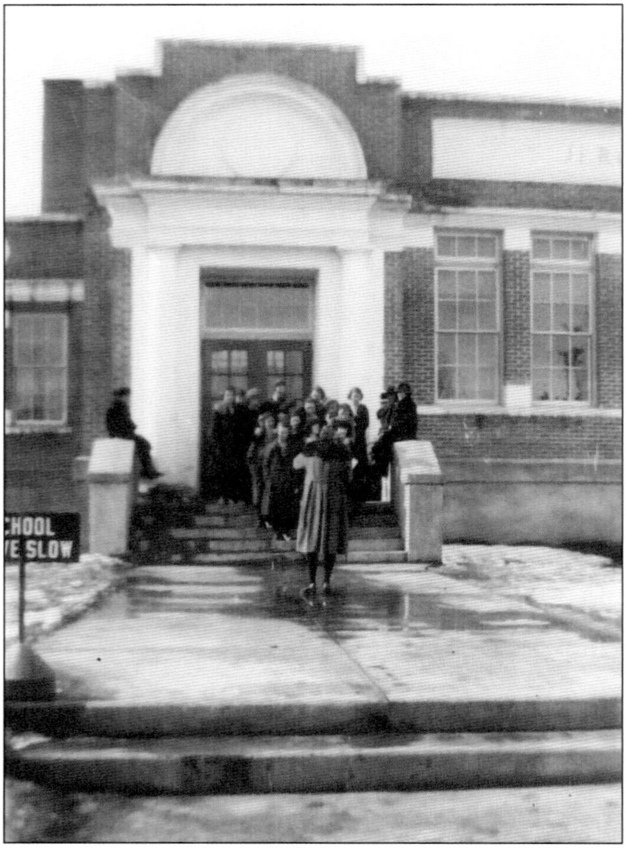

These students were photographed at Jerome High School in 1920.

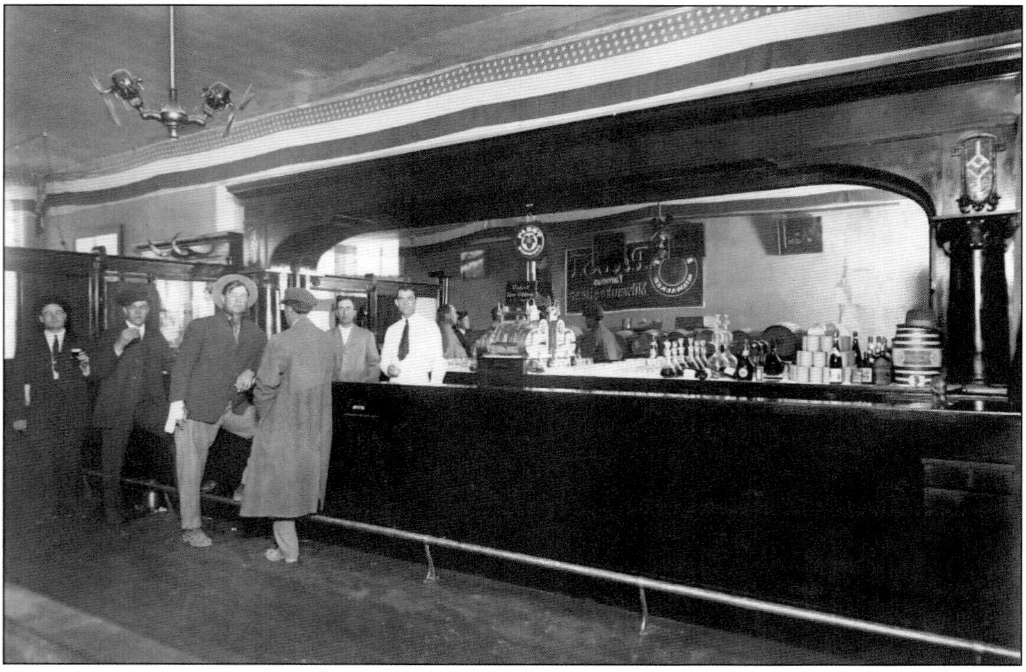

Several men enjoy a beer inside the Gem Buffet and Family Liquor Store.

These men partake in a quick beer break behind the bar.

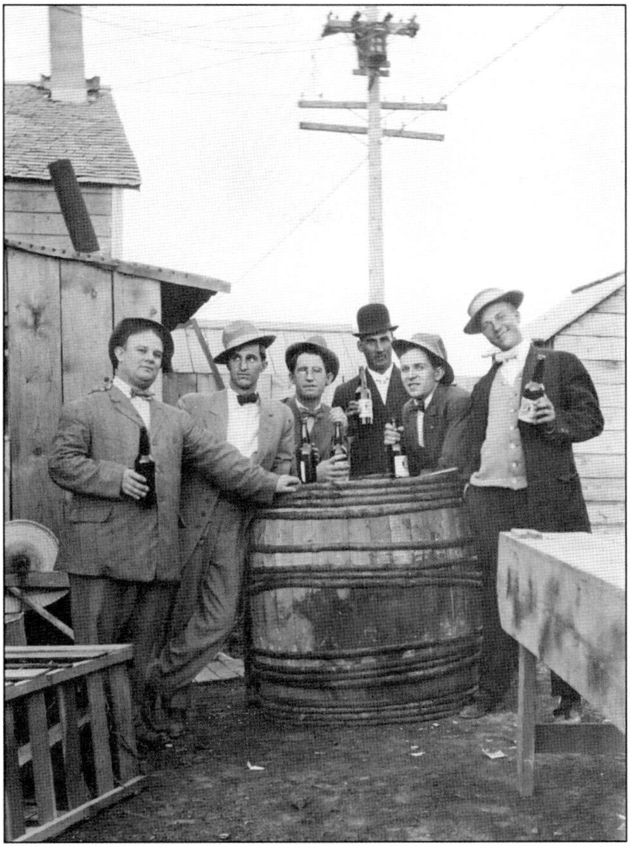

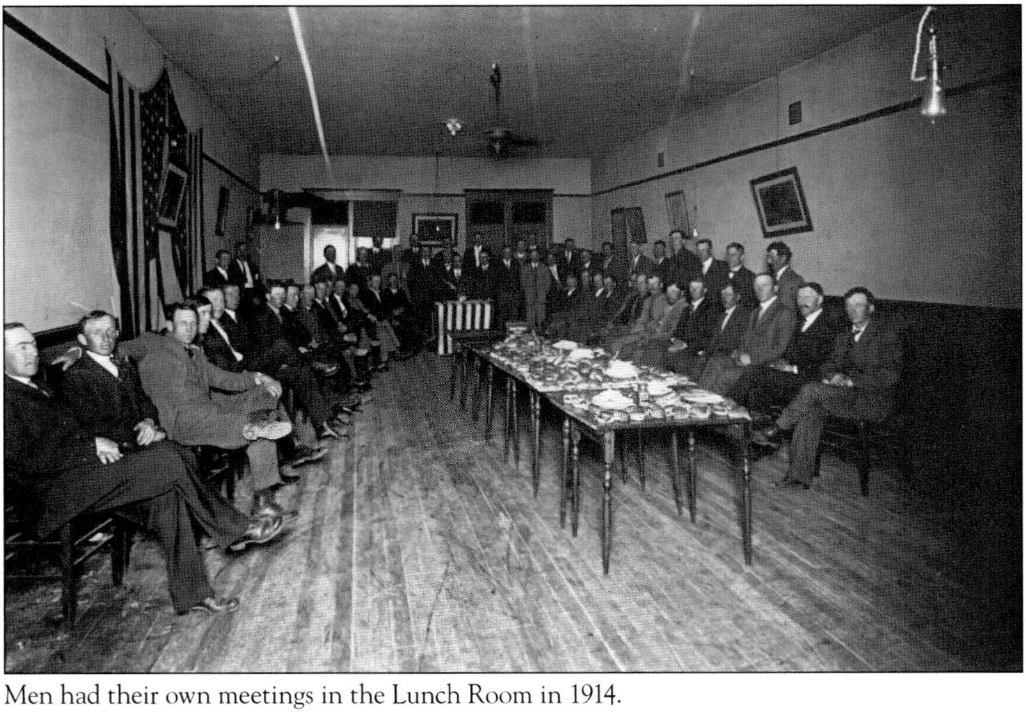

Men had their own meetings in the Lunch Room in 1914.

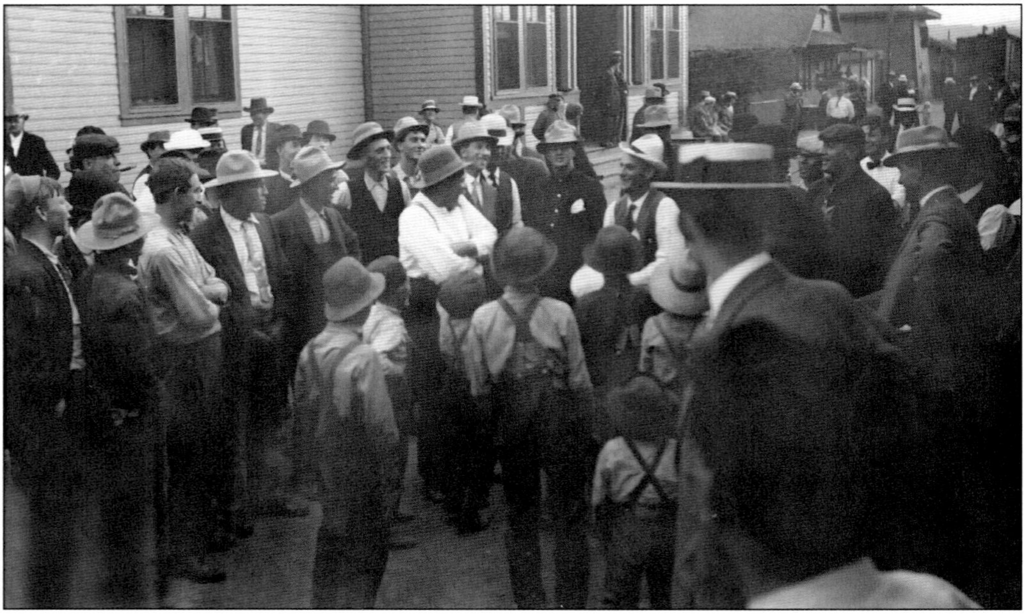

These local men and boys catch up with each other while the local women shop and socialize in the 1920s.

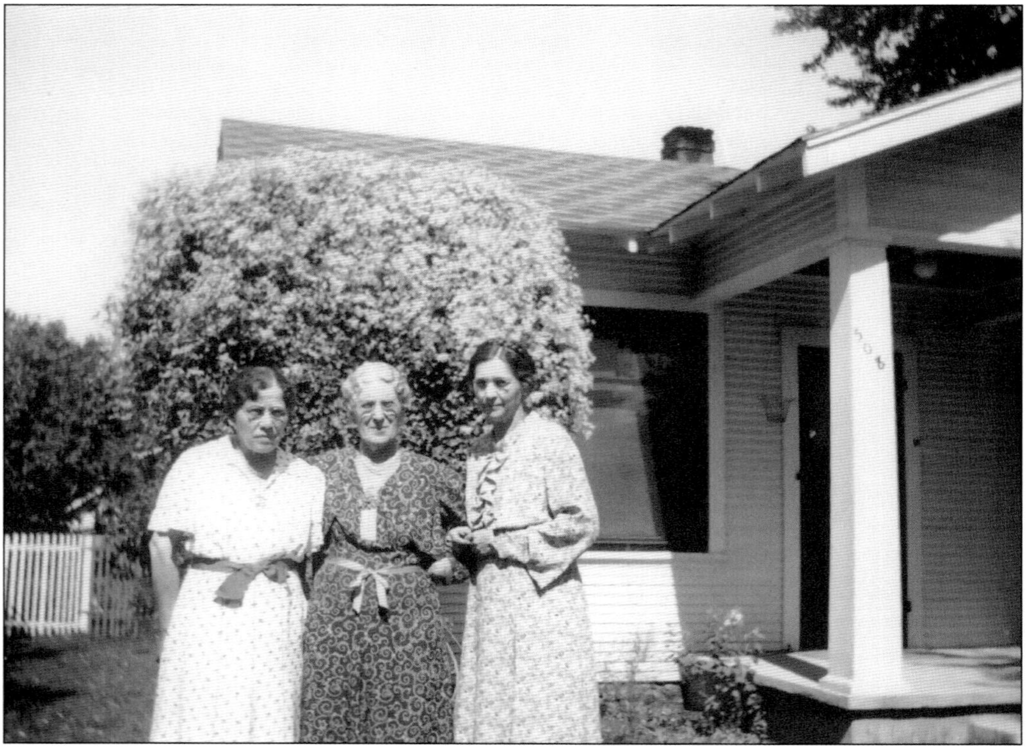

From left to right, locals Mary Speakman, Mrs. Stevens, and Bertha Fairman are seen here in 1939.

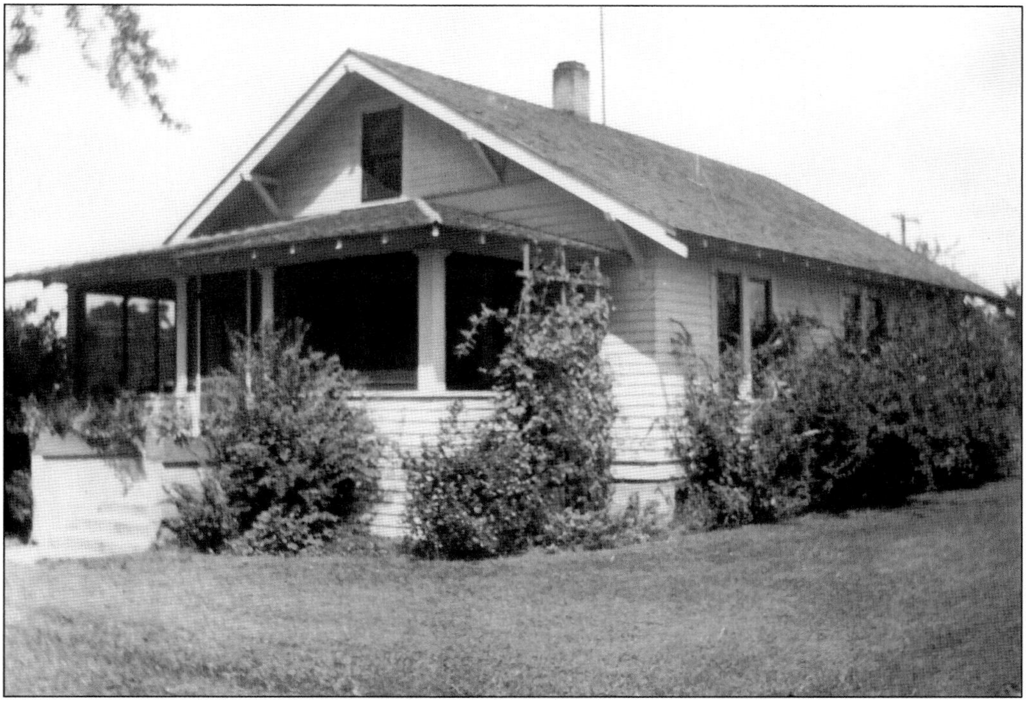

Bertha Fairman's home, pictured here in 1939, was located at 508 East Avenue A.

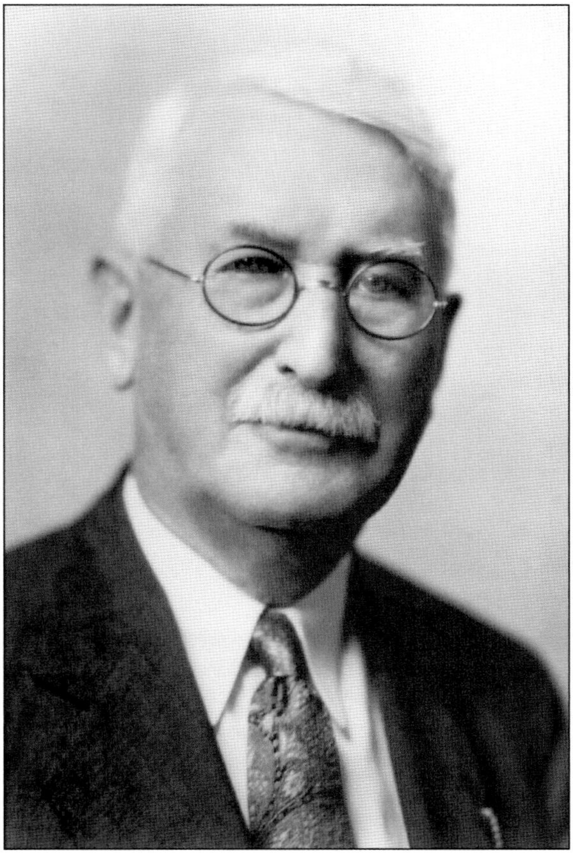

In 1913, Russell E. Shepherd worked on getting financing for the irrigation system, as well as for the Jackson Lake, American Falls, Milner Dam, and the Jerome Reservoirs. He and his wife, Nellie, lived on North Lincoln Avenue and donated their land to build St. Benedict's Hospital, at which point they built a new home on Seventh Avenue West across from the hospital. Shepherd also donated two blocks between First Avenue East and Second Avenue East, stretching from North Lincoln Avenue to North Elm (Buchanan) Street to the city. These blocks are now home to the town's library, post office, museum, tennis courts, playground, and National Guard office.

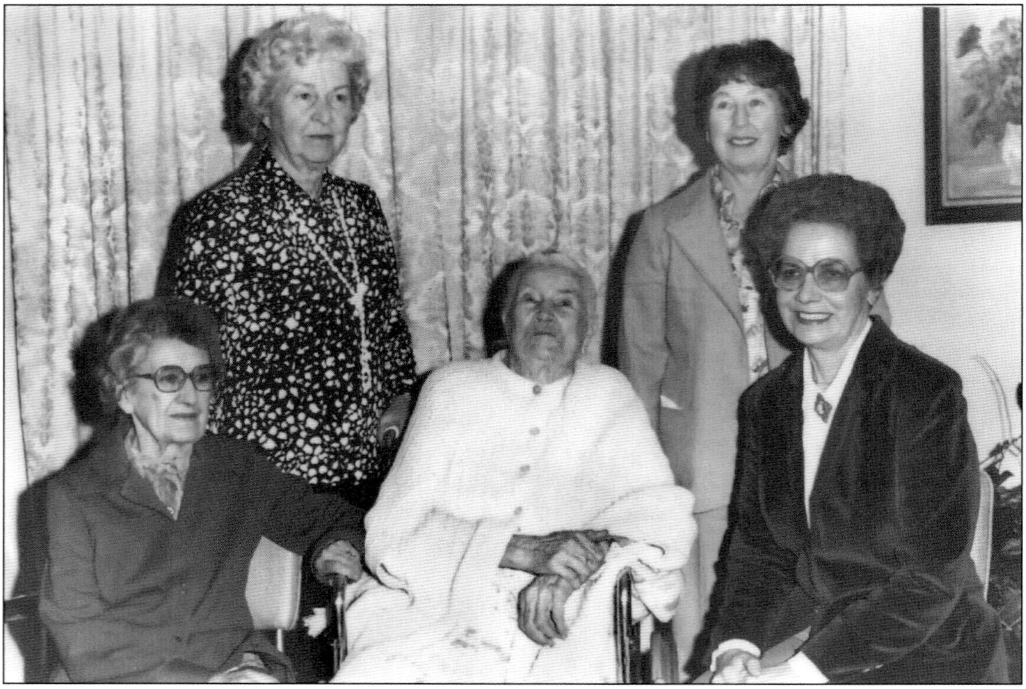

These women are the charter members of the Jerome Art Guild, which met at the Civic Club Library, where they displayed their paintings. Pictured from left to right are Ruth Brink, Carmen Davis, Dorothy Detweiler, Stella Walters, and Doris Fattig.

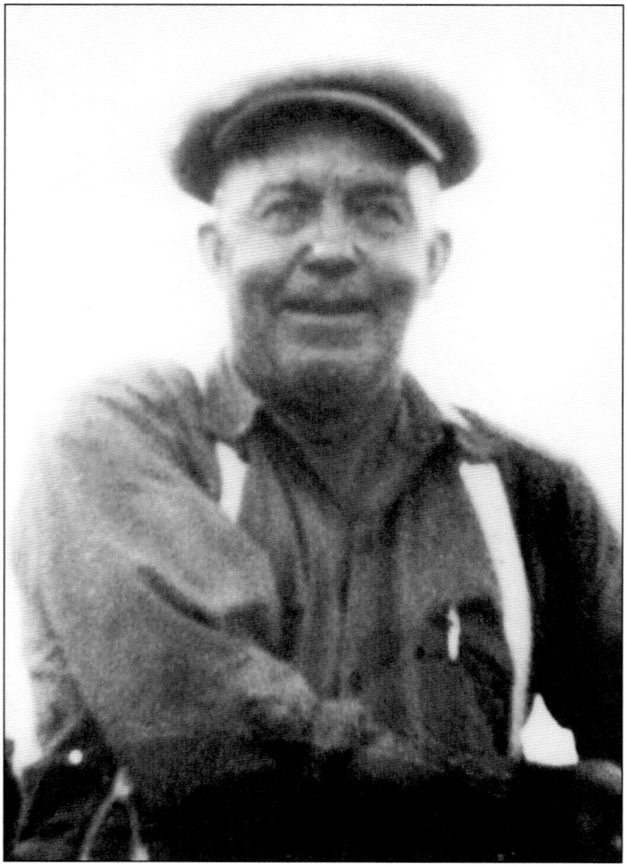

E.B. White was Jerome's first sheriff, serving from 1919 to 1923.

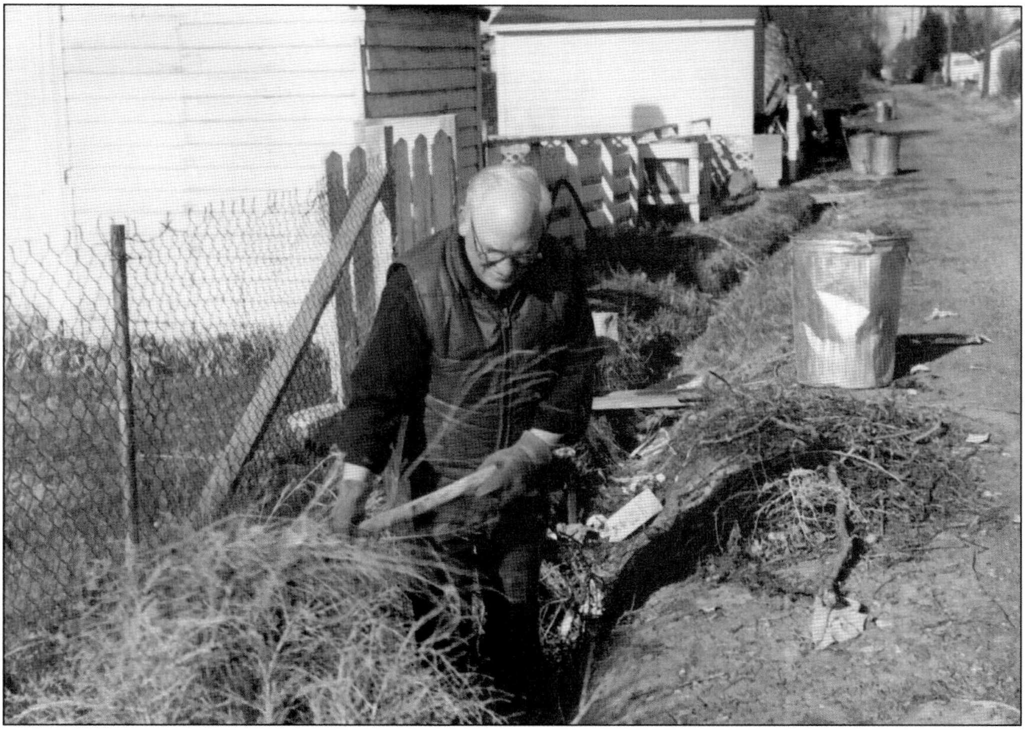

Marshall Everheart, seen here working in his backyard, was the owner of the sporting goods store just west of J.C. Penney's on East Main Street. He also sold hunting and fishing licenses, and as a sideline, cut keys.

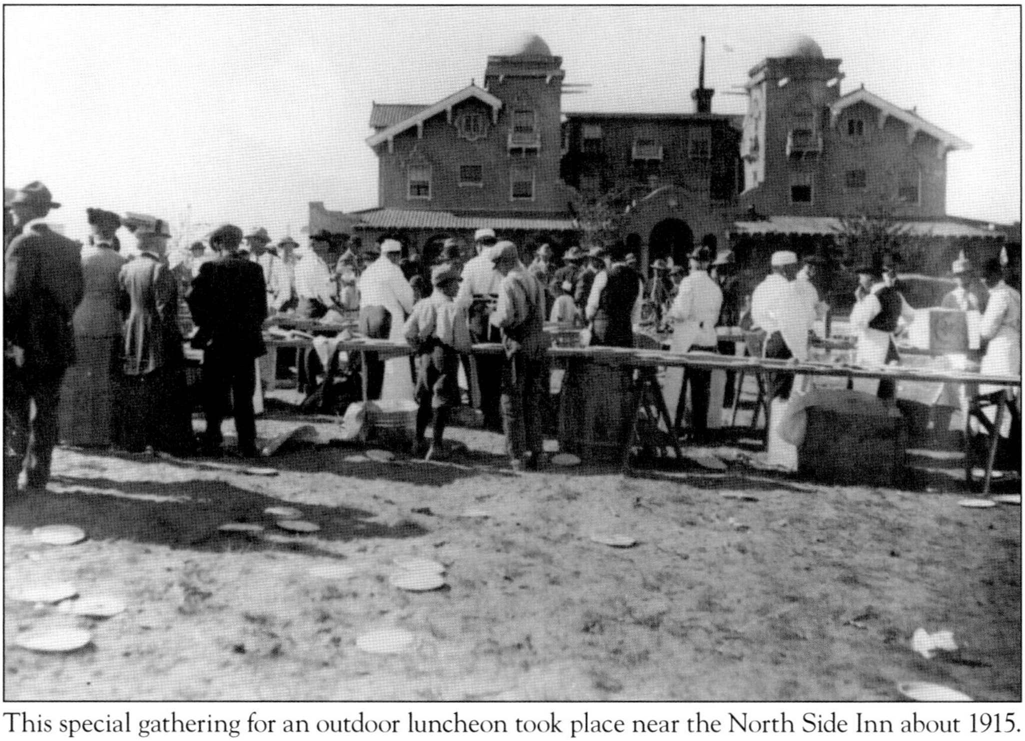

This special gathering for an outdoor luncheon took place near the North Side Inn about 1915.

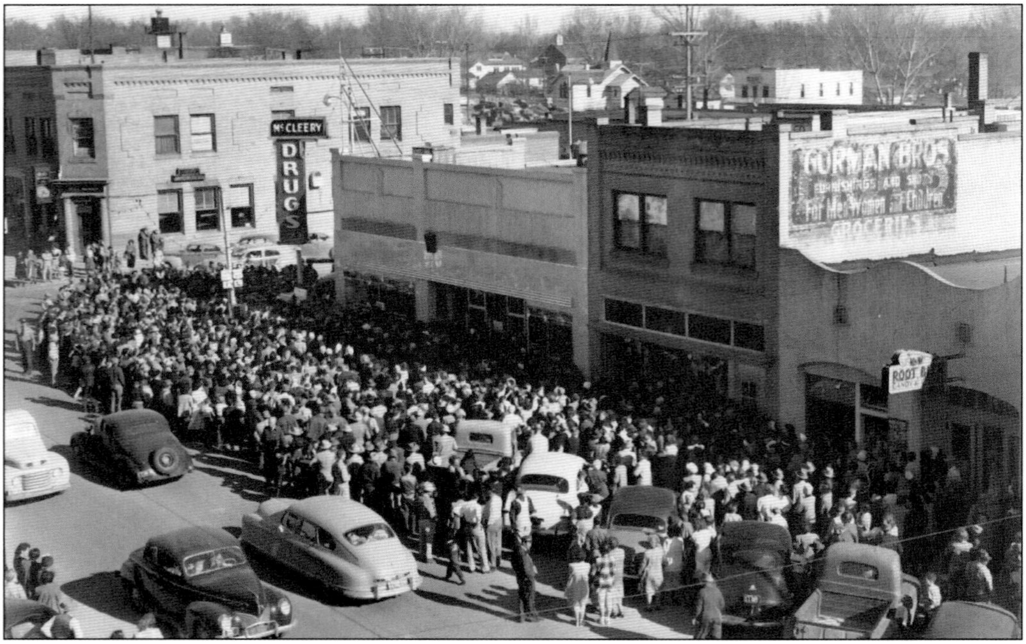

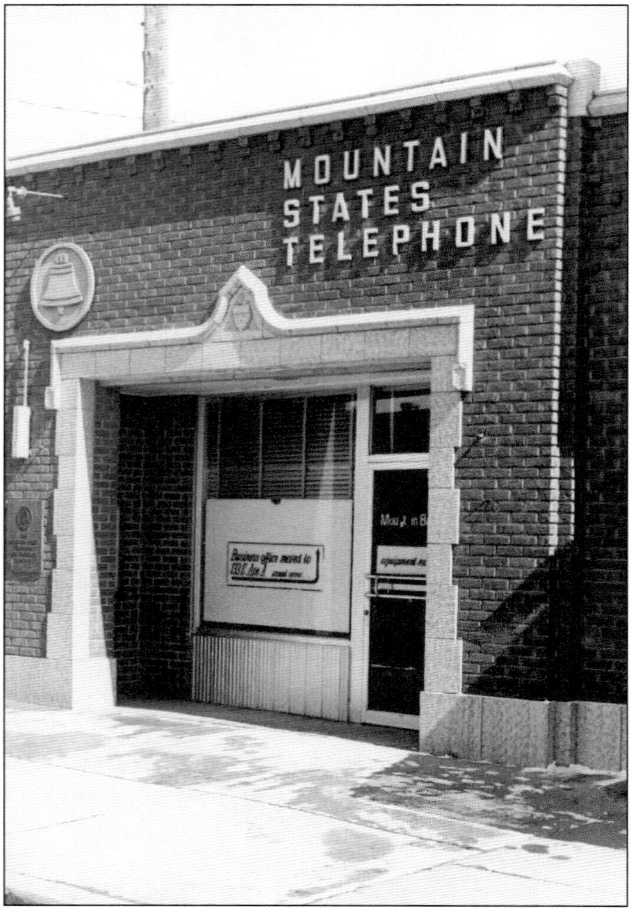

In this photograph, area residents gather at McCleery Drugs for reasons unknown; perhaps for the grand opening, as there is a new white range on the sidewalk in front of the store. McCleery Drugs also featured a lunch fountain, Christmas package–wrapping service in the basement, and a beauty shop on the mezzanine. On this day, some may have stopped at K&W for a root beer, candy, or a cigar.

Jerome had telephone service before the sale of city lots. When the Mountain States Telephone office moved from this building on South Lincoln to a building on East Avenue A, the city police department moved here.

Dorie Helms was a desk sergeant for the city police department in 1963. (Author's collection.)

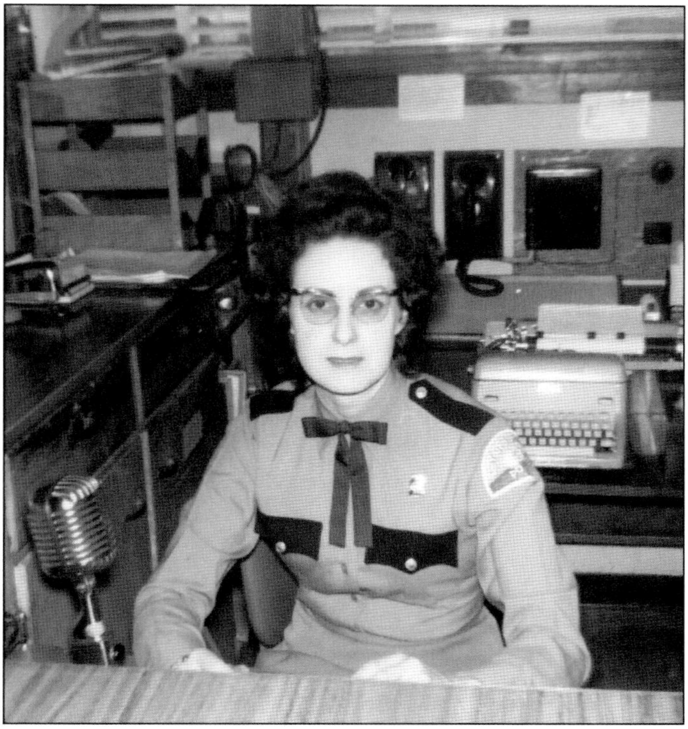

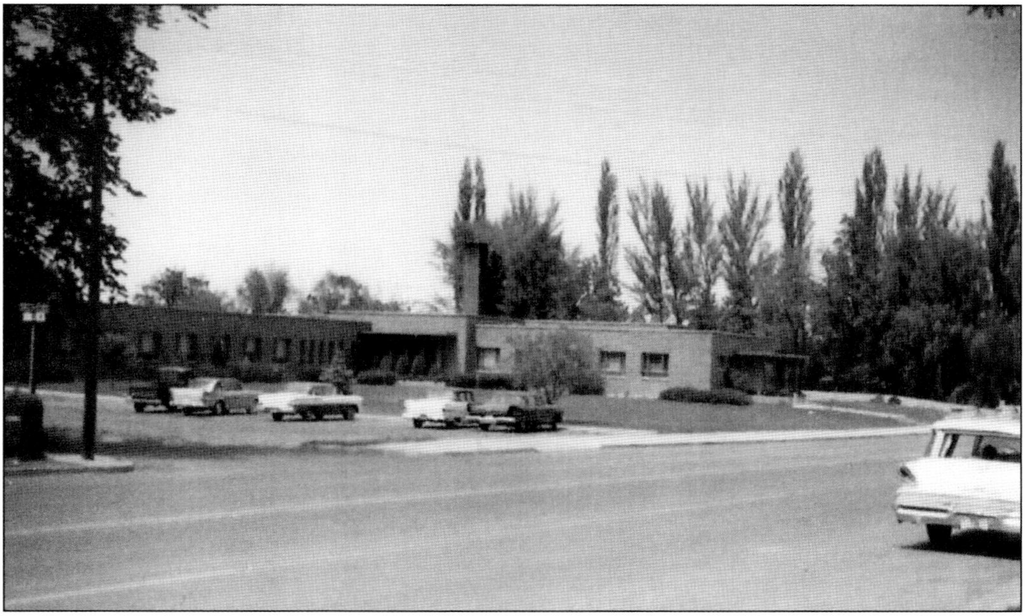

In September 1944, several businessmen planned to build a hospital in Jerome. At the time, residents had to travel 10 miles either west to Wendell's St. Valentine's Hospital or south to the Twin Falls County Hospital. Due to the war and supply shortages, the building was not completed in 1945 as scheduled, but in March 1951, plans were made and materials were procured. St. Benedict's Hospital opened March 18, 1952, with the Benedictine Sisters and other volunteers moving patients and equipment to Jerome from St. Valentine's Hospital, which closed the same day. This photograph was taken in 1959.

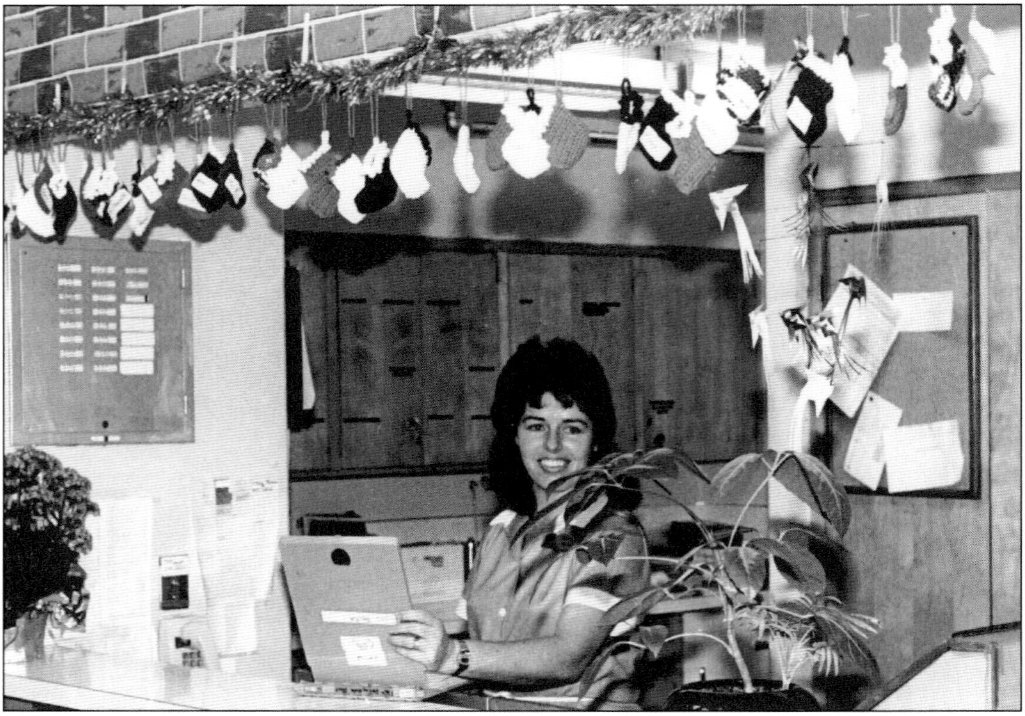

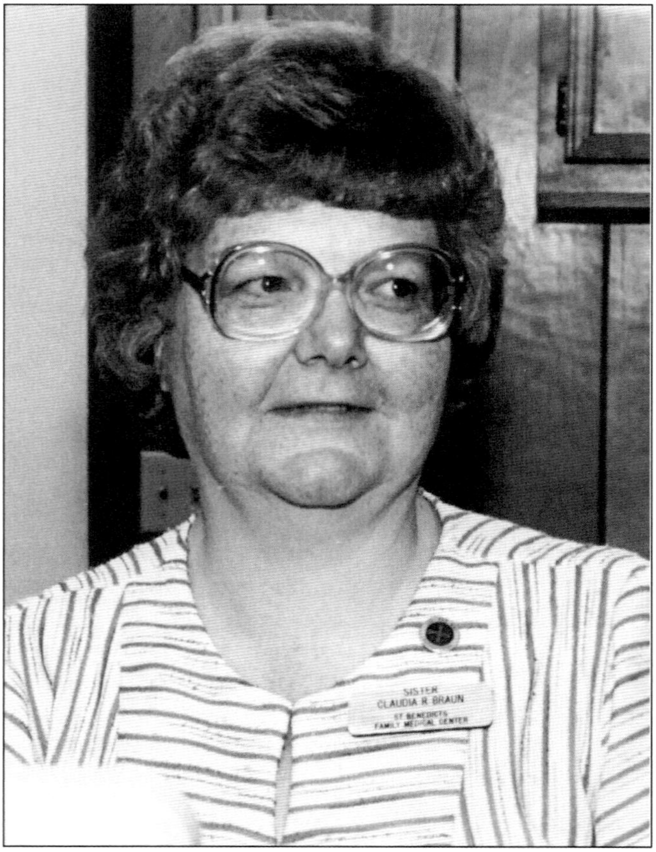

St. Benedict's Hospital added an attached long-term care unit. In this image, registered nurse Kathy Pike checks a resident's chart.

St. Benedict's Hospital was administered by the Benedictine Sisters of the Cottonwood, Idaho, monastery. Sister Claudia Rae worked in the accounting department and as a clerk in the nursing department, as well as in pastoral care.

Benedictine Sister Chanel worked in pastoral care in the 1990s at St. Benedict's hospital.

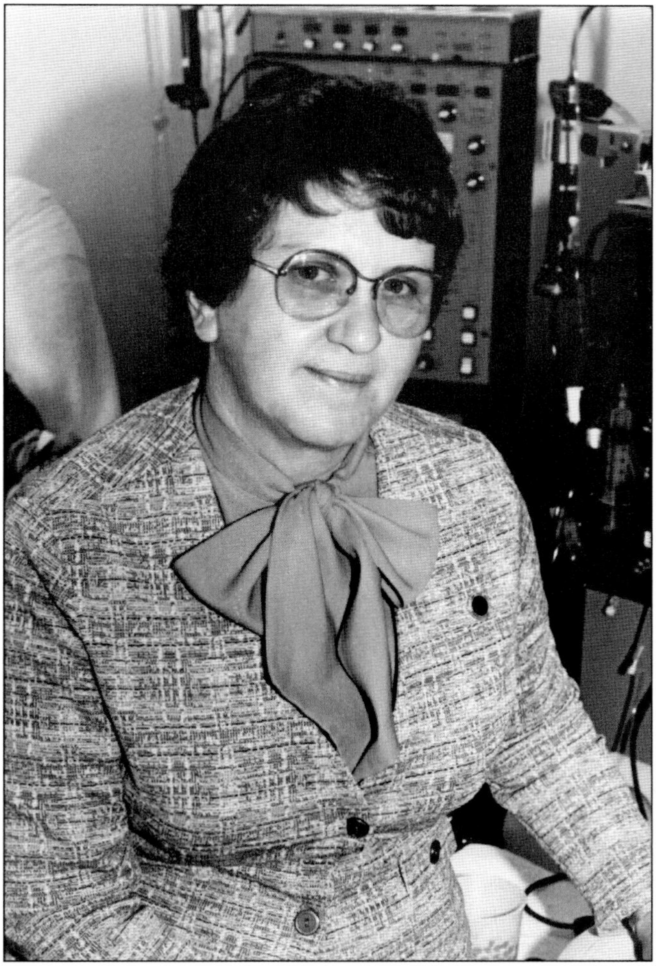

Pictured here is the only set of triplets born at St. Benedict's Hospital, Dale, Dawn, and Dona, children of Leslie and Peg Roberson. They were born on April 15, 1953.

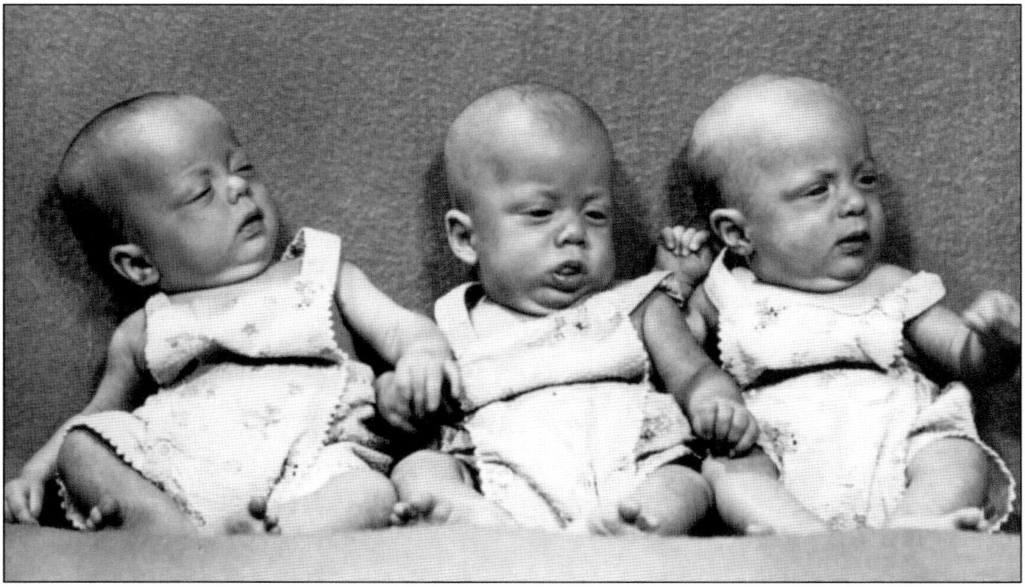

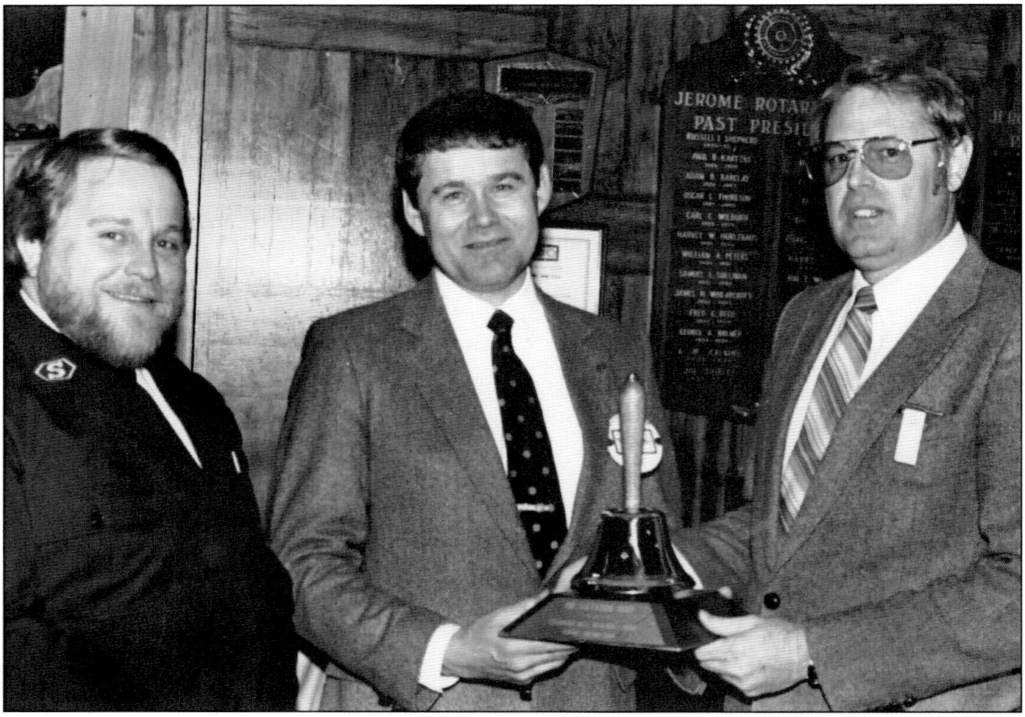

These civic leaders at a 1981 Rotary meeting are, from left to right, unidentified, Bob Campbell (an administrator at St. Benedict's Hospital), and Ed Robertson (Hove-Robertson Funeral Home director).

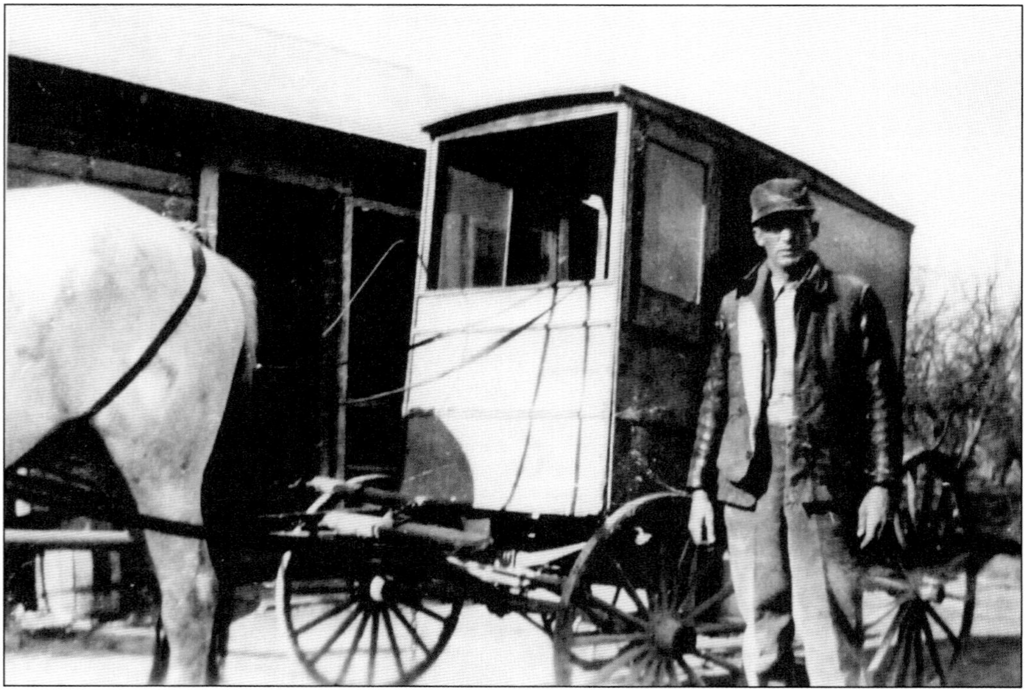

Albert E. Gould is shown with his horse-drawn wagon in 1927. He delivered produce and milk to restaurants and homes.

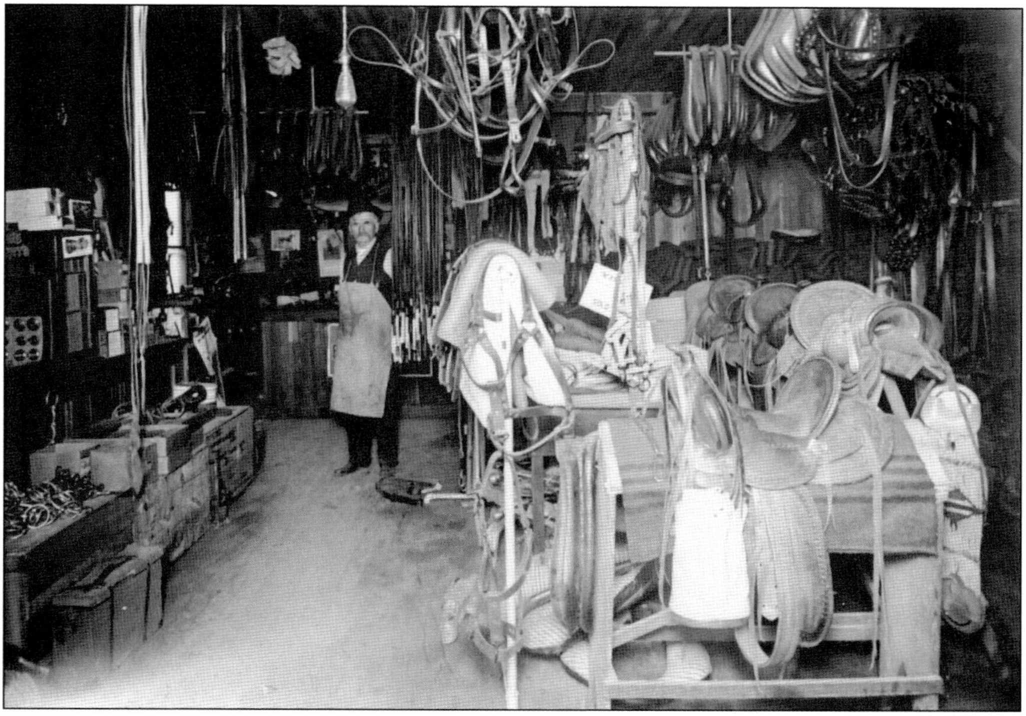

Pictured here is the interior of an early saddle and harness shop on West Main Street.

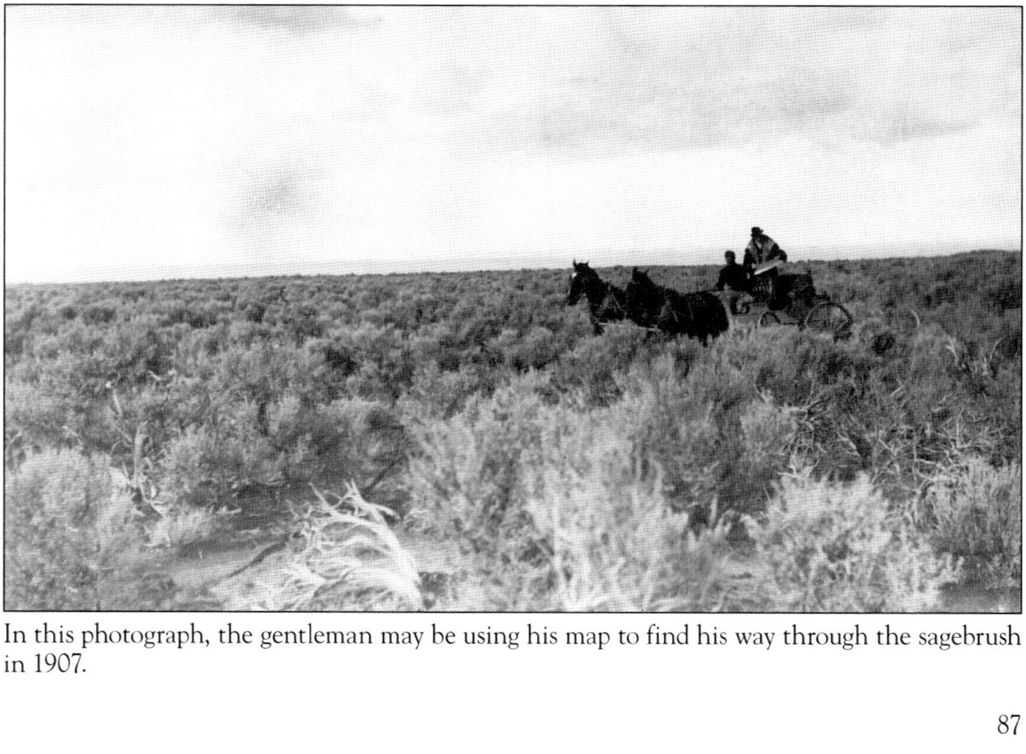

In this photograph, the gentleman may be using his map to find his way through the sagebrush in 1907.

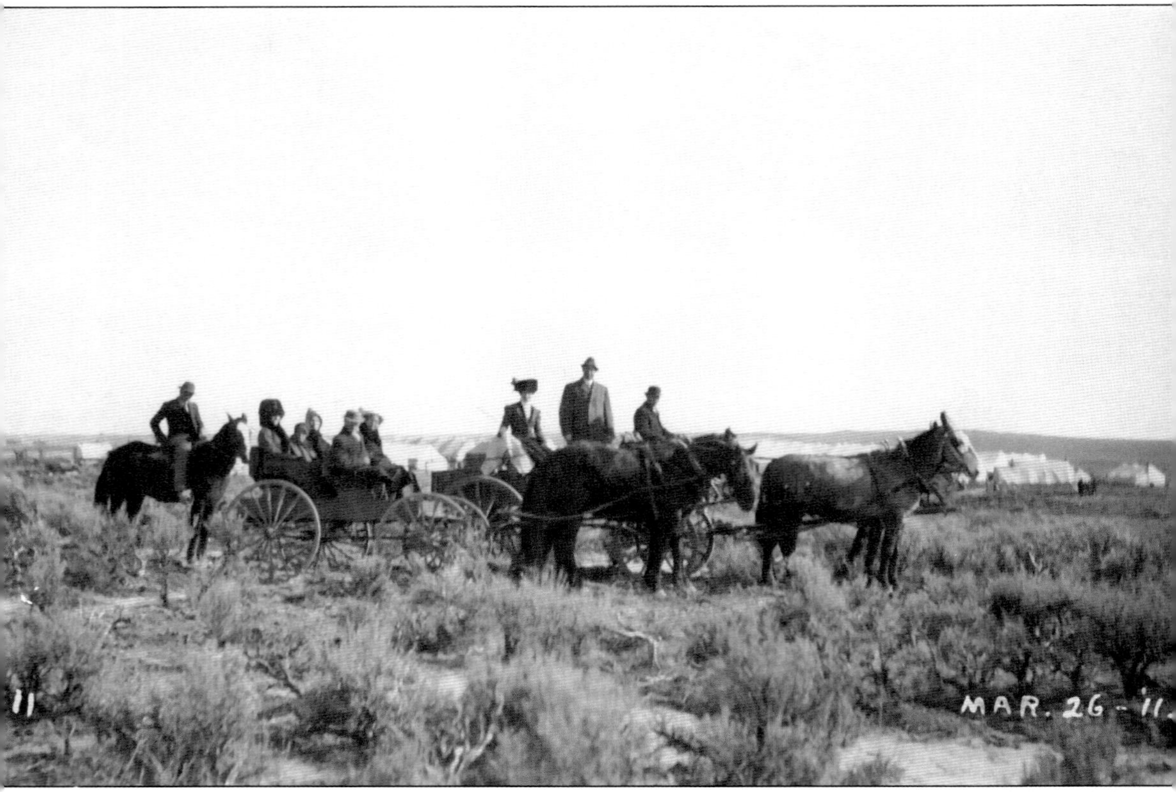

Clinton Smith and D.W. Sallady, owners of tourist wagons, pose with their families and the Ralph Wallace family near Jerome on March 26, 1911.

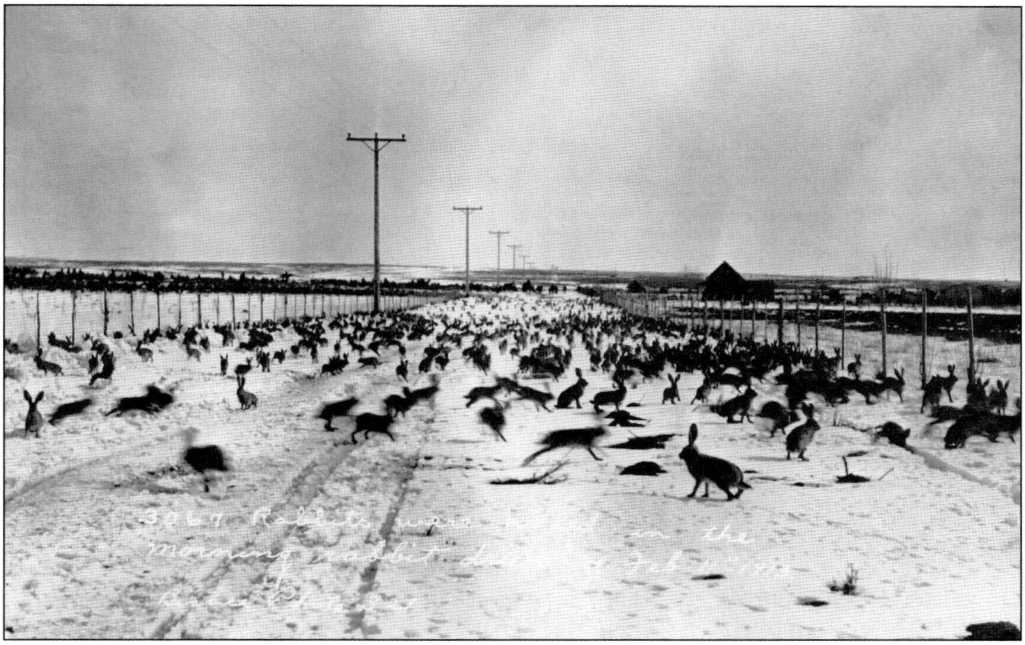

When the early settlers came to Jerome, they saw sagebrush, some coyotes, and lots of jackrabbits. Because the rabbits destroyed the crops, rabbit drives were formed. Men surrounded an area and drove the rabbits into a low holding pen. The rabbits were then clubbed to death. These drives were a weekly event from 1908 until the 1940s, and occasionally until the 1960s when the rabbit population increased in different areas around town. This photograph was taken on February 11, 1913, southeast of town. On that day, 7,500 rabbits were captured.

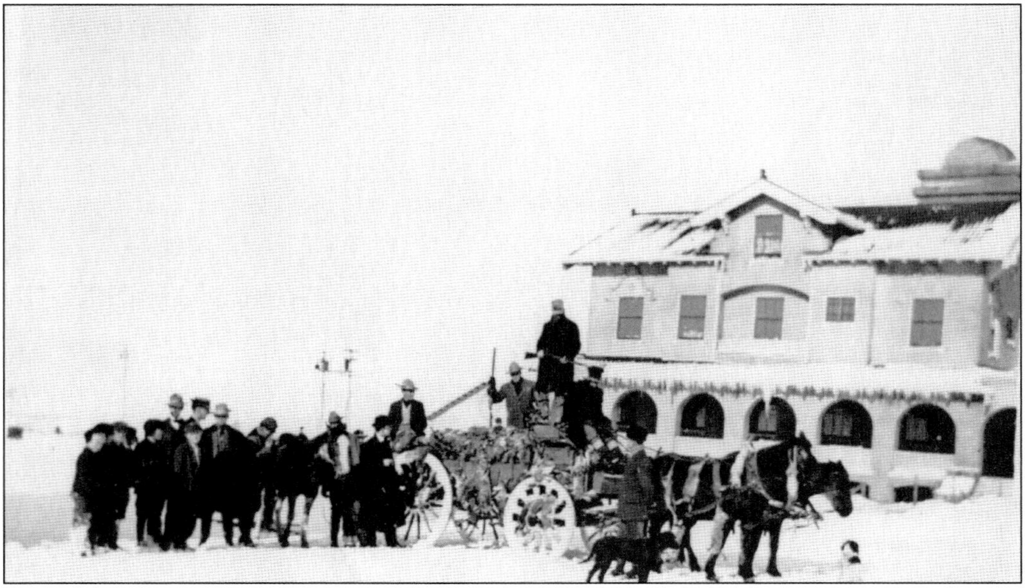

After the rabbit drive, pelts were taken by the wagonload to town and sold to a hide dealer. For ridding the area of a crop destroyer, the men received a small amount of money. Some people ate jackrabbits, but the meat was usually too tough.

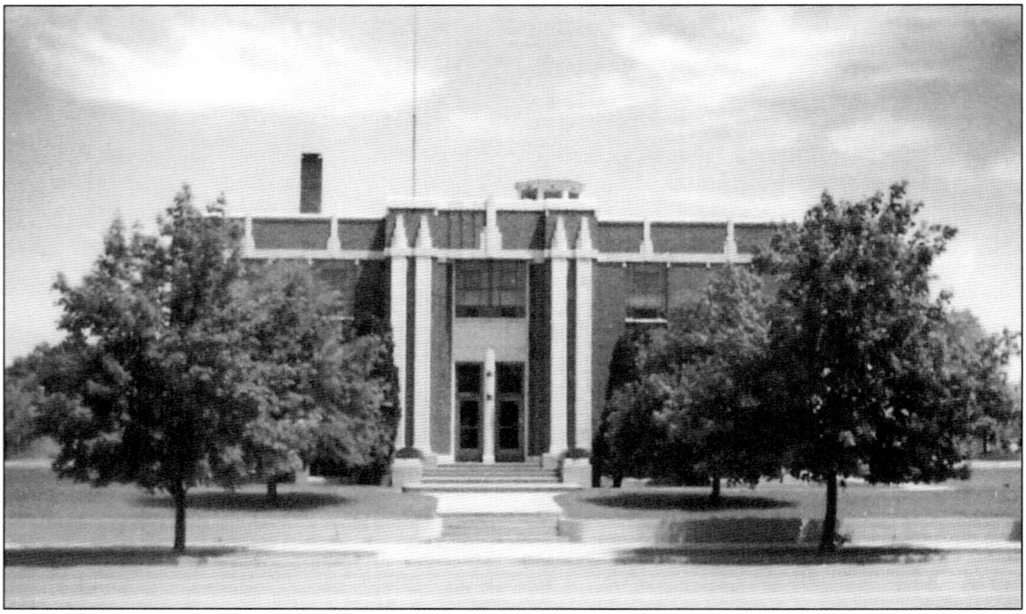

When Lincoln County was divided in 1919 to create Gooding County and Jerome County, Jerome became the county seat, as well as the 43rd county in the 43rd state. The courthouse was constructed on North Lincoln Avenue across the street from the high school. The county commissioners dedicated the courthouse on December 6, 1939. It took two days to move the heavy safe from the First Security Bank. This photograph was taken in 1959.

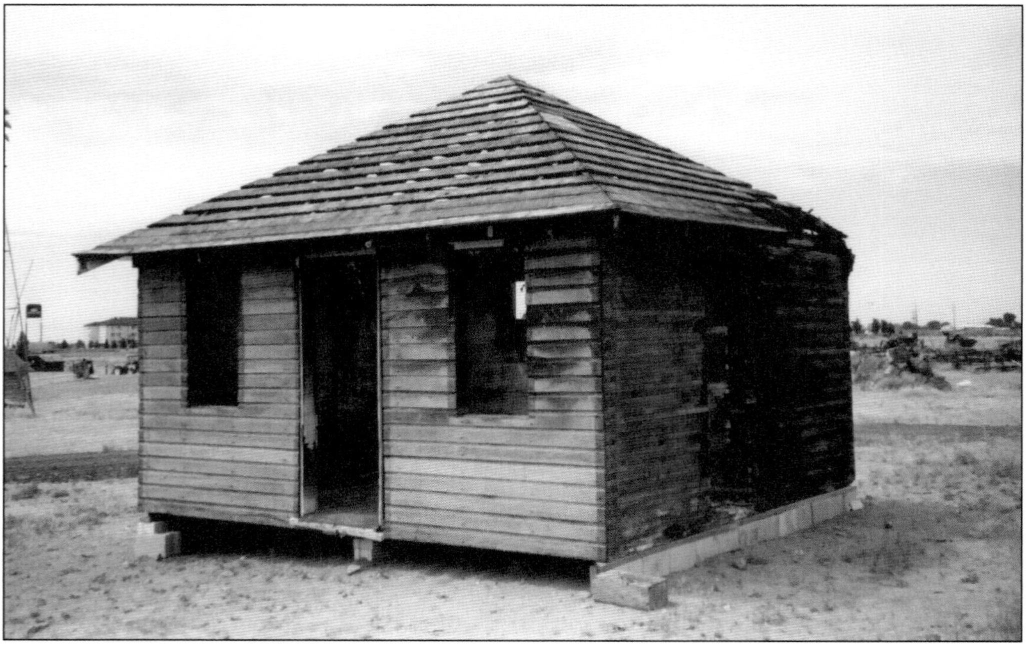

The first jail was a small building on East Avenue A. When the courthouse and the city police department were constructed in 1939, the old jail was used as a storage shed. In the early 1990s, the last owners were going to burn the building down, but when they realized the historical significance, it was donated to the historical society and moved to the Idaho Farm and Ranch Museum. (Author's collection.)

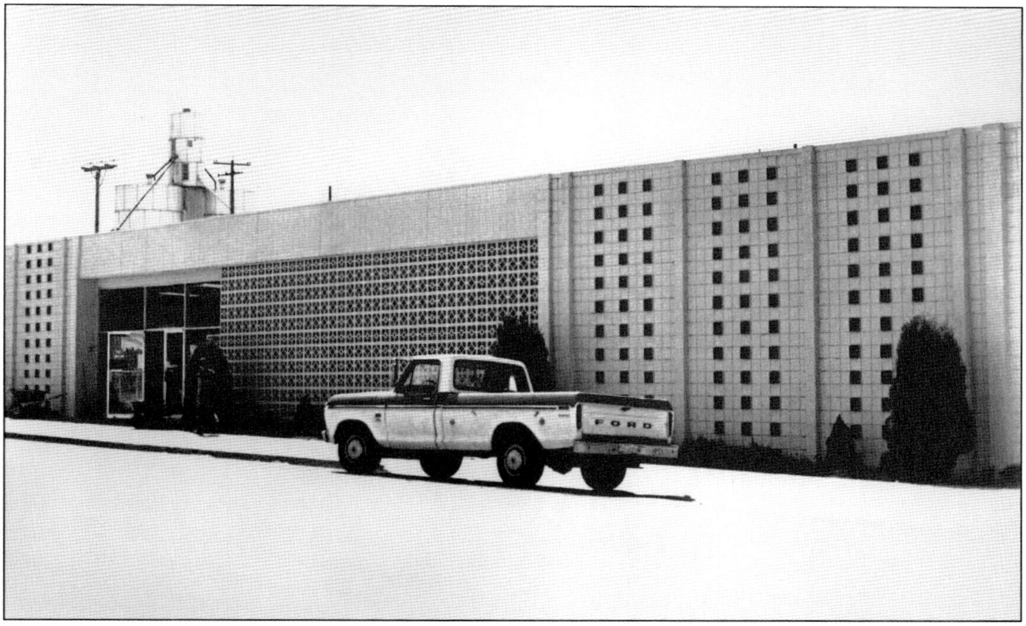

Volco Building Supply on West Main Street started making cinder blocks from the cinders near the Craters of the Moon National Monument and Preserve in 1943. Cinders did not work well, so the company used pumice, making it the first pumice block–production company in the United States, equaling the quality of pumice stone made in Italy. The cinder blocks were excellent, strong, and lightweight building materials. Volco also sold lumber, paint, and plumbing supplies.

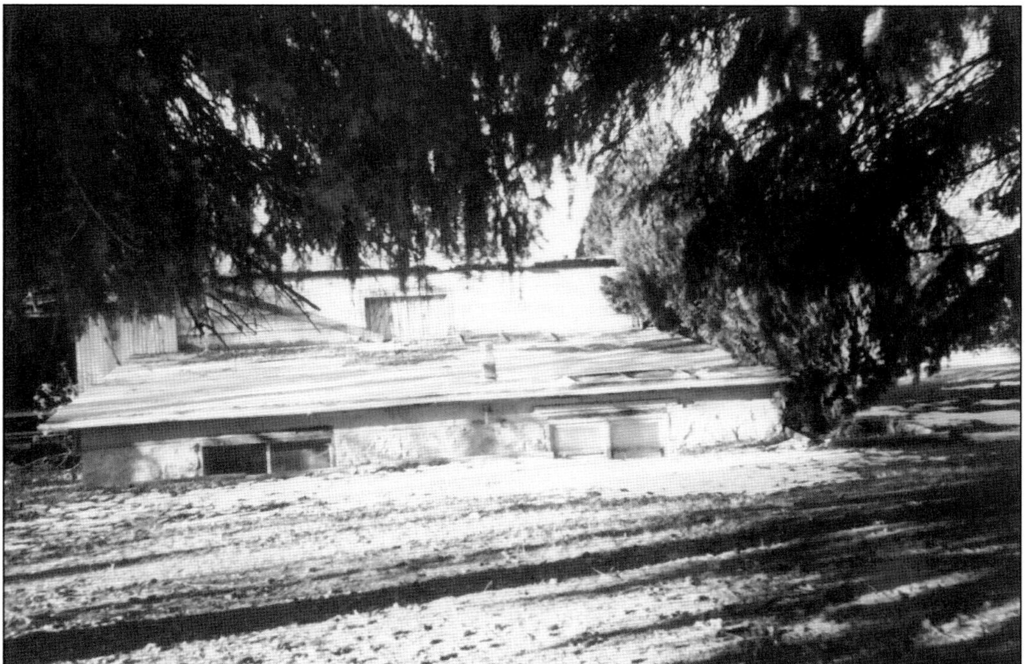

This unusual type of home, located west across North Fillmore from Jefferson School, was a basement house with living room, kitchen, bathroom, and two bedrooms and a stairway on the ground floor. At one time, Virgil and Betty Carpenter and their family lived here. (Author's collection.)

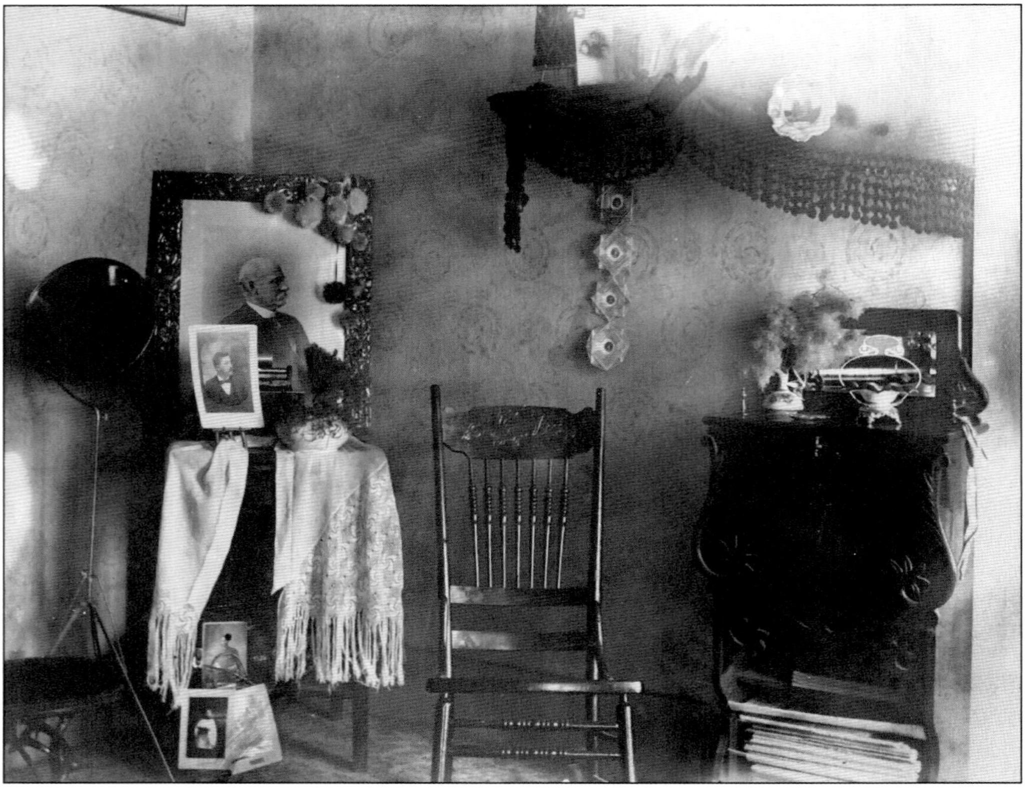

The people in the photographs within this image are unknown, but this picture was taken in Bob McCollum's home.

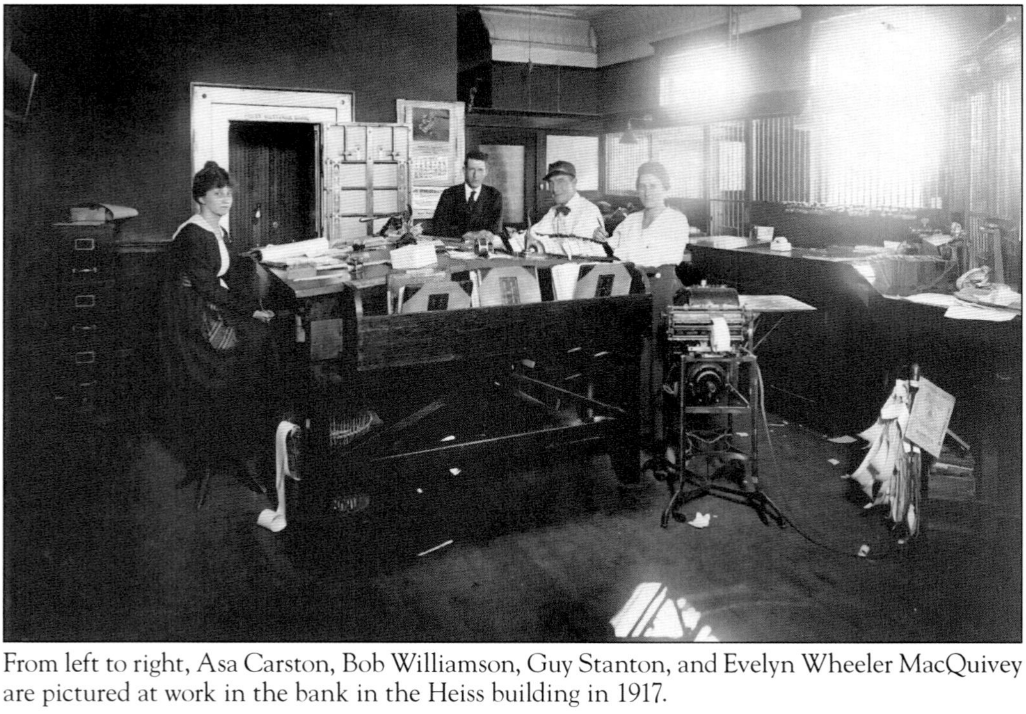

From left to right, Asa Carston, Bob Williamson, Guy Stanton, and Evelyn Wheeler MacQuivey are pictured at work in the bank in the Heiss building in 1917.

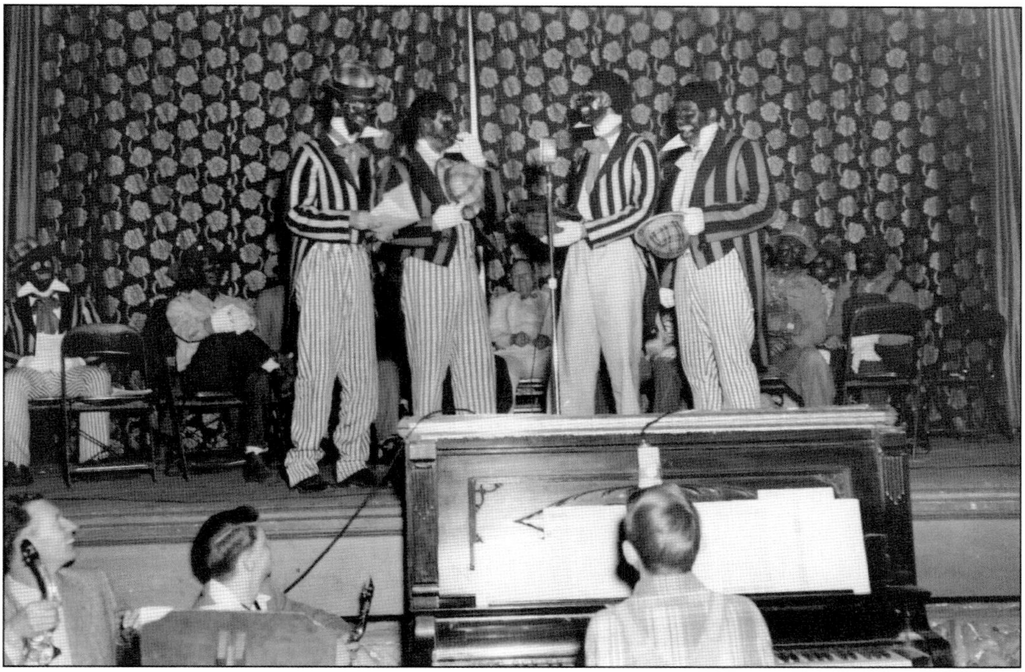

The Beetlee Bums were part of the entertainment for Farmer's Night in the 1940s at the Voris Theatre. The Bums were a local barbershop quartet in costume.

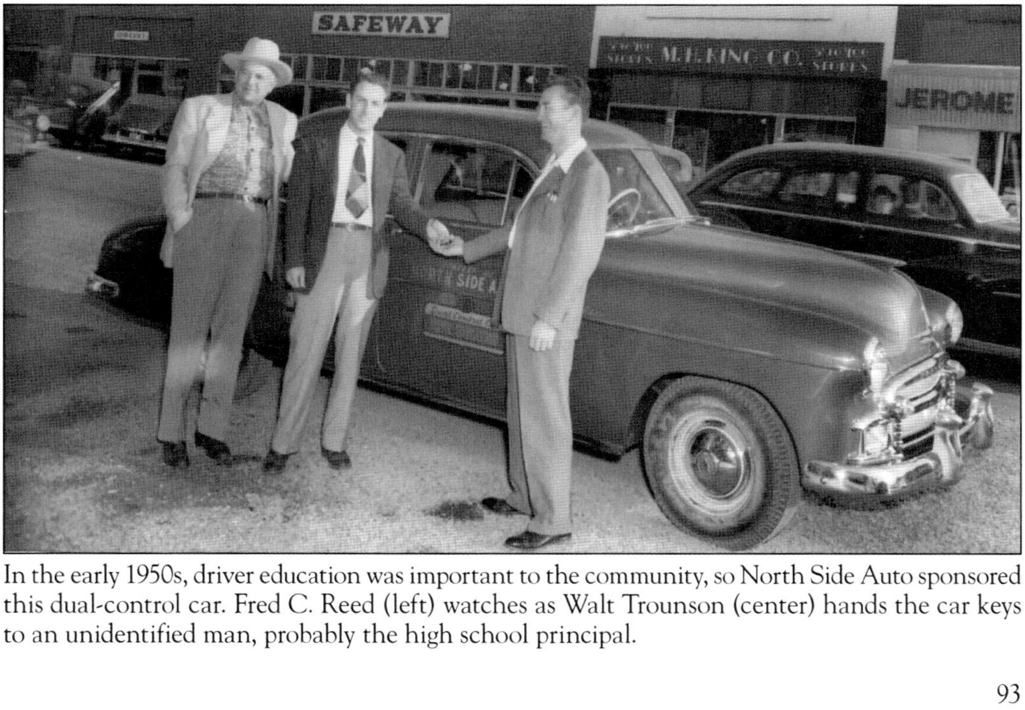

In the early 1950s, driver education was important to the community, so North Side Auto sponsored this dual-control car. Fred C. Reed (left) watches as Walt Trounson (center) hands the car keys to an unidentified man, probably the high school principal.

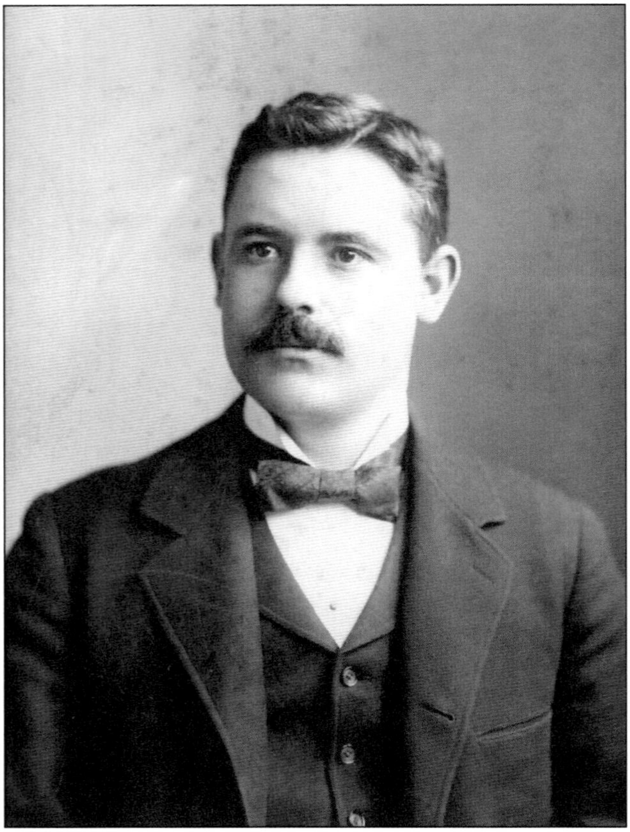

Edward Douglas Piper was the first doctor in town from 1908 to 1923.

Charlotte Roberson was the first woman clerk-auditor for Jerome County, serving from 1927 to 1947, and elected again as a write-in candidate in 1958. She retired in 1962 at age 74 and stated, "I still knew all the levies." She was happy to be in office when the courthouse was built in 1939, when the offices were moved from the First Security Bank building.

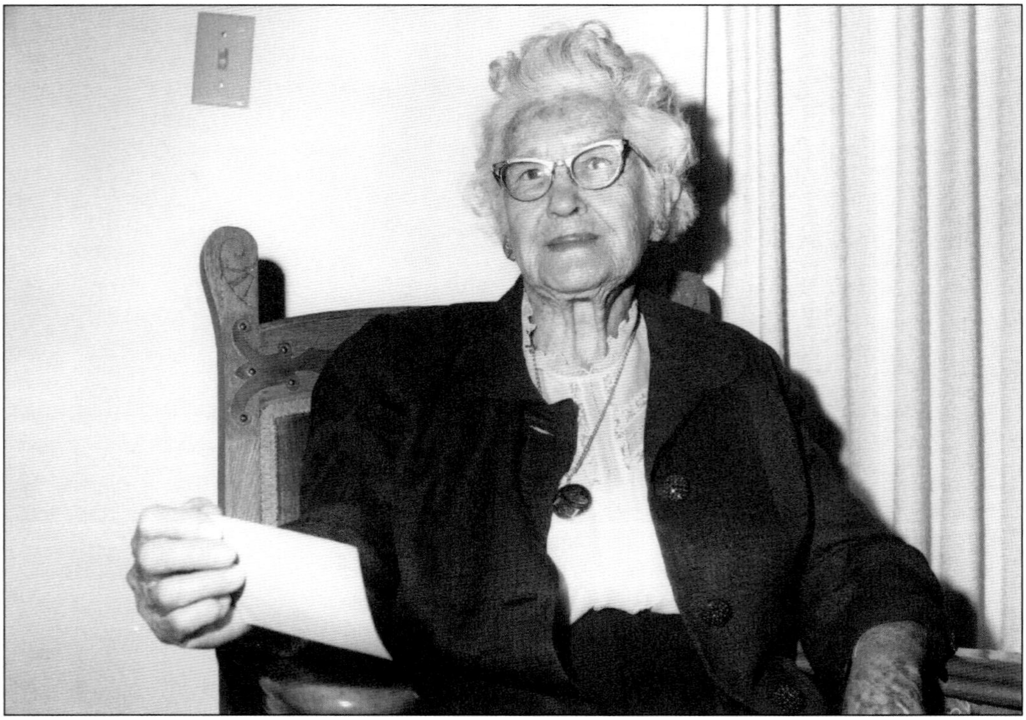

Stu Murrell was director of the Regional Idaho Fish and Game office in Jerome. He conducted gun safety classes for many years.

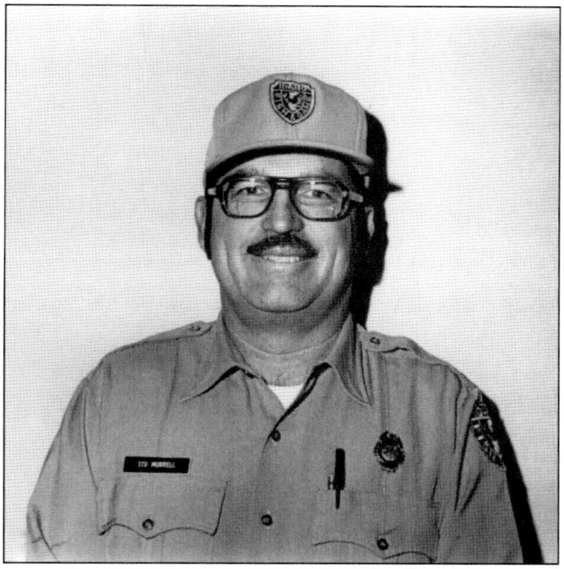

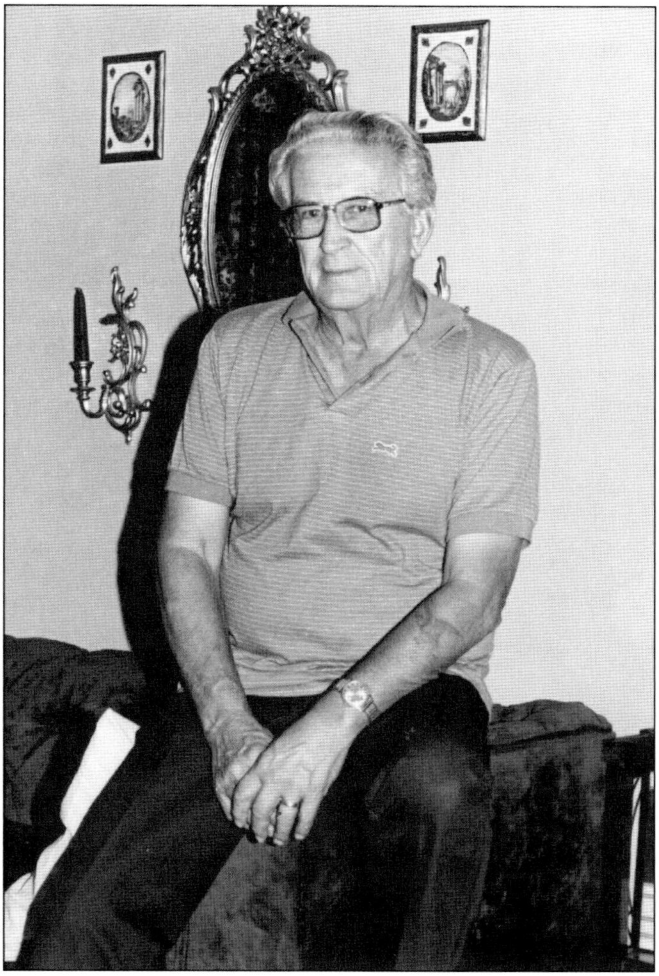

Lavere Gooch was a much loved athletic coach and teacher at Jerome High School.

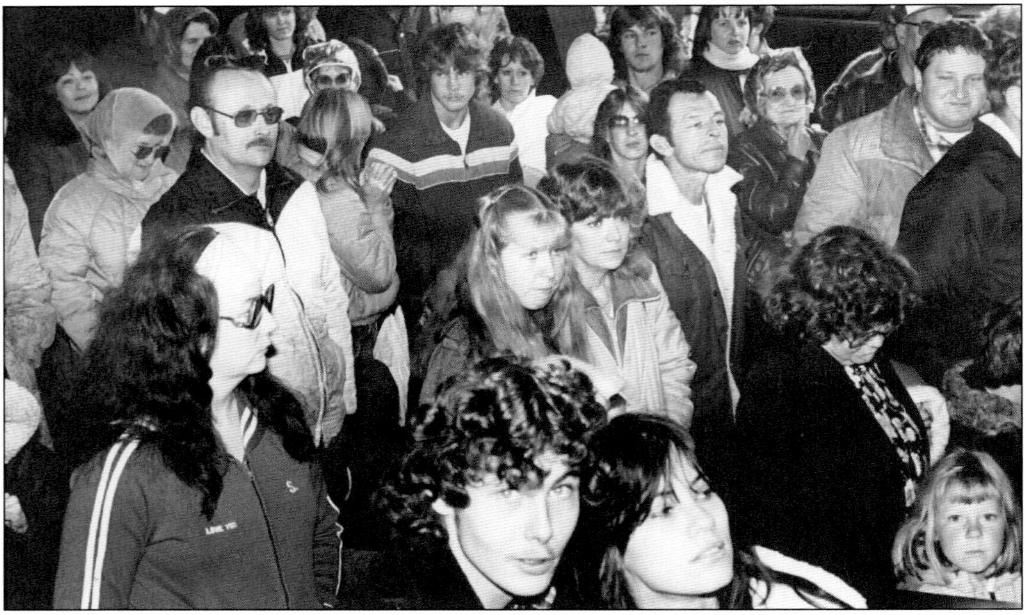

Beginning in early 1950, Gift Buck drawings took place every Saturday morning from Thanksgiving to Christmas Eve, enticing many residents. Jerome businesses gave customers one ticket for each dollar spent in the community businesses. Name, address, and telephone numbers were written on the tickets and placed into boxes at each shop. The boxes were then emptied into a large circular cage placed atop the fire truck parked at the northwest corner of Main Street and Lincoln Avenue. As Santa Claus handed out candy canes to the audience, city leaders drew tickets from the cage. The winners received certificates worth \$5, \$10, \$15, \$20, \$25, or \$50 worth of products at their choice of one of the participating businesses. This annual raffle was discontinued in the 1980s.

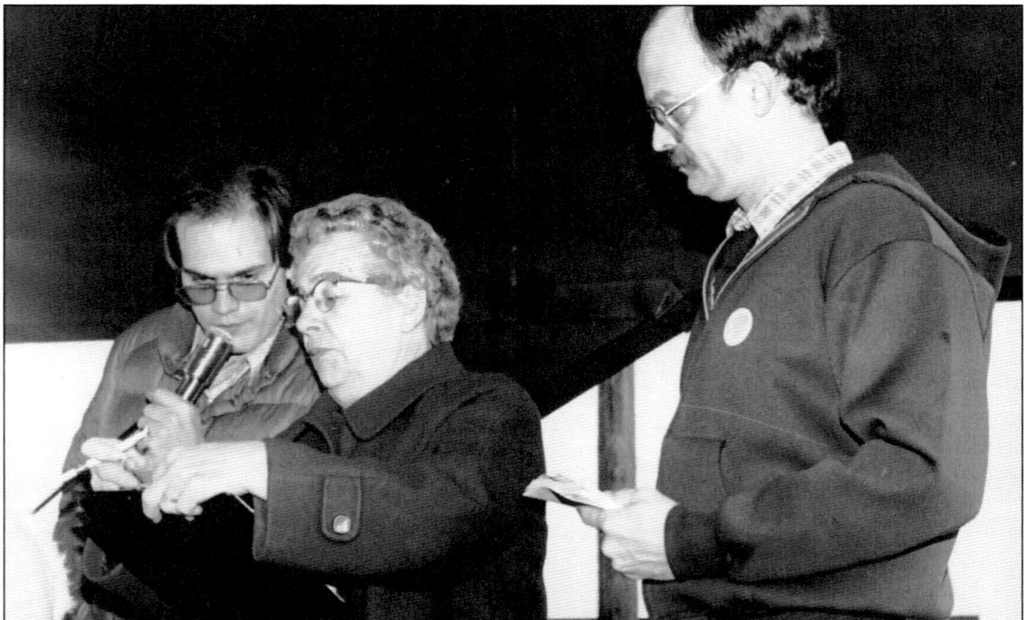

At the Gift Buck drawing, Paul Johnson announces a winning name that Ruby Grimes has drawn, as Bob Topmiller looks on.

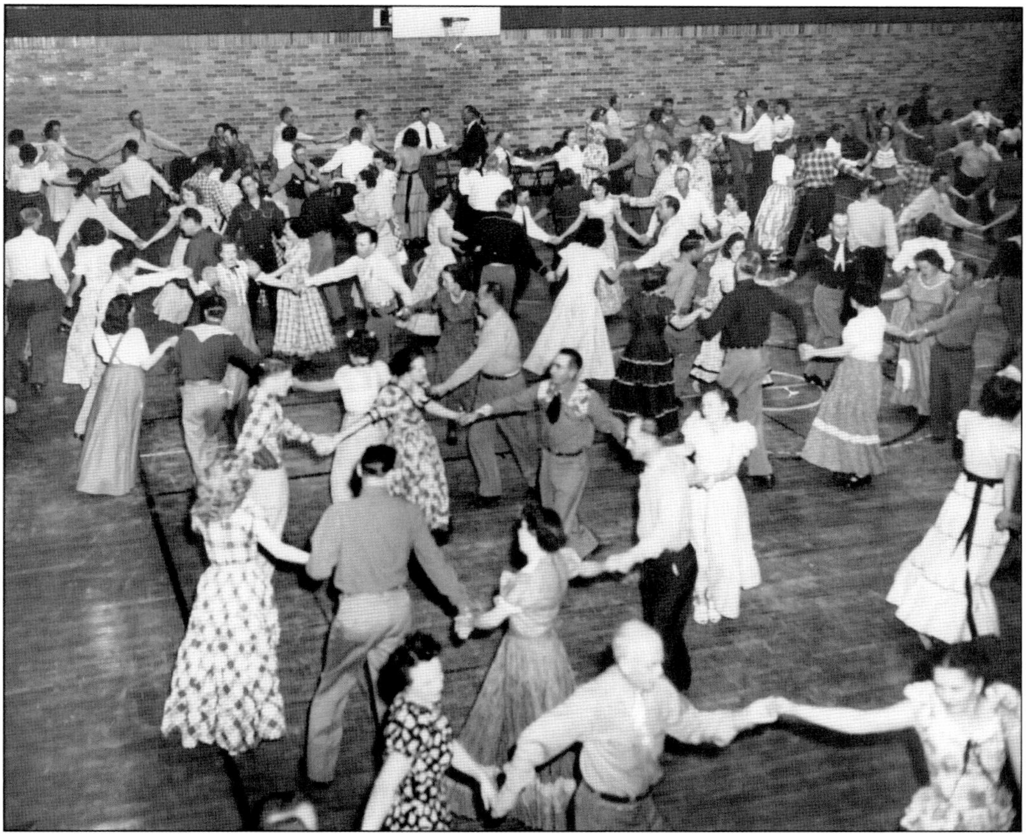

A fun activity for adults in Jerome is square dancing. This dance was held at the high school gymnasium in the 1950s. The Buttons and Bows Square Dance Club still holds lessons and dances in Jerome, along with another club, Magic Valley Singles.

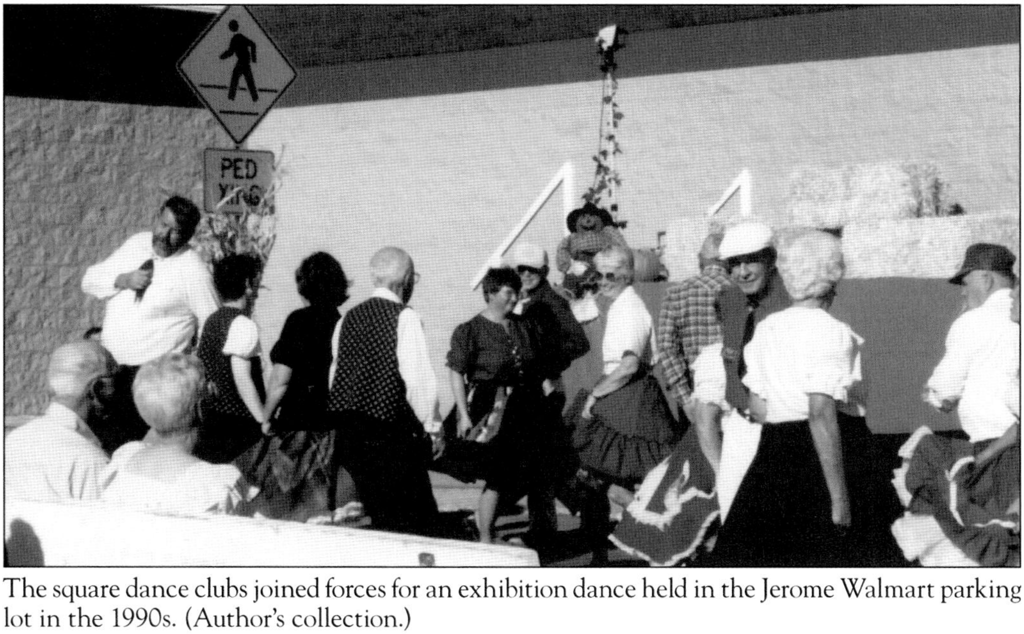

The square dance clubs joined forces for an exhibition dance held in the Jerome Walmart parking lot in the 1990s. (Author's collection.)

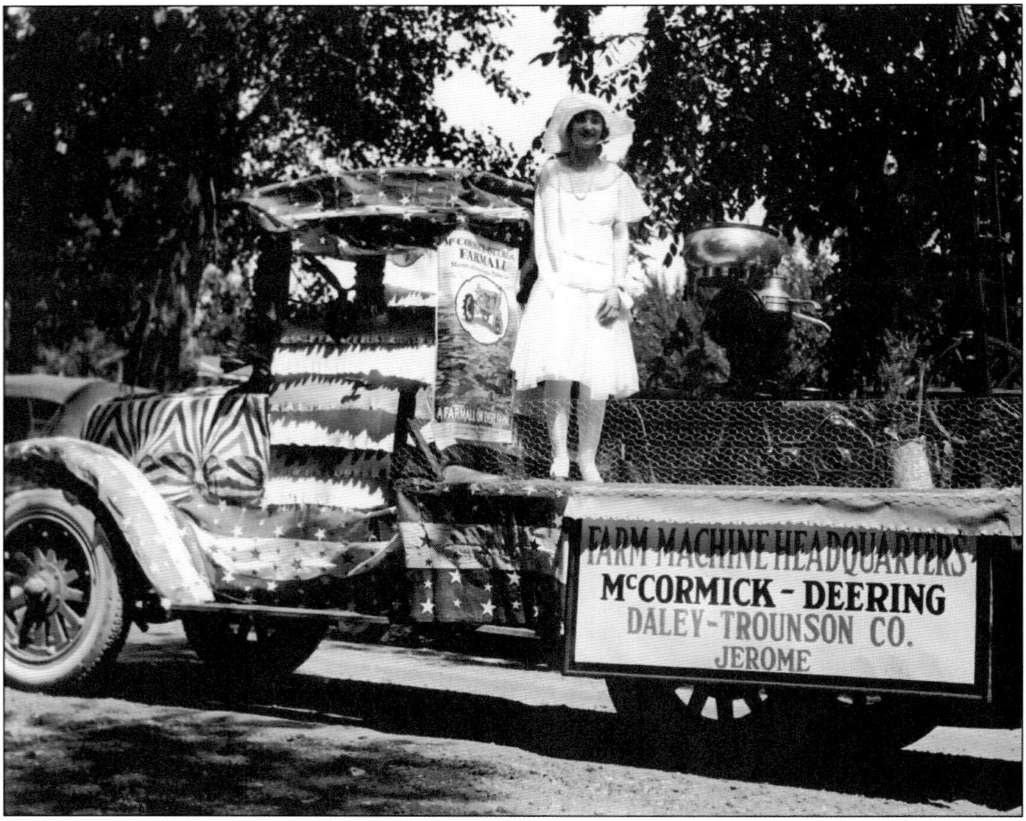

This 1930s parade float features a lovely young lady and a cream separator from the Daley-Trounson farm machine company.

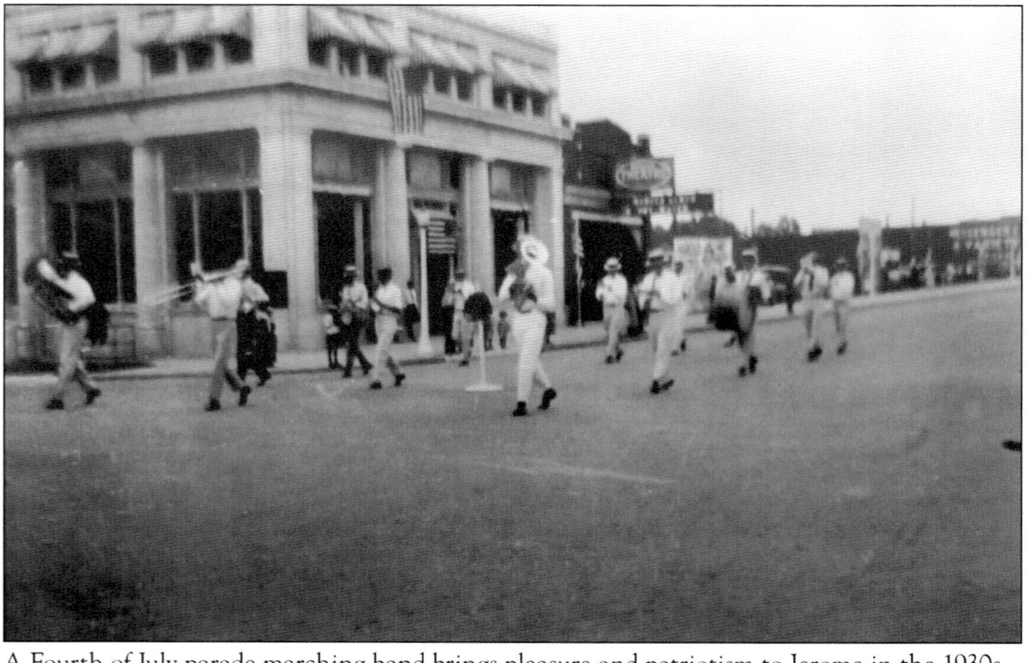

A Fourth of July parade marching band brings pleasure and patriotism to Jerome in the 1930s.

Patriotism in Jerome has always been prevalent, as is shown in this Fourth of July parade in the early 1950s. Flags are placed in special containers along the sidewalks. A baseball team participates in the parade, as does what could be the sheriff's mounted posse. Note that the parade travels from the North Park to the west end of town, and then turns back east to the South Park where a Ferris wheel and other festivities are set up for the public.

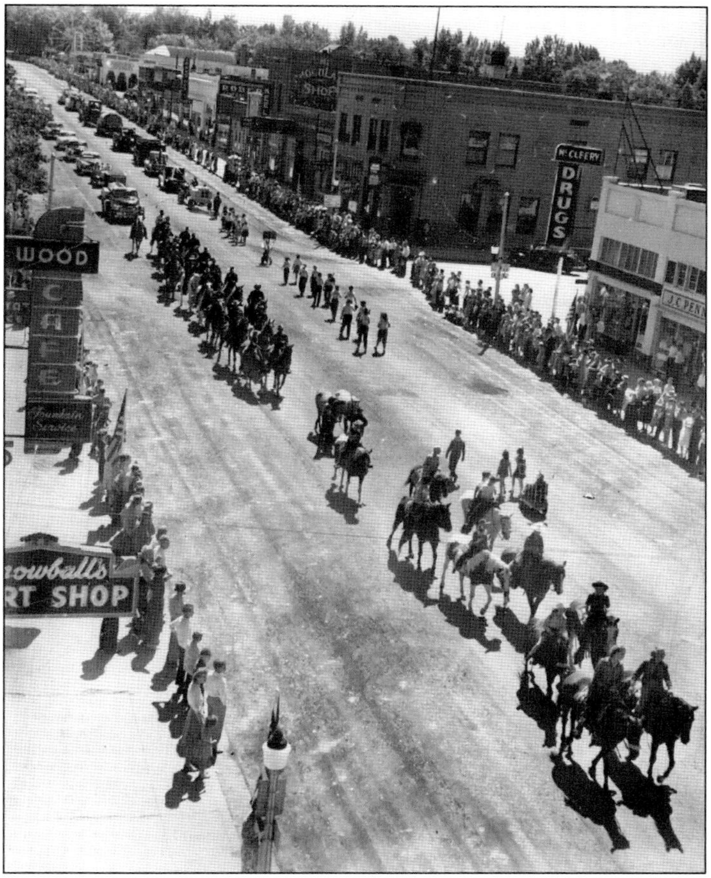

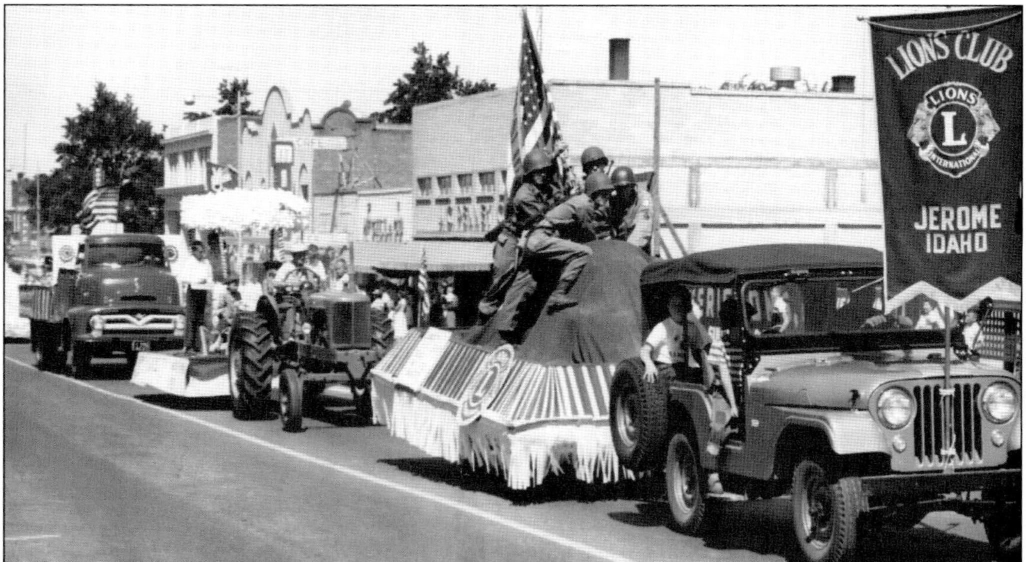

This early-1950s parade on Main Street focuses on the Lion's Club float honoring the US military at Iwo Jima. The J.C. Penney building and McGill's Five and Dime Store are visible in the background. The first bowling alley opened in the basement of the Mint Café.

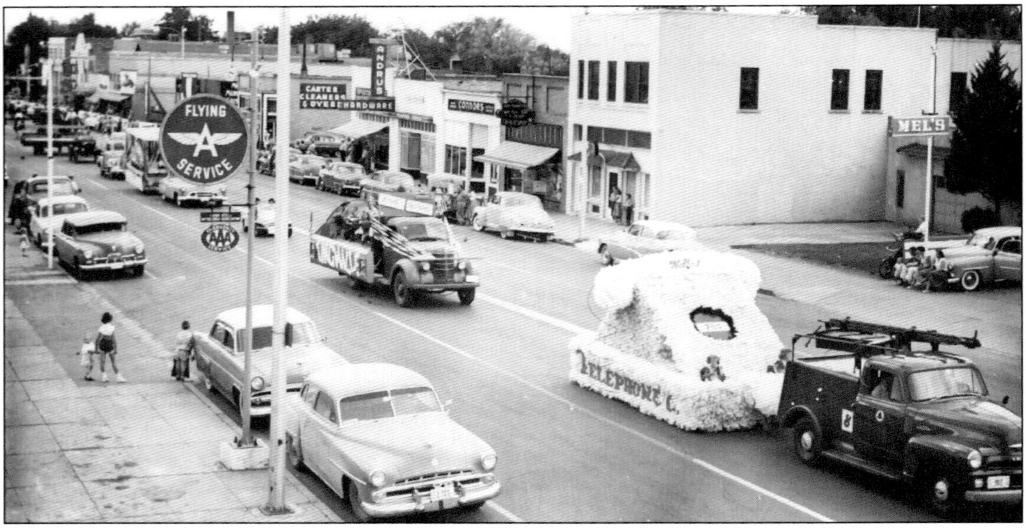

This photograph of a parade in the 1950s shows businesses that are no longer operating in these buildings.

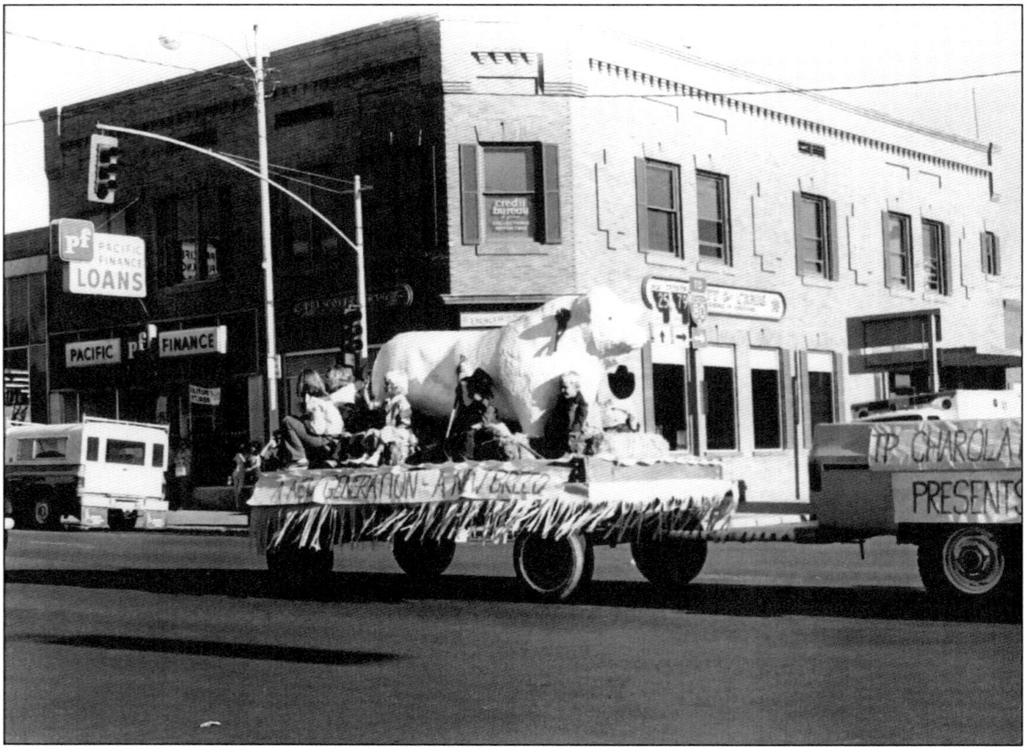

Many local ranchers had floats in the parades, such as this one depicting Tom Prescott's Charolais cattle.

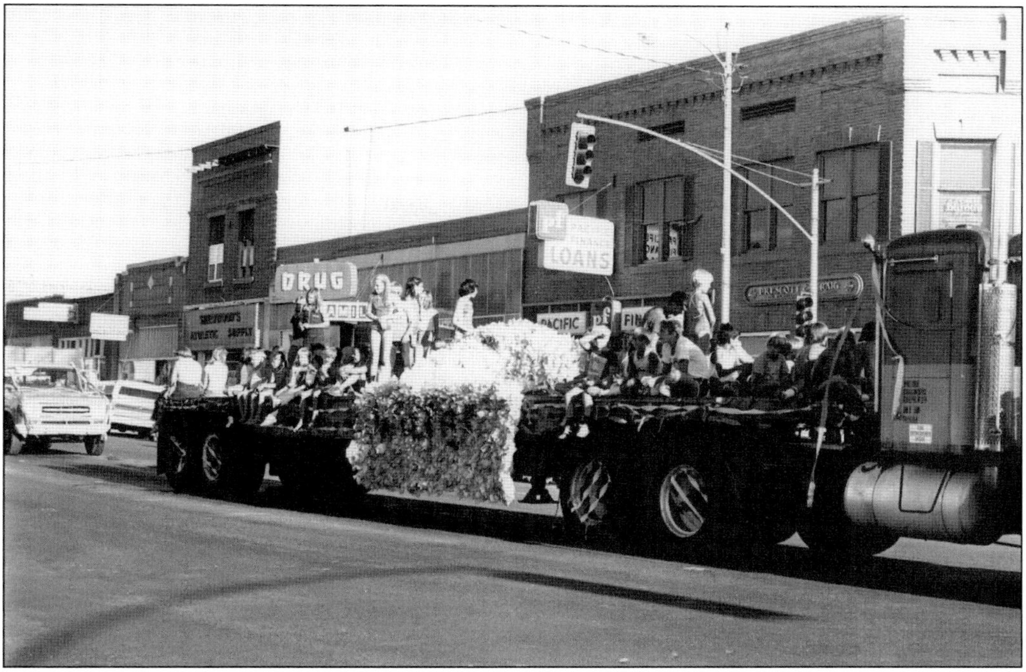

Children love parades, whether they are watching from the sidewalks or participating themselves.

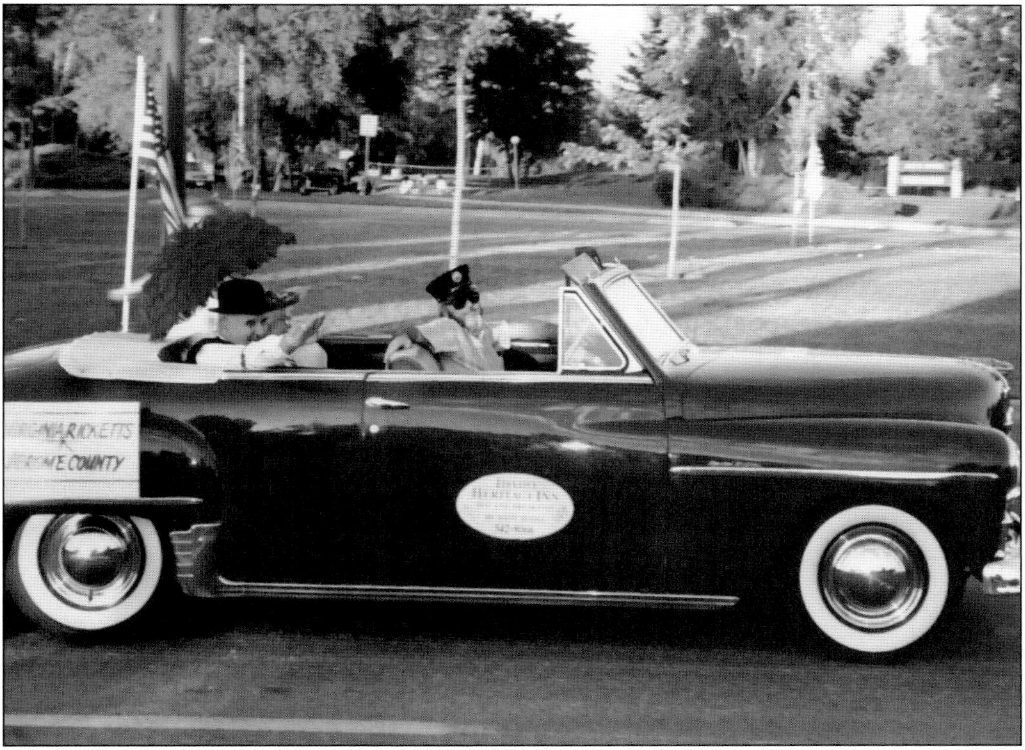

Local historians and curators of the Jerome County Historical Museum Clair and Virginia Ricketts, seen in the back of this convertible, were the grand marshals of the Fourth of July parade in 1990.

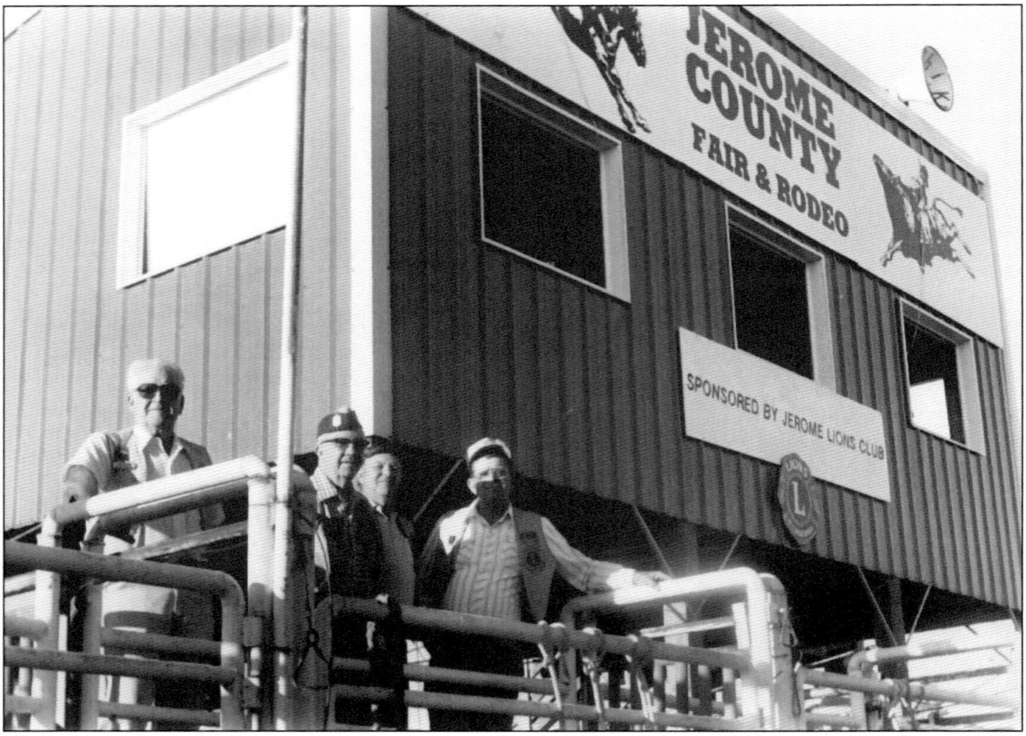

The county fair and rodeo is an exciting event that the residents look forward to each year. The Lions Club sold rodeo programs and ran the concession stand for many years.

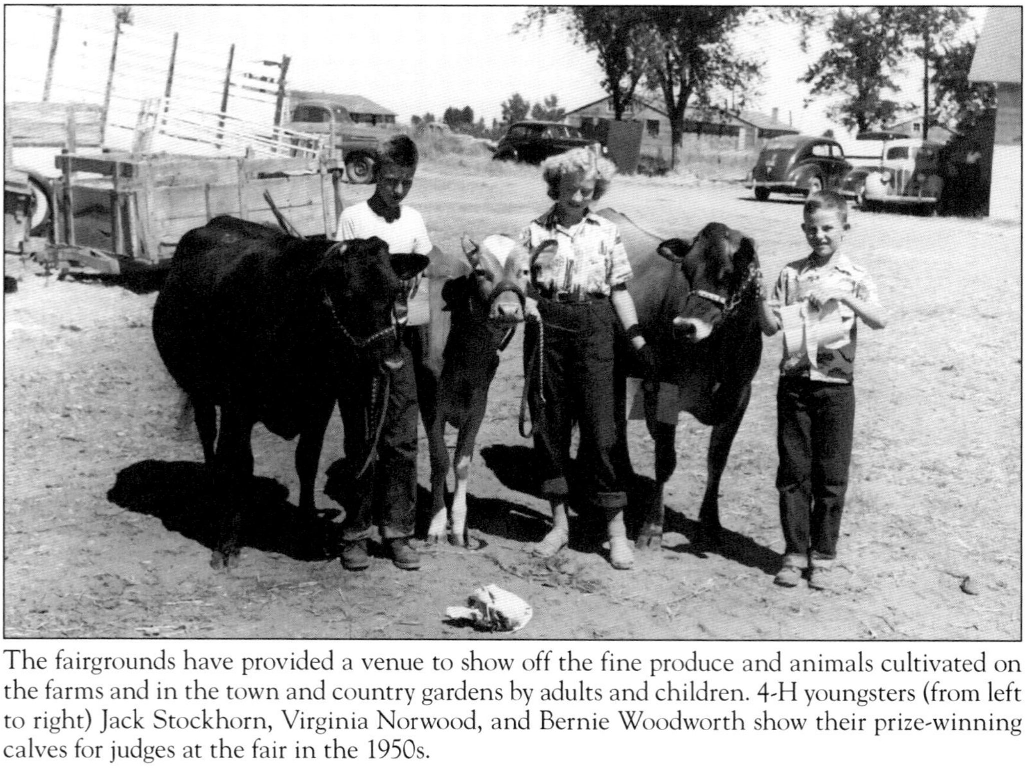

The fairgrounds have provided a venue to show off the fine produce and animals cultivated on the farms and in the town and country gardens by adults and children. 4-H youngsters (from left to right) Jack Stockhorn, Virginia Norwood, and Bernie Woodworth show their prize-winning calves for judges at the fair in the 1950s.

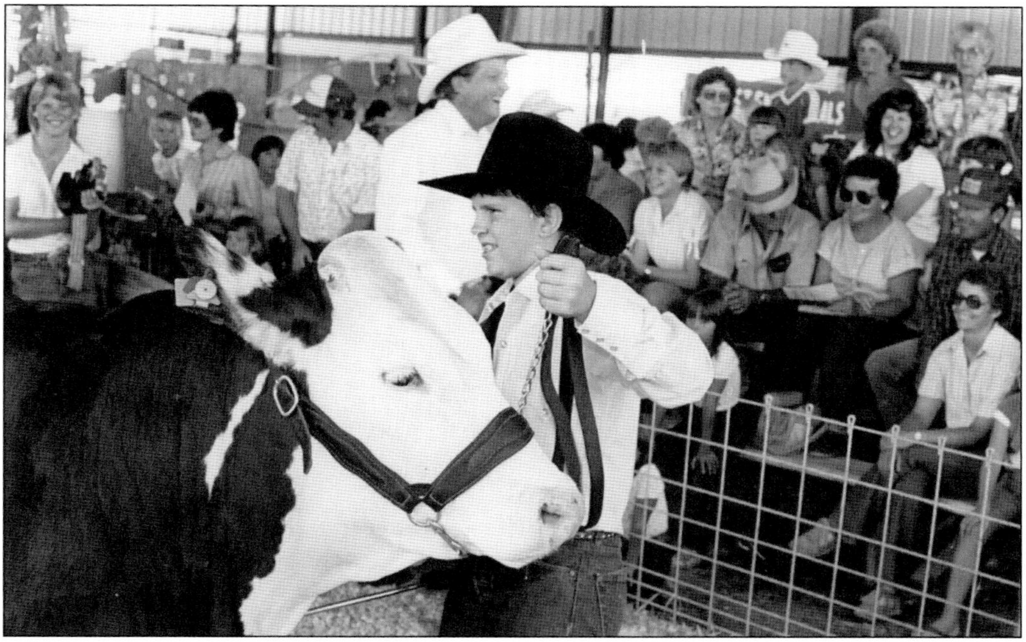

After the 4-H youngsters raise their animals through the summer and show them at the fair, the animals are then put up for auction, which helps train the children to understand the business. All the money earned from the auction went to the child to repay for the care and feeding of the animal, as well as putting a few dollars into their own bank account. Jerry James, wearing the white western hat in the center, is the auctioneer.

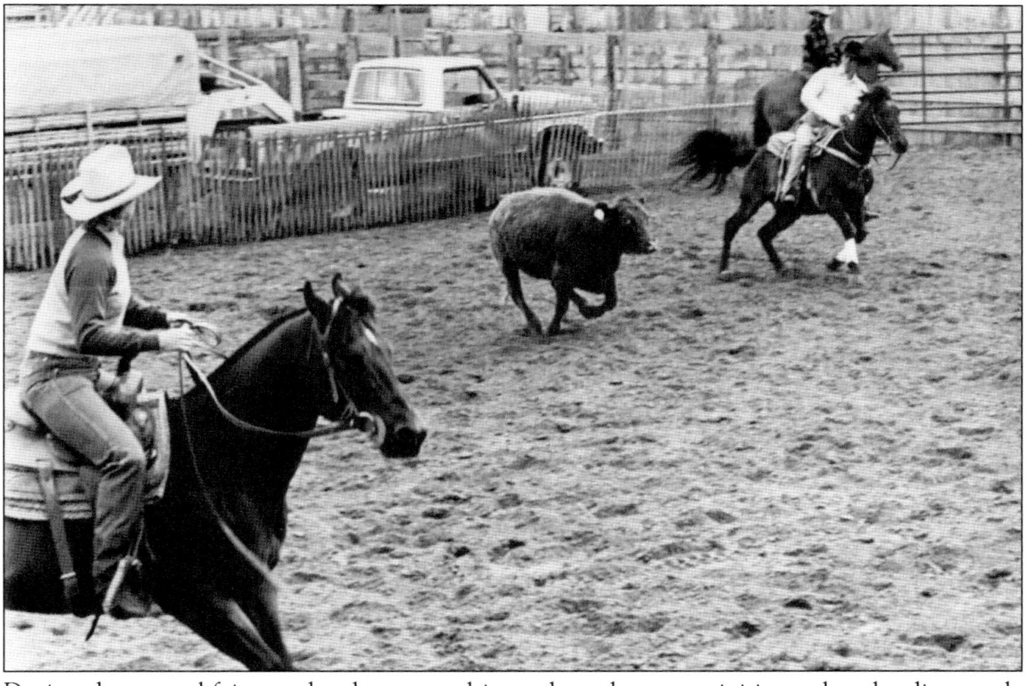

During the annual fair, a rodeo, horsemanship, and ranch-type activities such as herding cattle take place. These cowboys and cowgirl herd a calf into a holding pen at the other end of the arena after the calf-roping event.

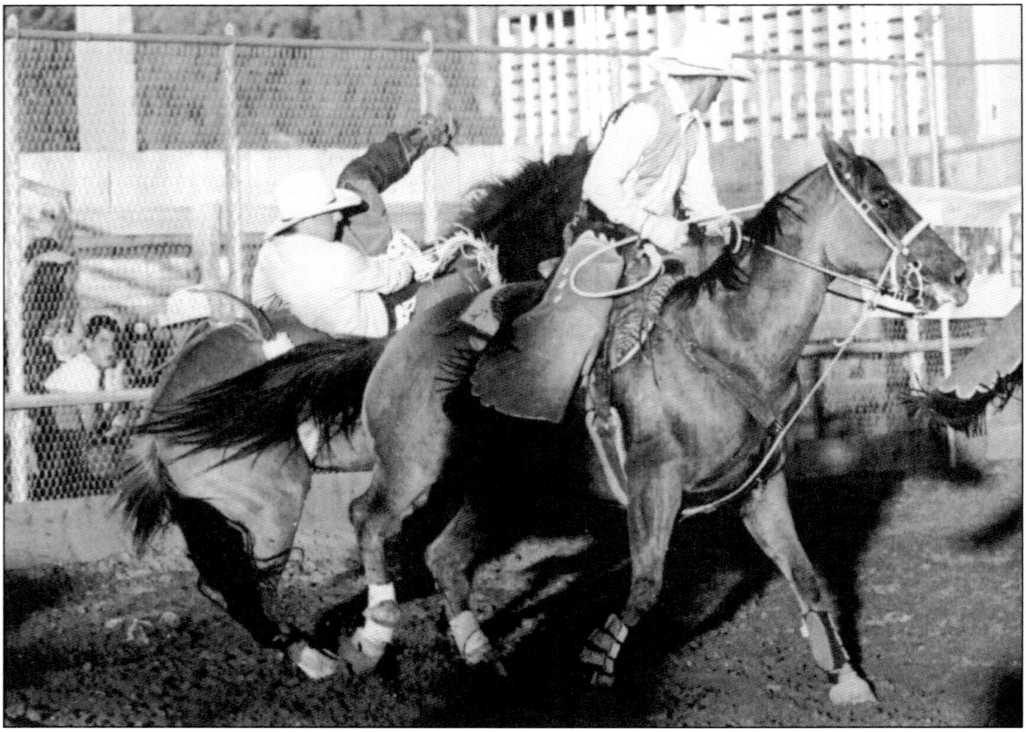

Another attraction at the rodeo is saddle bronc riding. The pickup man in the foreground is ready in case the bronc-riding cowboy needs to quickly move from the bronc onto the pickup man's horse.

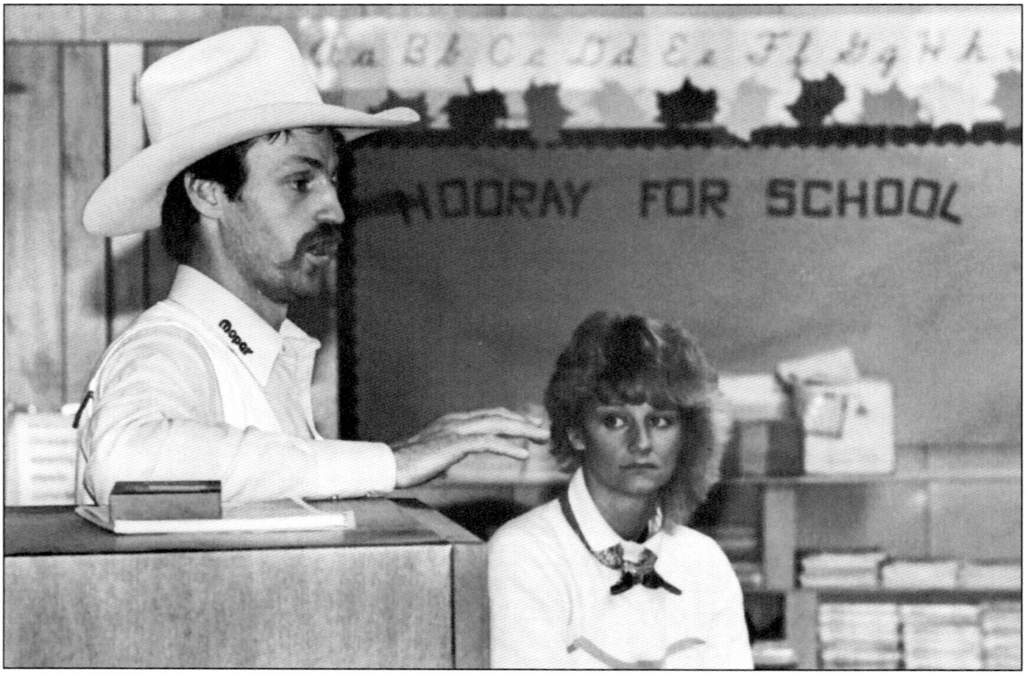

Mickey and Laurie Young tell a classroom about raising rodeo stock, as well as bucking horses and calves for roping. At one point, they also operated a natural herb store on Main Street.

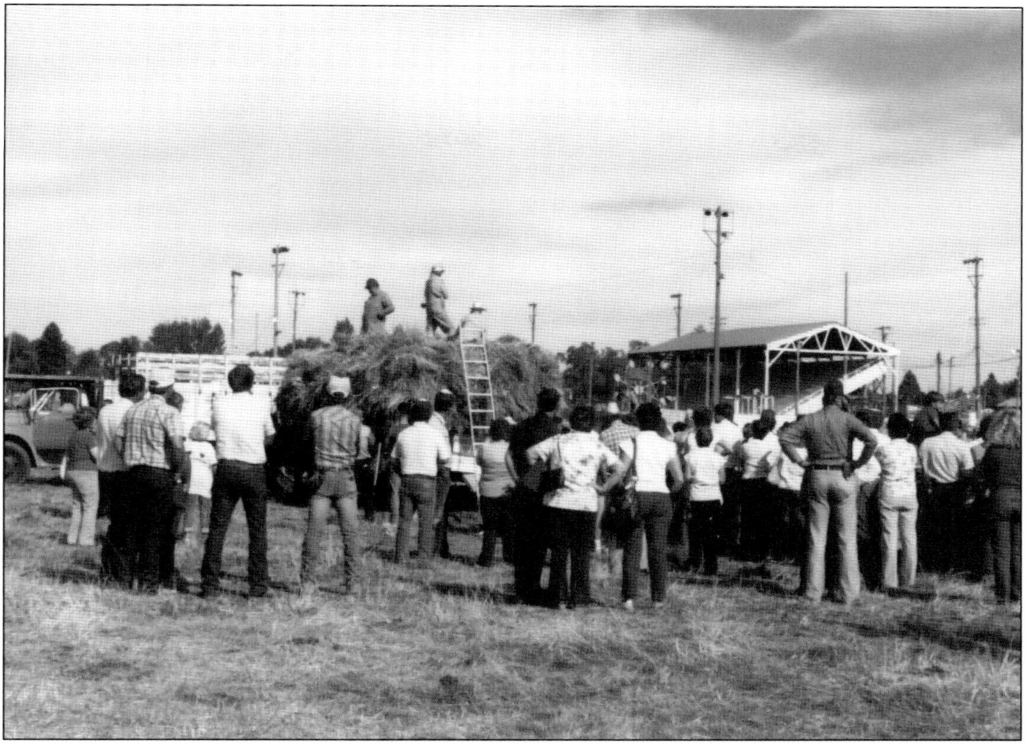

So that younger generations will understand how their farming ancestors worked, a haying demonstration was held at the fairgrounds. The rodeo grandstand is seen in the background.

Each year, a Miss Jerome County Rodeo Queen is chosen who then competes for Miss Rodeo Idaho; whoever wins that crown competes for Miss Rodeo America. Idaho has had five Miss Rodeo Americas and one Miss Rodeo USA. Jerome has the distinction of having three county rodeo queens go on to become Miss Rodeo Idaho, and all three of them went on to become Miss Rodeo America. Karen Lavens James (pictured) carried the three titles in 1960, 1961, and 1962.

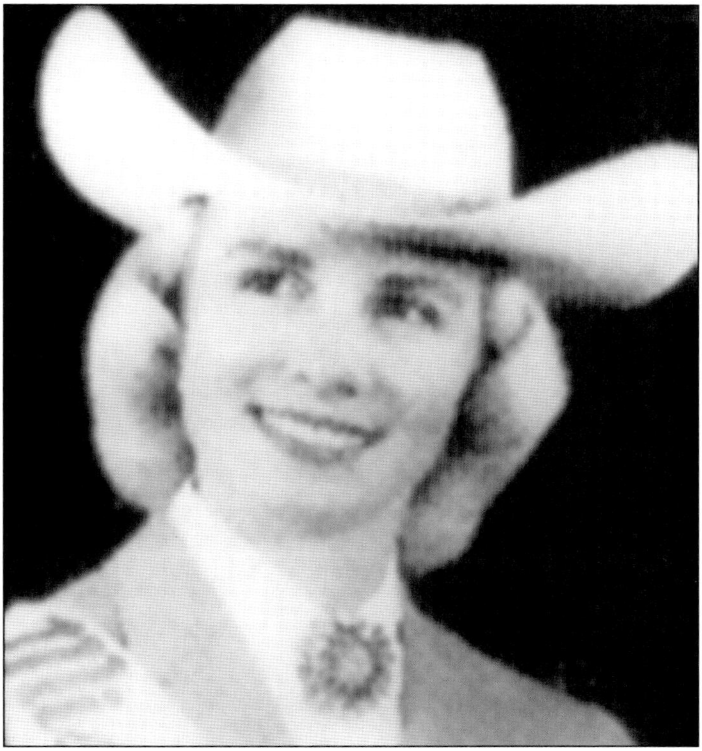

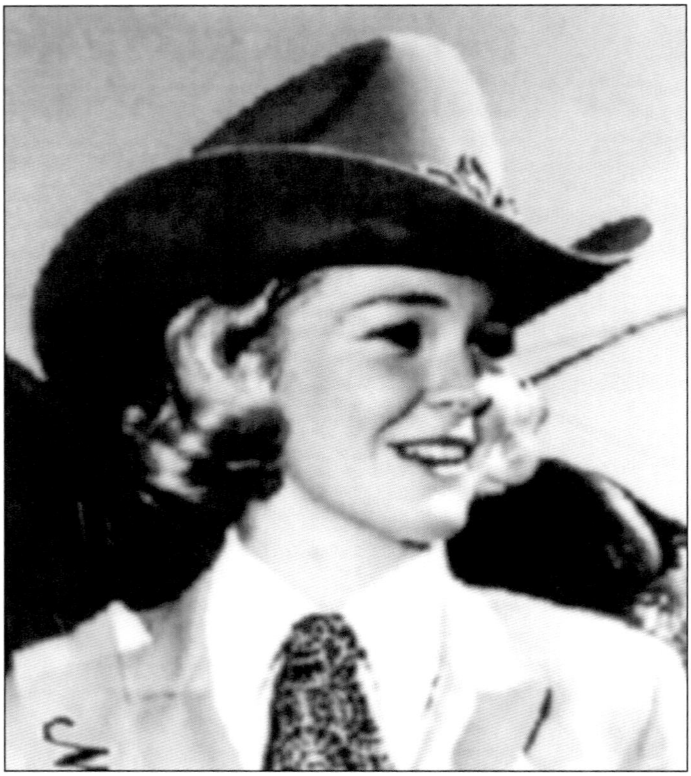

Lana Brackenbury Parker carried the three rodeo queen titles in 1969, 1970, and 1971.

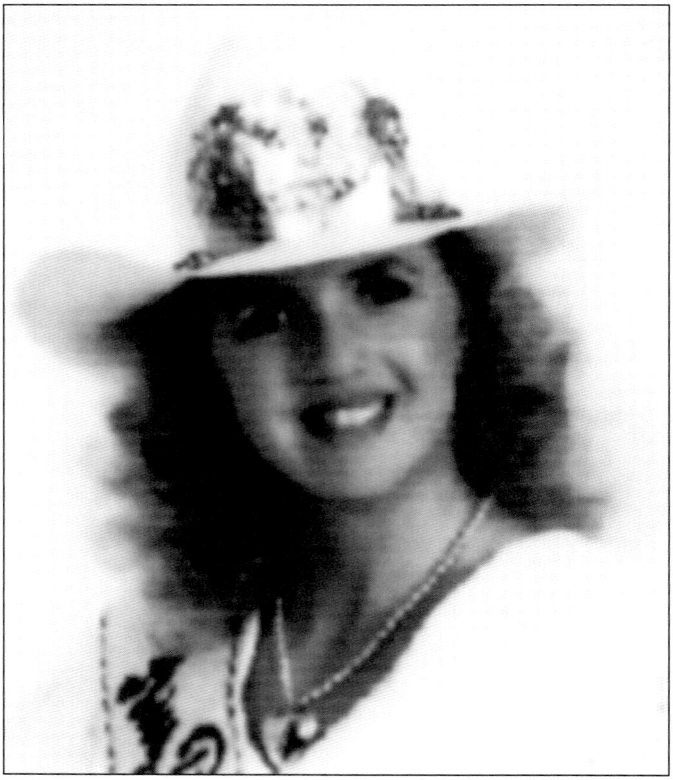

Joni James Smith carried the three rodeo queen titles in 1988, 1989, and 1990. She had the additional distinction, with her mother, Karen Lavens James, of being part of the only mother and daughter duo Miss Rodeo America queens in the history of the competition.

When the household had more garden produce and meat than could be eaten, it was donated to the community canning kitchen, where it was cooked in large amounts and then spooned into tin cans and sealed with lids. It was then marked with indelible pen and taken home by the gardeners. The kitchen began in 1947 and operated until 1980. There was a membership charge to belong to the canning kitchen, and the gardener paid a small fee per can to pay for the electricity and water for the kitchen.

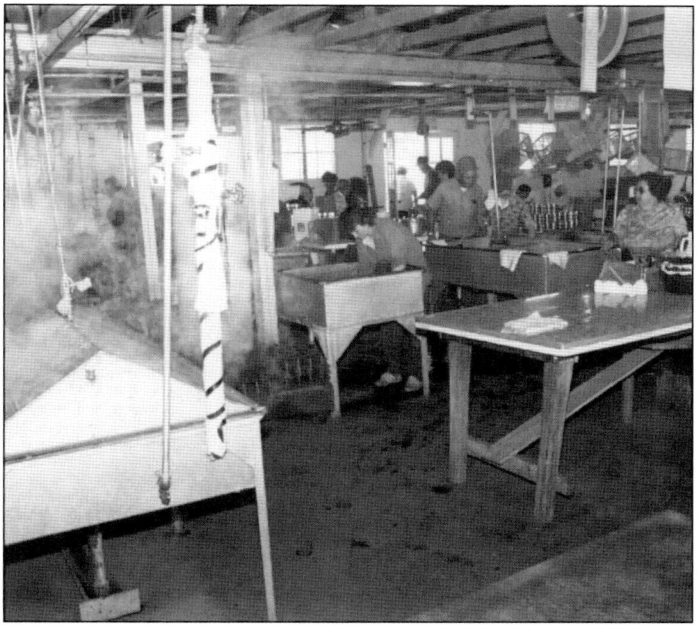

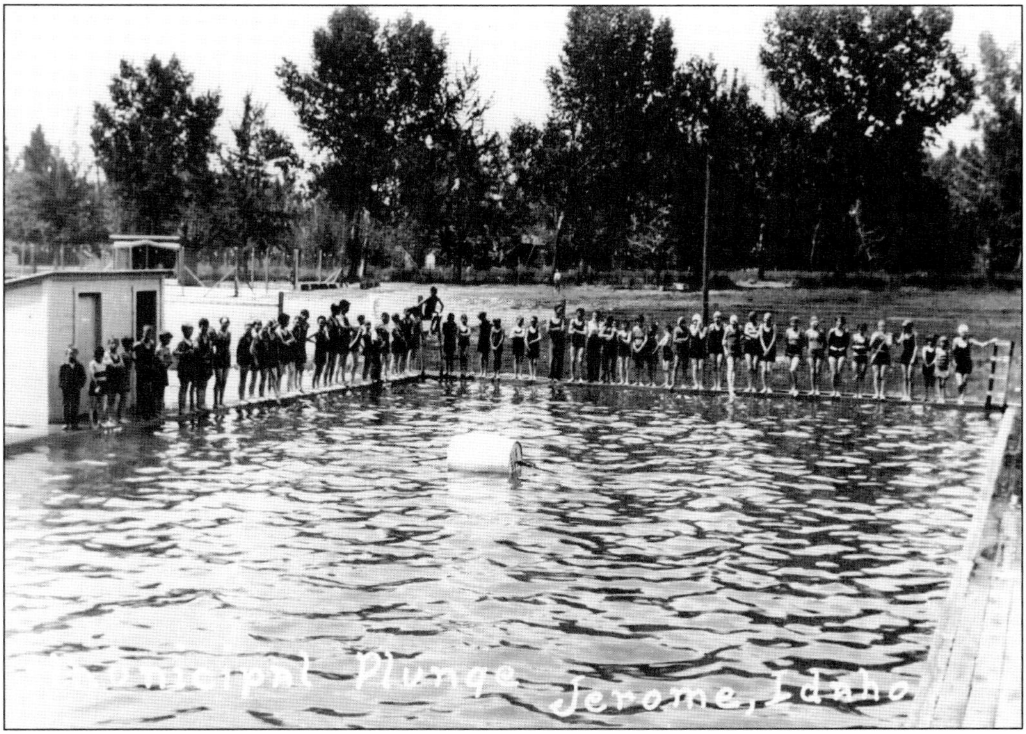

Between 1923 and 1947, Jerome children swam in this pool, located on the north side of the first block of East Avenue A. It was 16 feet by 24 feet and sloped from one foot to ten feet deep. When this pool was no longer needed, it was filled in with dirt, and a paved parking lot was placed over it. In November 2002, while replacing a water line, this forgotten pool was rediscovered by city workers, filled in properly, and resealed with asphalt.

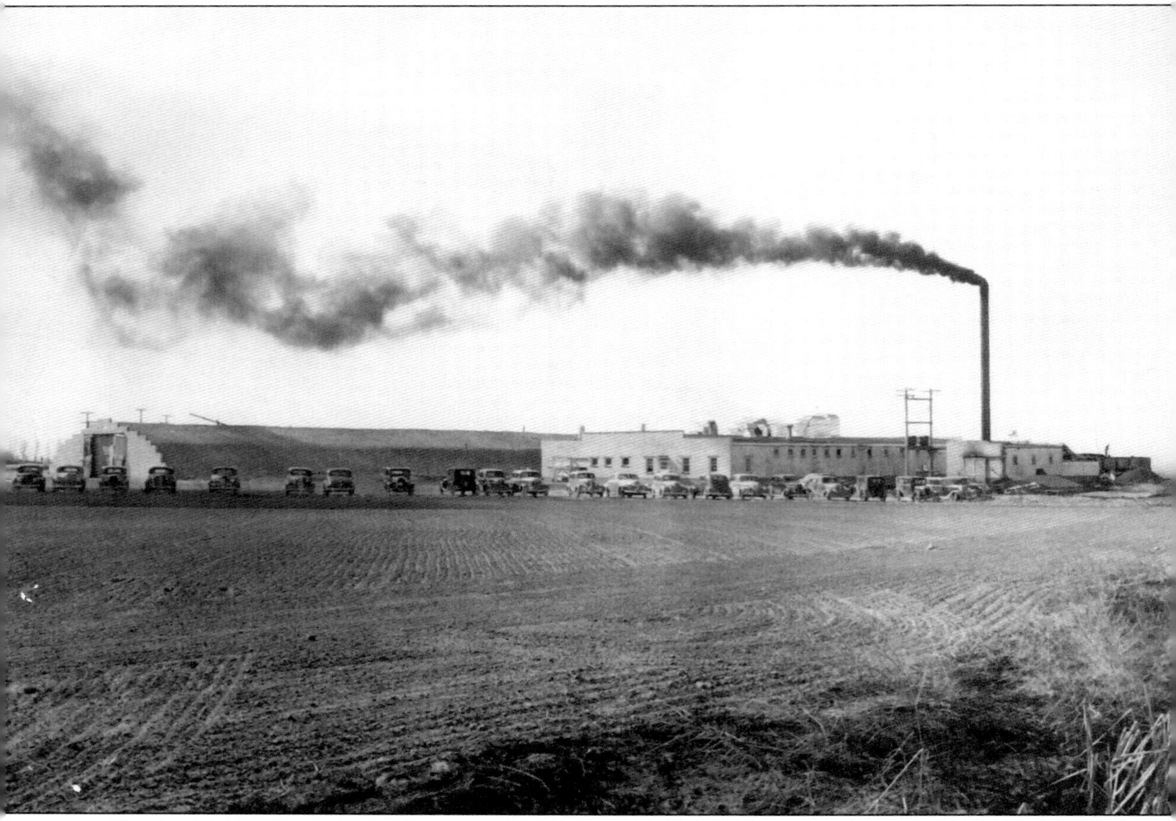

Charles Marshall was an early potato farmer in the Jerome area who discovered in 1934 that by processing the potatoes at his own plant south of Jerome, he could increase his earnings, help other local potato farmers, and employee local people. A large potato storage cellar is seen behind the plant.

Five

Irrigation

The north side of the Snake River Canyon was dry, sagebrush-covered land. It wasn't until the idea of building a dam and canal system came to light that anyone considered settling this area. With financing from eastern US millionaires, the dream became possible. The town of Milner was erected on the south side of the river as a construction camp for the dam, but with other towns thriving downriver, Milner became a ghost town in 1920.

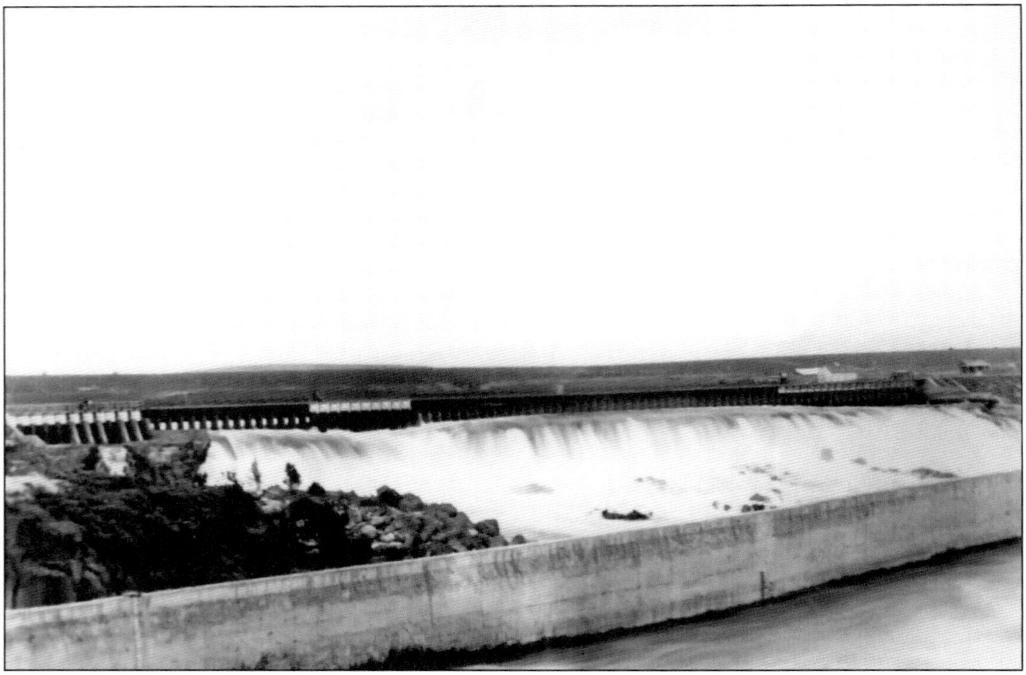

Milner Dam was envisioned in 1900 and completed in 1905. It was built on an area of the Snake River that was almost level with the countryside before it dropped into the deep canyon for the next 90 miles. Canals were then dug on the south side of the Snake River in 1906 and on the north side in 1908. The dam was 28 miles southeast of Jerome.

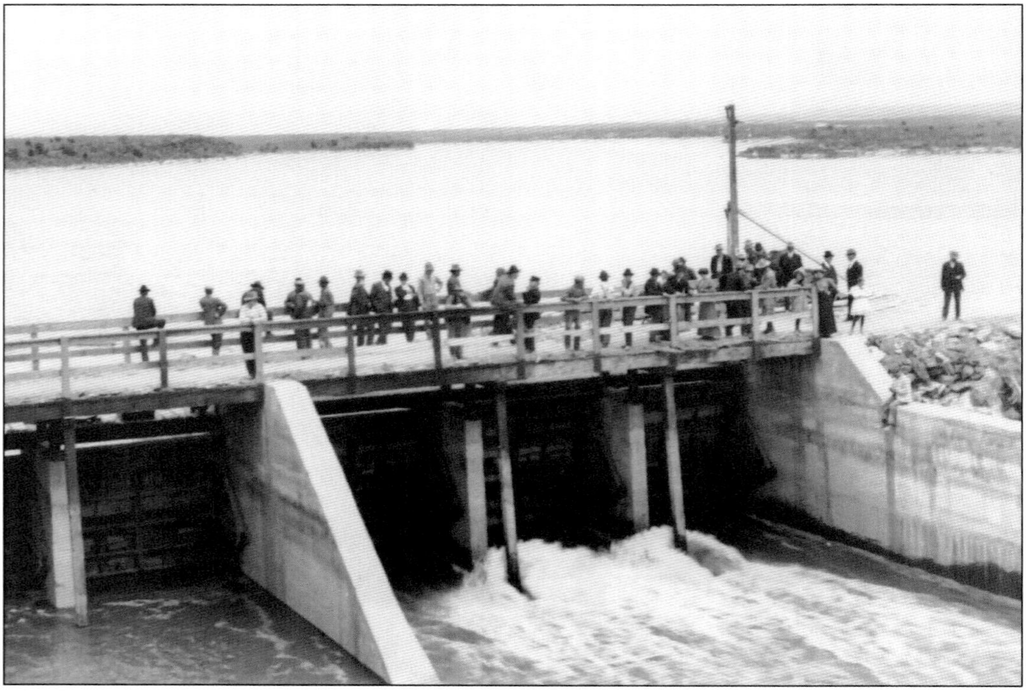

The financiers of the Milner Dam watch the water flow from the Milner Dam Reservoir into the North Side Canal on Sunday, April 10, 1909, at 1:27 p.m.

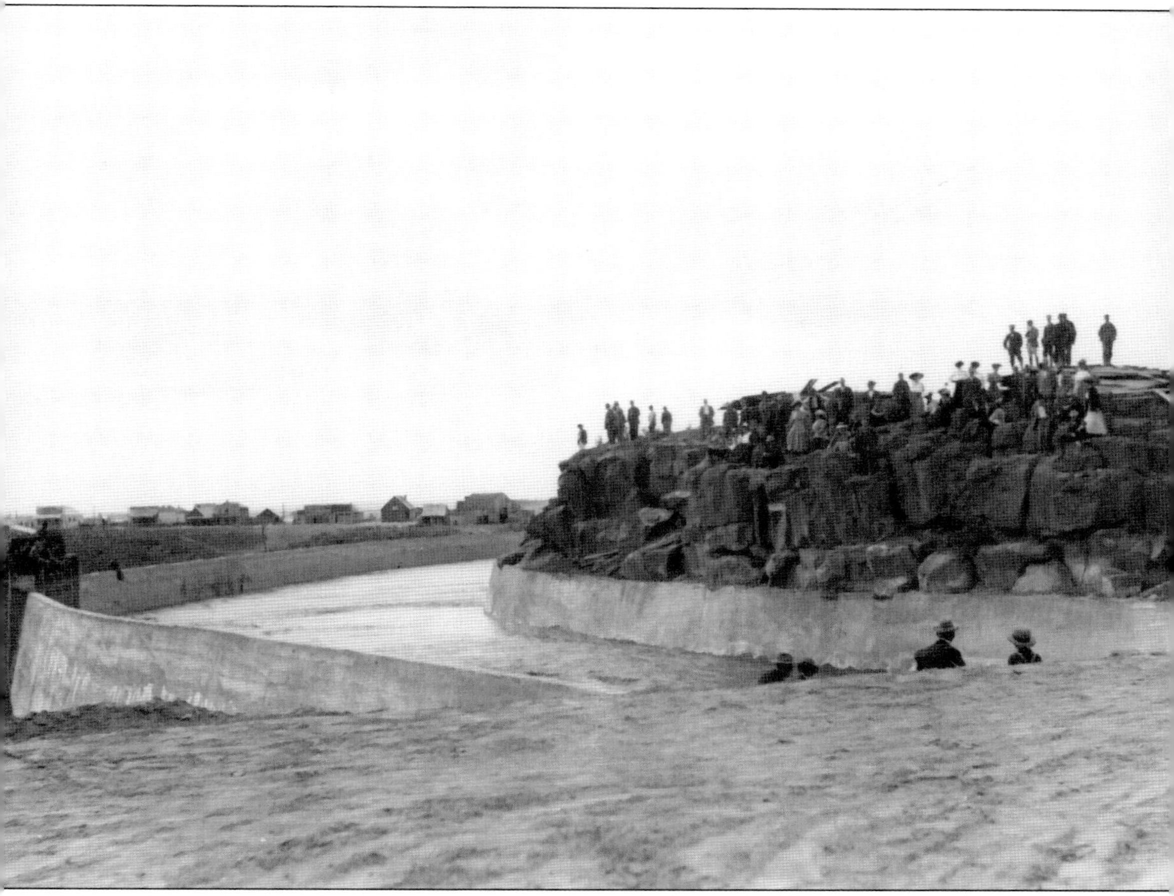

The land in this area is mostly basalt rock, so the North Side Canal was dug using horse teams, handpicks, shovels, and dynamite. The first time the water was sent through the canal in 1908, it disappeared through the cracks and crevices in the basalt rock. After a cement liner was added, the water was again turned into the canal on April 10, 1909. The men in the foreground stand on bare ground above the canal. Milner is seen in the background.

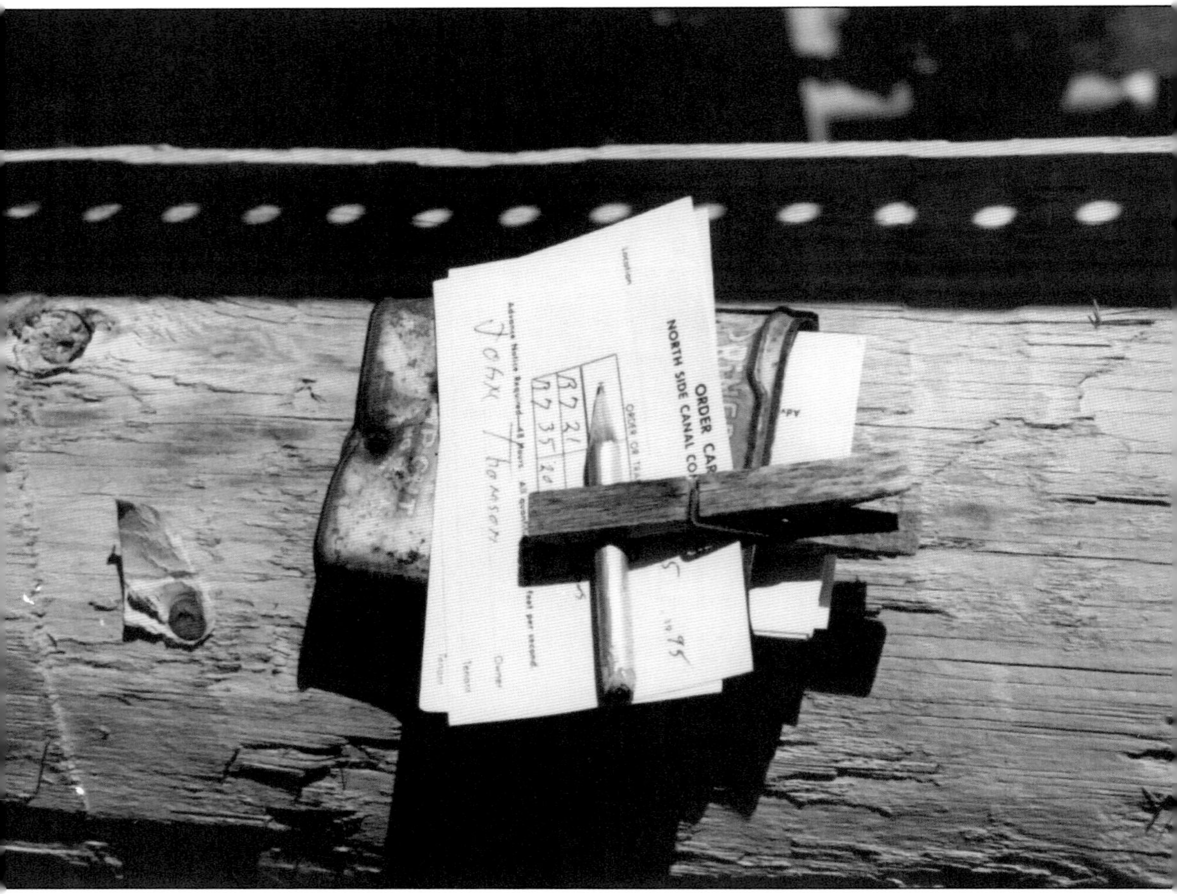

With the water in the main canal, laterals were dug to transfer water to the farm ditches. The laterals were closed off with headgates. Each farmer purchased water shares per acre of land to be irrigated from the North Side Canal Company. The ditch riders made sure that each farmer received his appropriate amount of water through the headgates. Different amounts of water were needed for the crops at specific times throughout the year. When ordering water, a farmer left a notice for the ditch rider on a fence post near the headgate. Blank cards were left in an old Prince Albert tobacco can nailed to the fence post, and the current order was attached to the can with a clothespin.

Six

Blue Lakes Ranch

When Ira B. Perrine was introduced to this area by Charles Walgamott in 1884, he decided it was his Utopia. The trail down into the canyon was only wide enough to walk and lead his pony and 25 head of dairy cattle to the river. He built a house and barn and planted poplar trees, fruit tree orchards of cherries, apples, peaches, and plums, and a vegetable garden with strawberries and raspberries. By 1891, his fruit was so fine, he took some examples to Paris, France, and received first prize, as well as additional prizes many years after that. He decided if the river water helped his orchard and garden grow so well, the river could water farms on the rim. With his office in his home, he convinced wealthy businessmen to finance the greatest irrigation system in the new state of Idaho. His descendants still reside in this area.

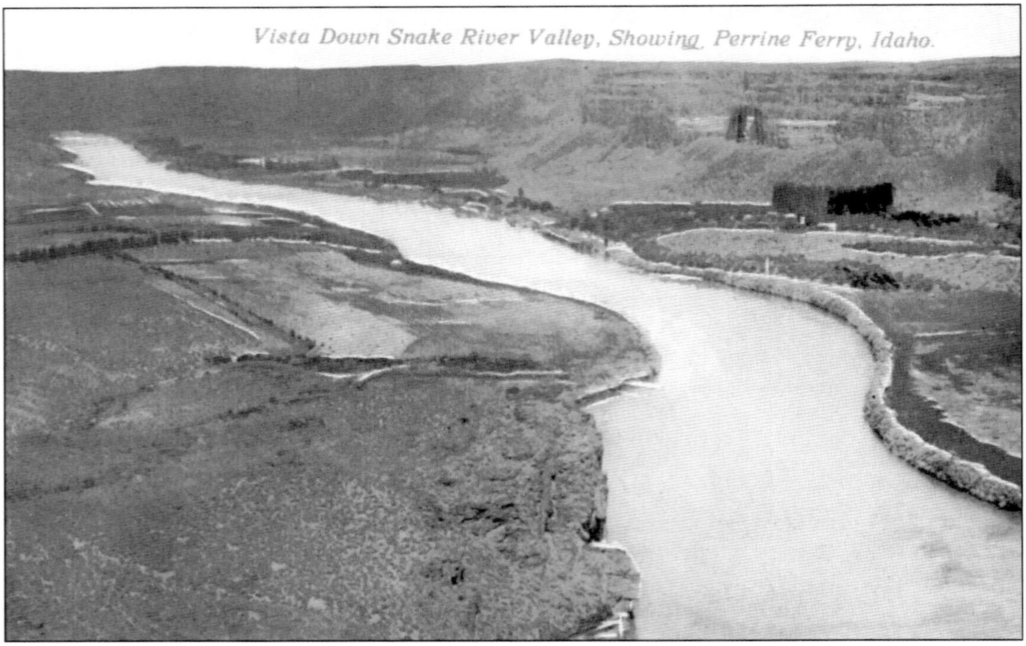

This portion of the Snake River runs in front of Ira Perrine's home. Perrine's ferryboat, which is not visible in this photograph taken from the south canyon rim, was used to freight people, animals, and produce across this portion of the Snake River between 1884 and 1900. The Perrine family donated the ferryboat bell to the Jerome Centennial Committee in 2007, and it is now housed at the Jerome Senior Center.

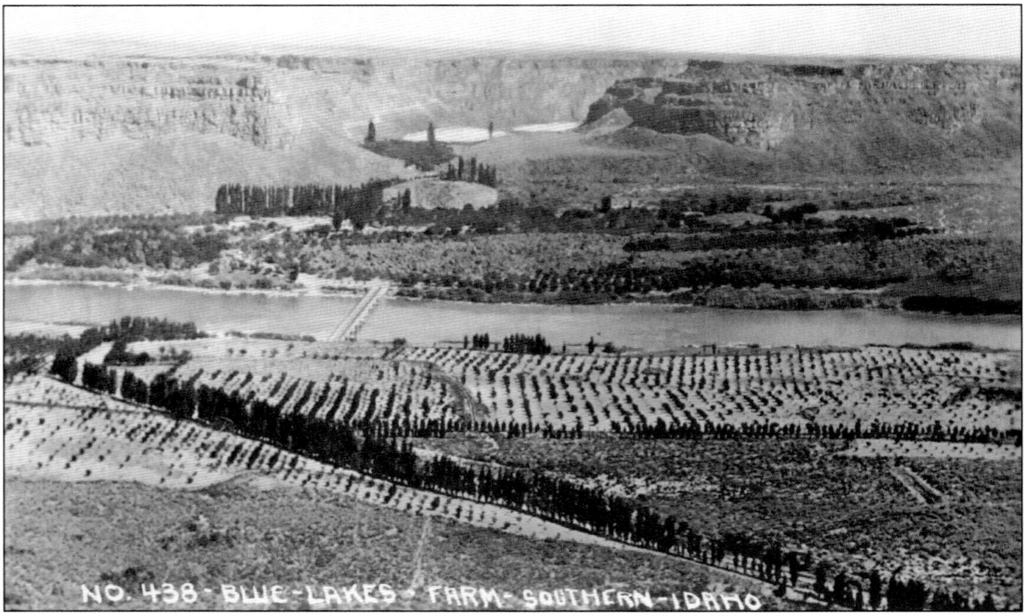

This photograph was taken from the top of the south rim. The Blue Lakes are seen in the background with the north rim road snaking down the side of the canyon. Ira B. and Hortense Perrine's home is in the center of the image toward the right on the north side of the Snake River. About 1900, Perrine retired his ferryboat and built a wooden bridge across the river. In 1927, a new rim-to-rim toll bridge was constructed just above Perrine's ranch.

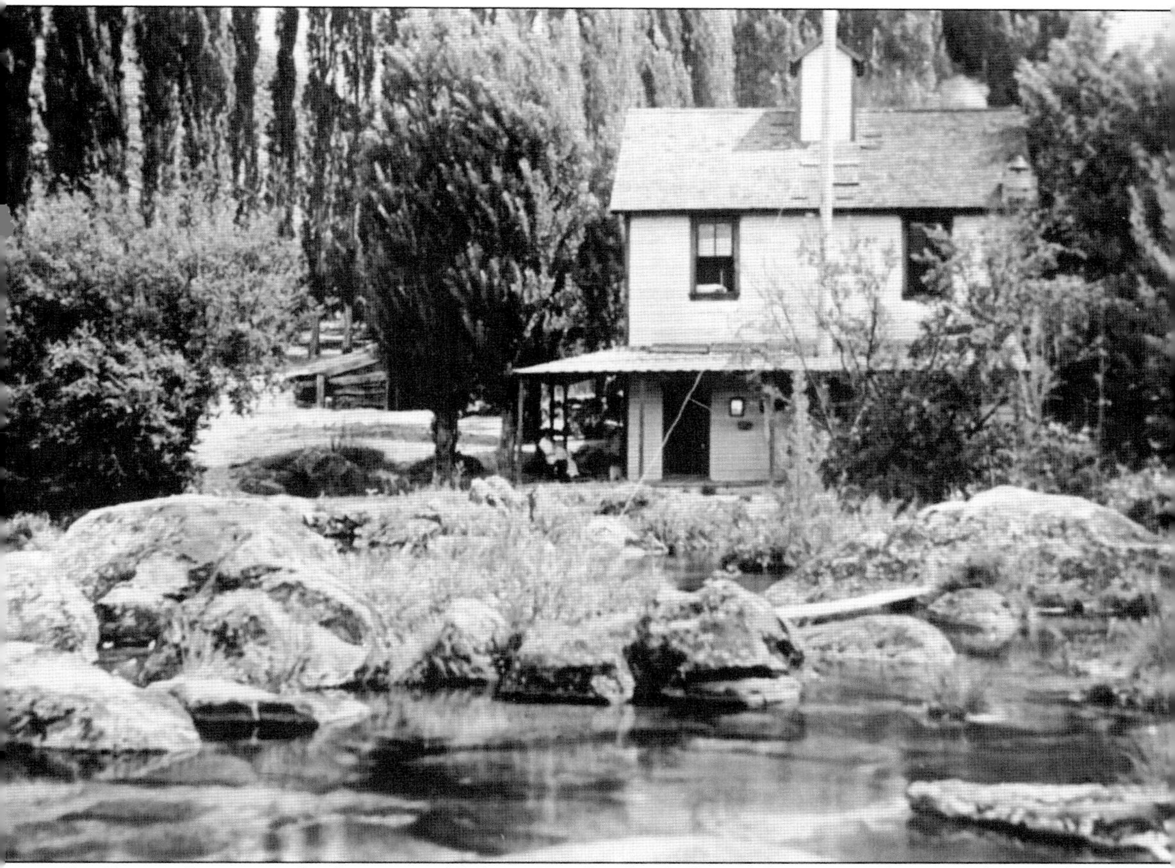

The Perrine home was built next to Alpheus Creek, which flowed from an underground natural well. A post office was established in the home with Hortense Perrine as postmistress. The home was visited by many state and national dignitaries, as well as local people who came for garden parties and picnics.

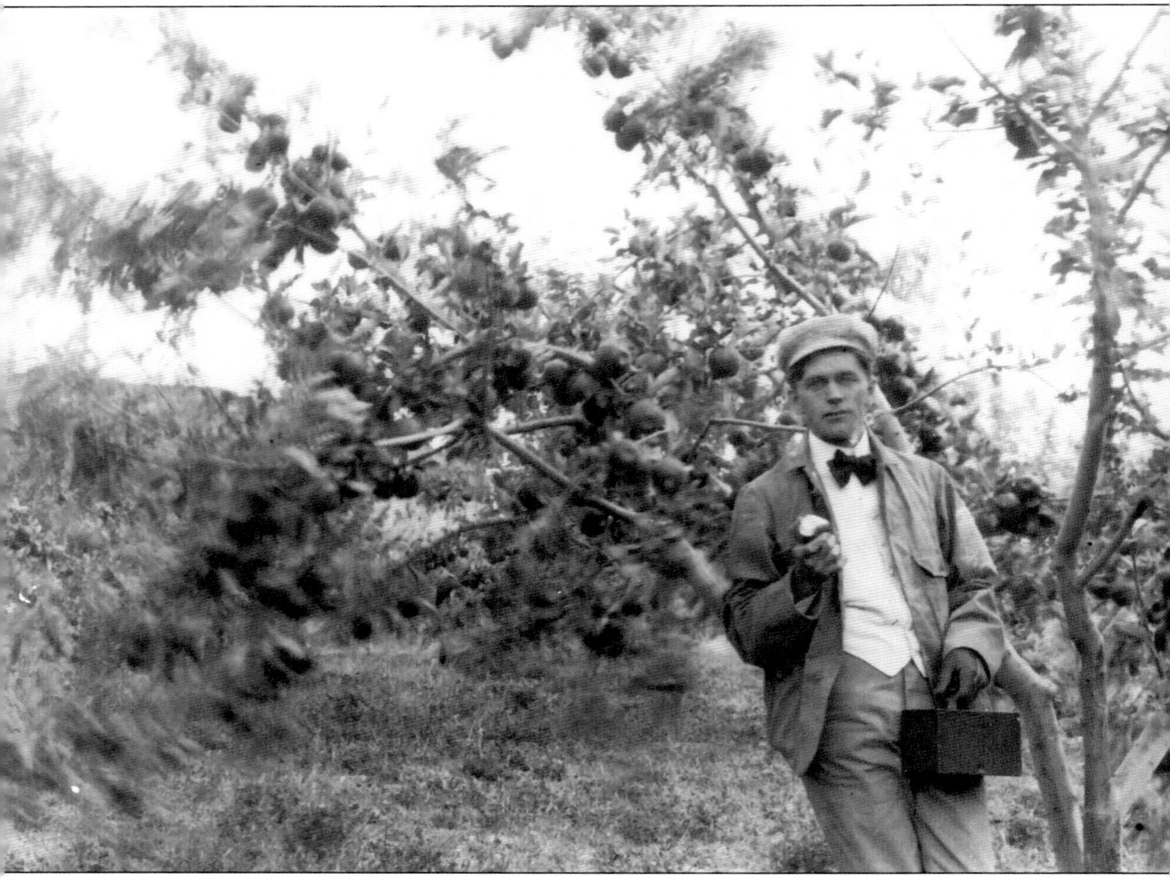

Rob Spafford is pictured here in Perrine's apple orchard in 1907. Some of these trees still grow on the Perrine ranch and produce great fruit.

Seven

Jerome's First Farmers

When prospective farmers were promised relatively cheap land and water to irrigate the arid desert land under the 1894 Carey Act, hundreds of people flocked to the north side area. After purchasing the land, part of the requirement was to "prove up" a portion of the land. A structure had to be erected, commonly called a "prove-up shack." The owner had to live on the land and at least have five acres plowed and planted for five years. This was to prove that the owner and family were going to actually work the land, not just buy it on speculation and quickly sell it for immediate monetary gain. Orchards, gardens, and crops were planted; however, the vegetation came across obstacles. Sagebrush has very deep, wide-spreading roots searching for underground water, and there were basalt rock ledges in most areas, as well as arid, shallow volcanic ash topsoil. Additionally, a myriad of rabbits and yellow-bellied marmots (also known as "rock chucks") loved to eat the tender shoots of trees and other crops. With the irrigation canals delivering water to the area, persistence in grubbing the sagebrush, and plowing and fencing, these obstacles have been overcome, and the farmers have excelled in crop production.

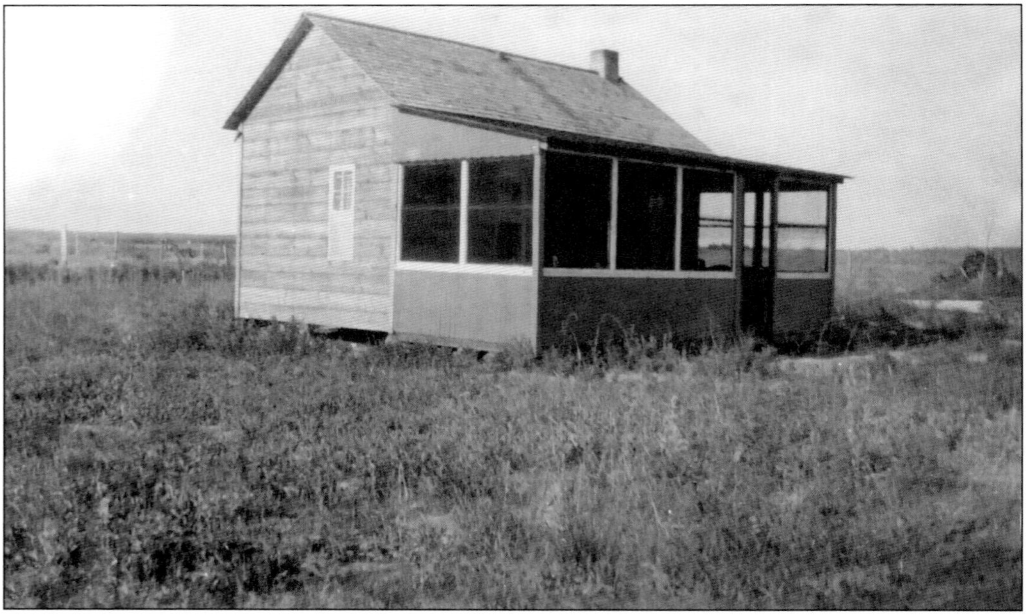

Percy G. Fairman's prove-up shack, situated north of Jerome in 1909, met the requirements for land ownership. Usually, these houses were very small, perhaps only one or two rooms. Some homes actually had kitchens, parlors, and more than one bedroom. Almost no early home had bathrooms, and some had only a pump handle for water in the kitchen.

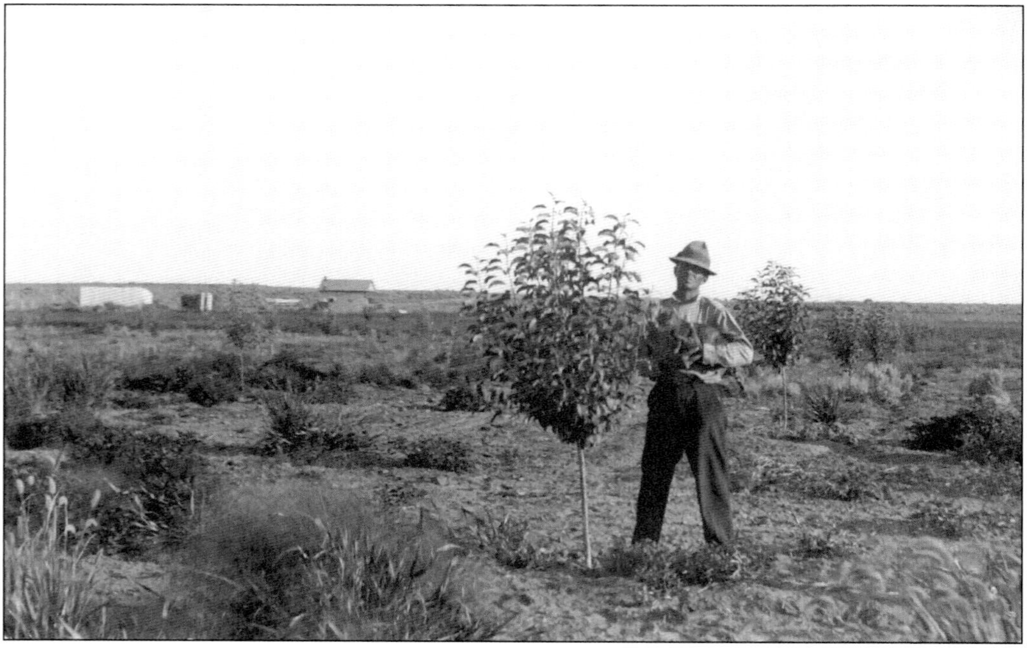

The deep snowfall of the 1909–1910 winter provided the rabbits a close-up area to "girdle" the new trees, eating the leaves off their bottoms. Percy G. Fairman shows the damage that rabbits caused in 1910.

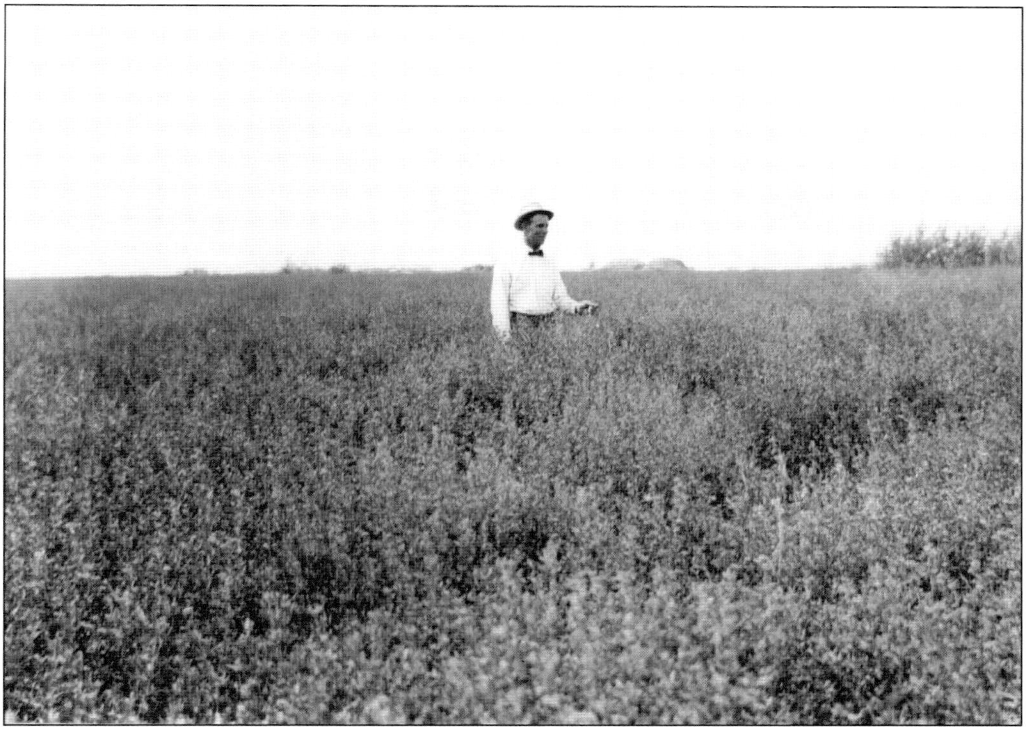
A Jerome-area farmer shows off his first stand of alfalfa, which is a favorite crop in this area, not only for immediate farm use, but also to sell outside of the area.

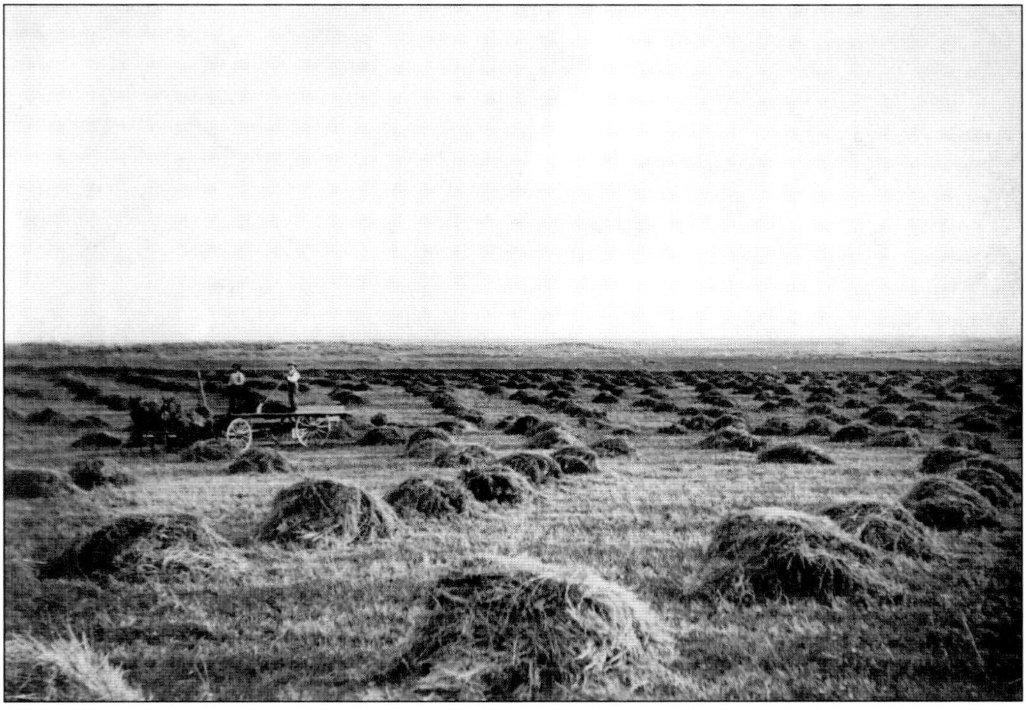
Two men have cut and "mini-stacked" the alfalfa to dry. They will now fork the hay (as the dried alfalfa is called) onto the horse-drawn wagon and haul it to a stack closer to the barnyard.

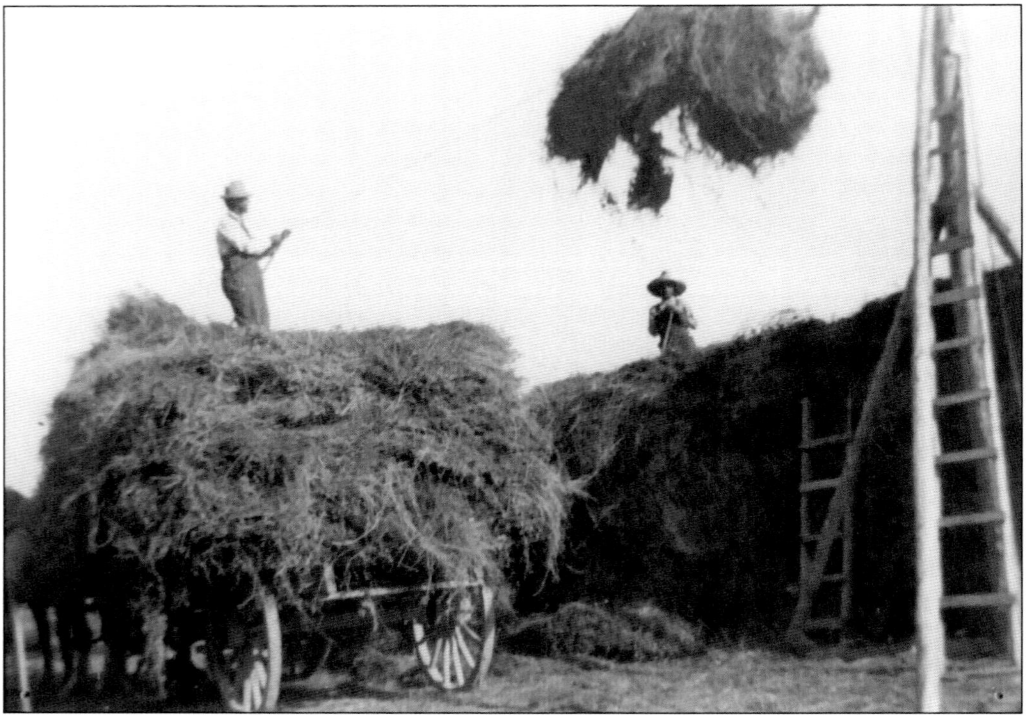

After the hay wagon is full and driven to the barnyard, the hay is transferred by four-foot-wide, four-pronged forks attached to cables to the main stack. The man on the main haystack then spreads the hay evenly across the top of the stack so it will not fall over.

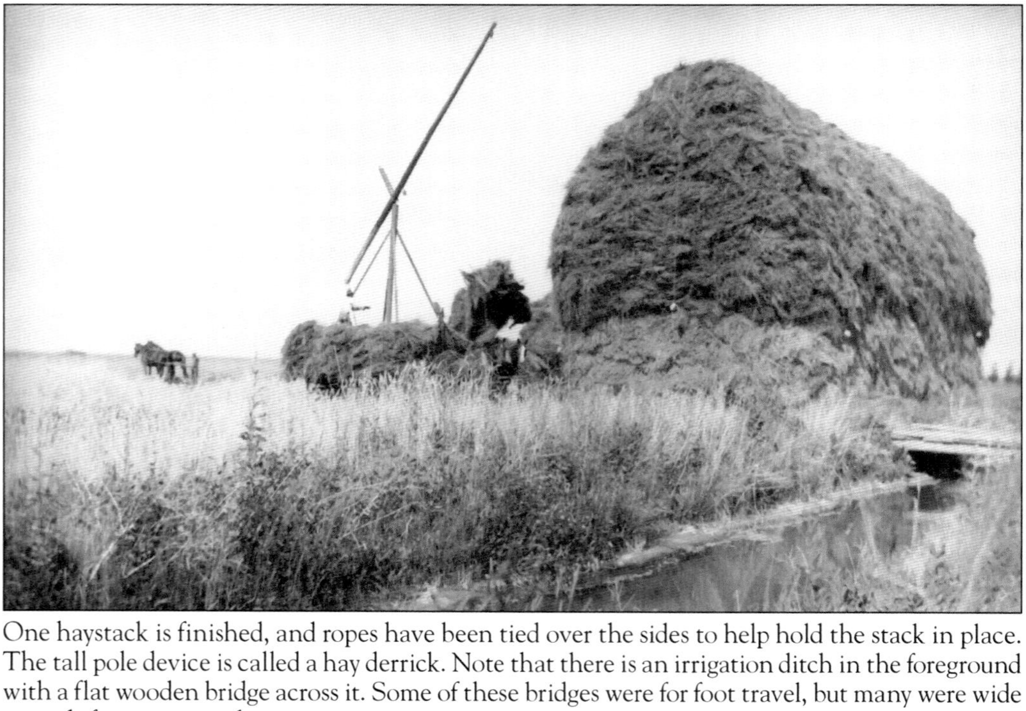

One haystack is finished, and ropes have been tied over the sides to help hold the stack in place. The tall pole device is called a hay derrick. Note that there is an irrigation ditch in the foreground with a flat wooden bridge across it. Some of these bridges were for foot travel, but many were wide enough for a team and wagon to cross.

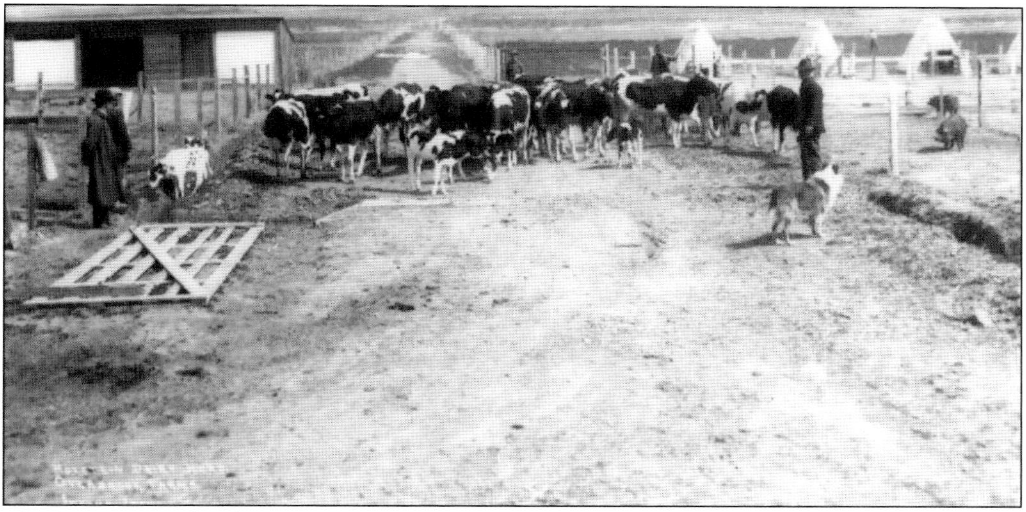

The Jerome area has been home to dairy and beef cattle since the beginning. One of the first dairy herds was at the Overbrook farm. In this photograph, Holstein cows and calves are being moved from a pasture area to a corral, perhaps in preparation for milking. The stacked hay will be fed to the cattle after the milking.

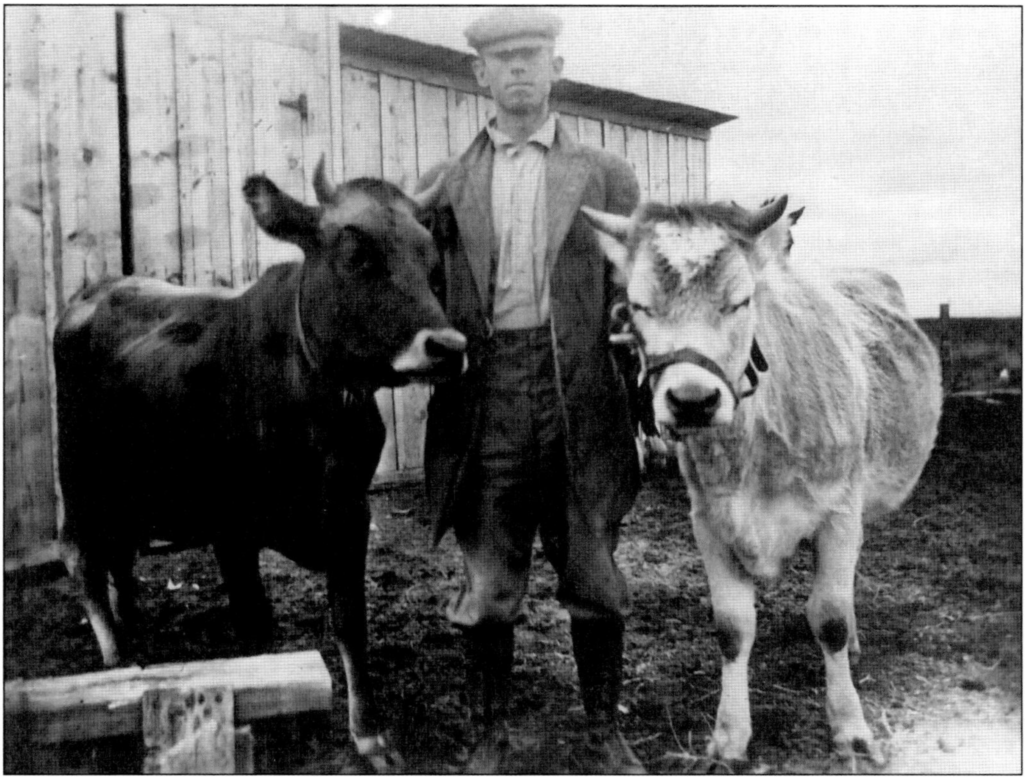

Another breed of dairy cattle on the Jerome farms was Jersey, which provided higher butterfat milk. Ralph Wallace, pictured here, is very proud of his Jersey herd.

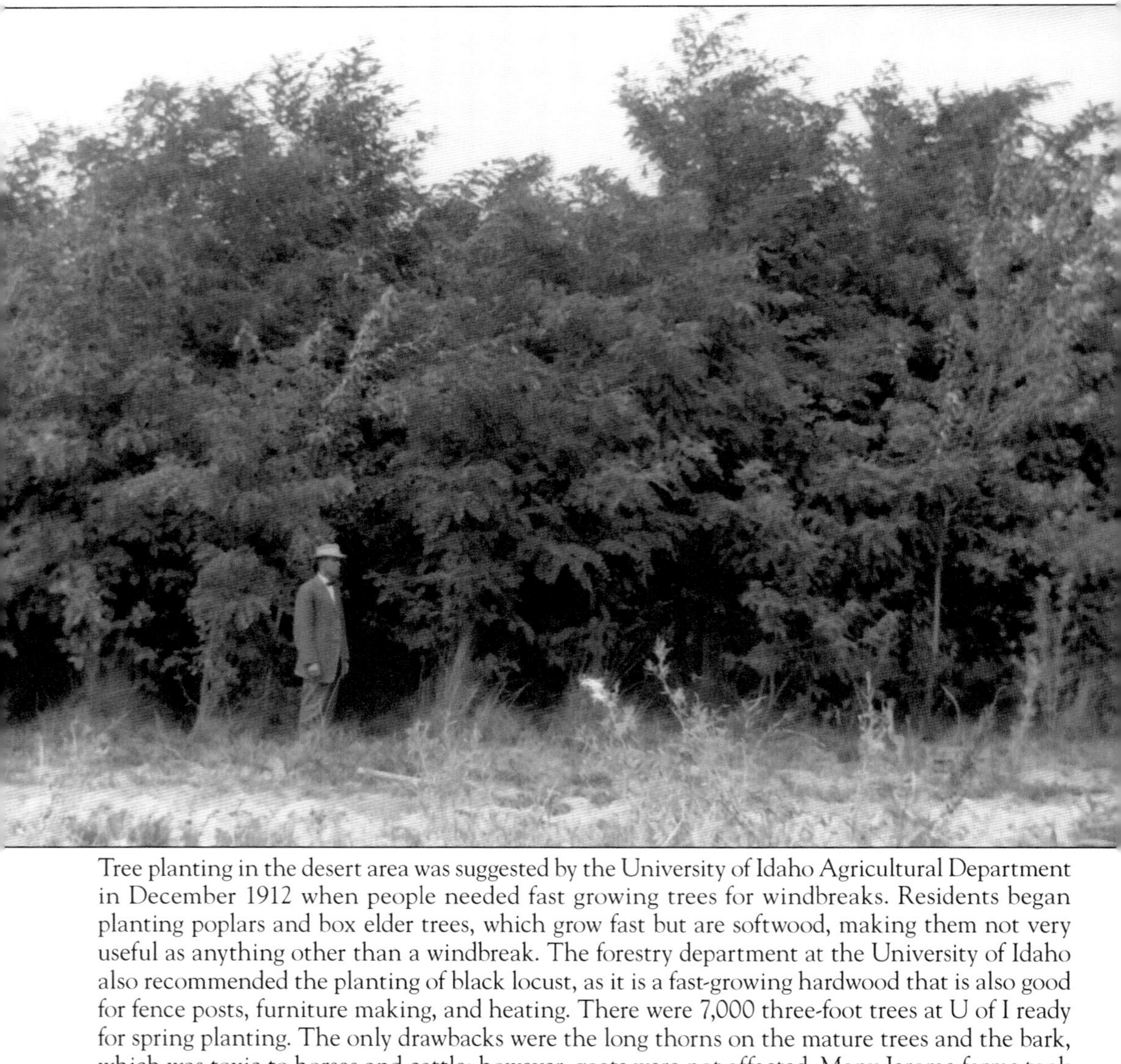

Tree planting in the desert area was suggested by the University of Idaho Agricultural Department in December 1912 when people needed fast growing trees for windbreaks. Residents began planting poplars and box elder trees, which grow fast but are softwood, making them not very useful as anything other than a windbreak. The forestry department at the University of Idaho also recommended the planting of black locust, as it is a fast-growing hardwood that is also good for fence posts, furniture making, and heating. There were 7,000 three-foot trees at U of I ready for spring planting. The only drawbacks were the long thorns on the mature trees and the bark, which was toxic to horses and cattle; however, goats were not affected. Many Jerome farms took advantage of this suggestion, and some windbreaks still stand in the area.

Eight

Japanese-American Internment Camp

December 7, 1941, and the next four years affected the Jerome area in a difficult way. Many Jerome residents were drafted and joined the military. Others stayed, continuing to raise crops, some for the local market and some for the military. In the summer of 1942, President Roosevelt and his advisors determined that all persons of Japanese descent should be moved from the Pacific coast to inland internment camps. Ten internment camps (also called relocation centers) were constructed in different US states, and one was situated just 13 miles east of Jerome in the area known as Hunt. Out of the 100,000 persons relocated, 9,385 were transported from Puyallup, Washington, by train to Jerome. The first 600 arrived on August 10, 1942, and were housed for a week at the Jerome County Fairgrounds until the Morrison-Knutson Company completed the barracks buildings at the camp. By September, the remainder of the Japanese Americans arrived at the camp. Even though they were in the middle of a desert area, the internees made the best of their time and place; they had a garden to supplement the government meals and raised chickens for eggs and meat. They also had a school, a newspaper, a store, and access to medical care. Even though they were under armed guard with a barbed-wire fence surrounding the camp, they were allowed to have passes to work in the fields of the local farmers. In 1943, the US government determined the men were eligible for US military service, so the 442nd Infantry Regiment Combat Team was formed and sent to fight for their country in Europe. This unit was the most decorated of World War II and suffered the most casualties. The camp was closed November 1, 1945, but many of the internees remained in this area as very productive citizens.

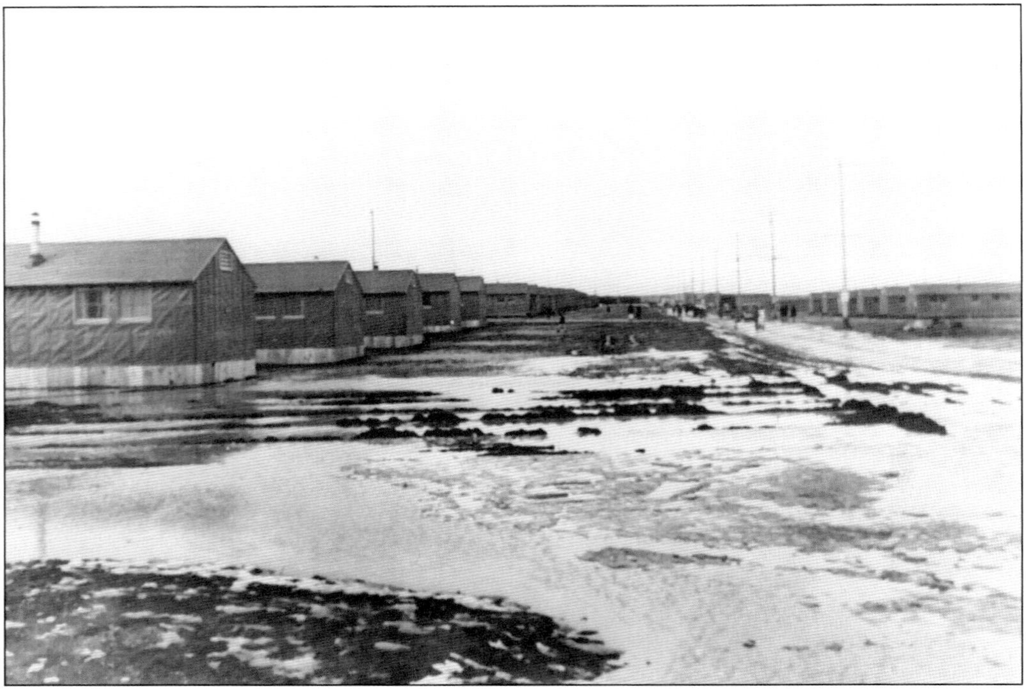

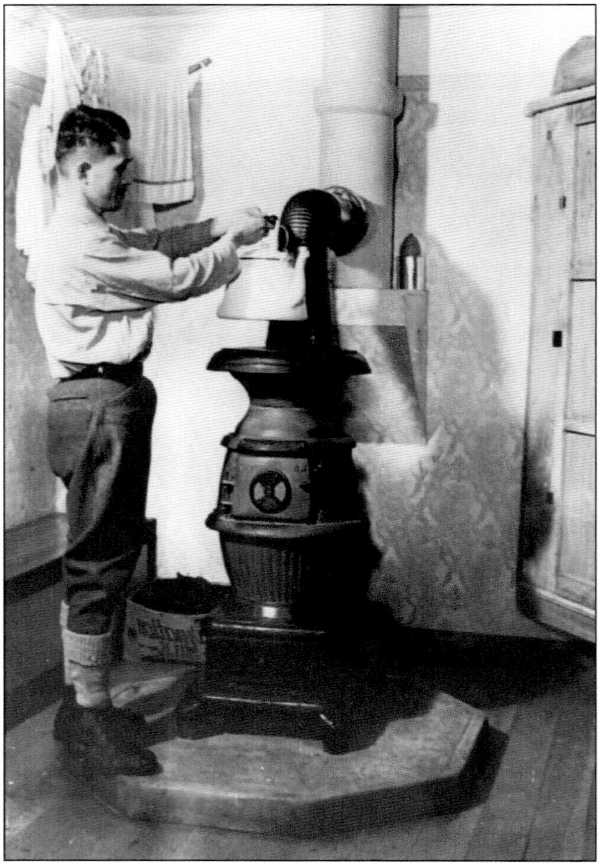

Some of the 550 wood-frame and tarpaper-covered buildings on over 300 acres of land that were homes for the Japanese American internees are shown here. In December 1942, some of the snow had melted into icy puddles.

Inside the barracks were three apartments, each with an outside door, one bare lightbulb hanging from the ceiling, wooden floors, and one potbellied stove for heat. There were also iron cots for beds. The gentleman pictured here heats water for tea or a quick wash. The residents ate in a mess hall and did laundry in one of the barracks. Restrooms and showers were in another barracks.

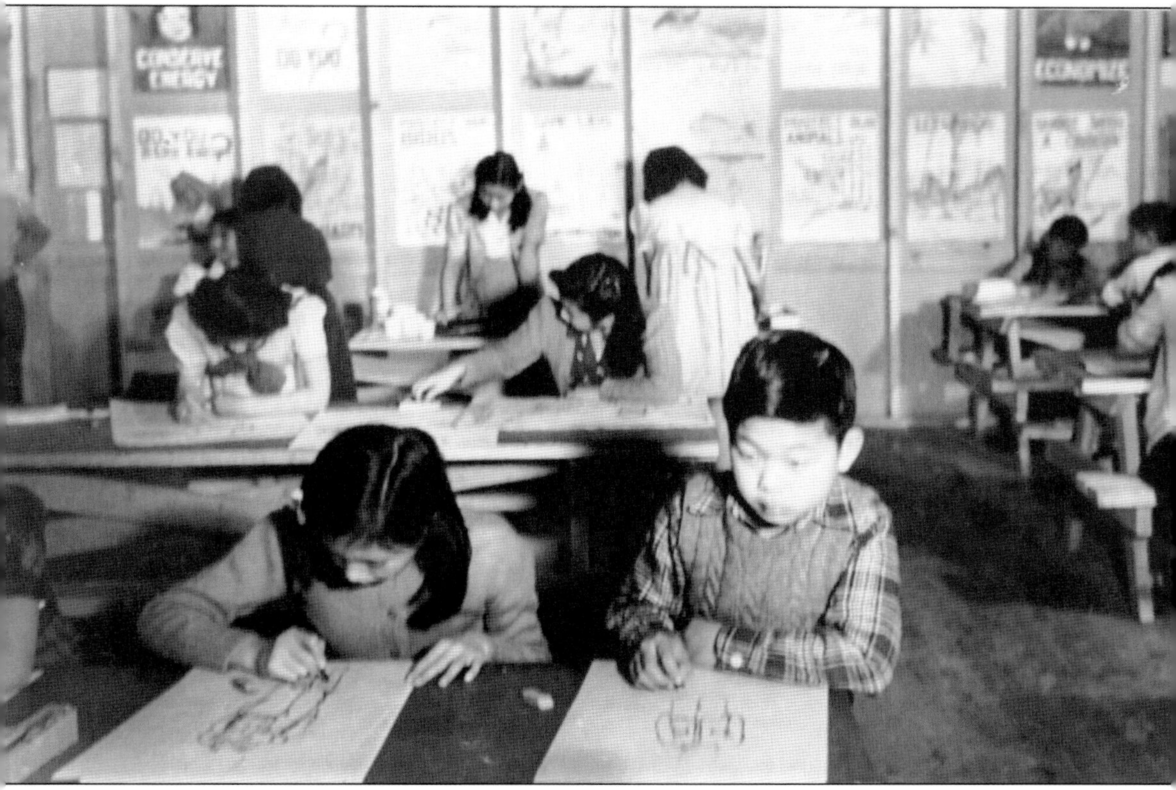

These children continued their schooling at the camp. It was the largest school in Jerome County, with 1,200 students registering on November 14, 1942. The first high school graduation commencement on July 23, 1943, had 210 graduates who, before coming here, had attended 52 different high schools in Oregon and Washington. The school's fourth and last commencement was on June 1, 1945. During the history of the camp, 3,881 students attended Hunt High School, with 695 graduating.

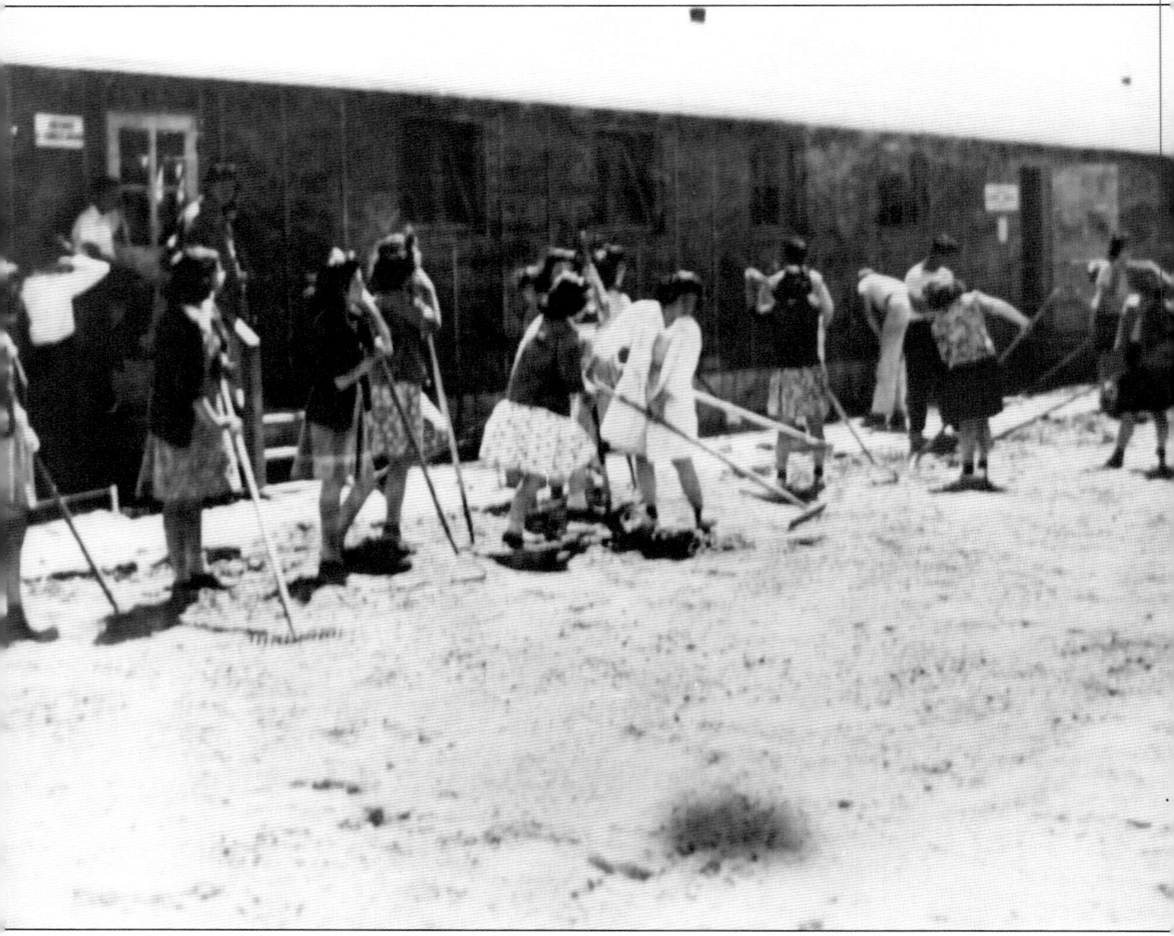

Even though the US government provided food for the camp, the residents planted gardens to supplement their meals. There was a potato cellar near the garden where they could store root vegetables for the winter.

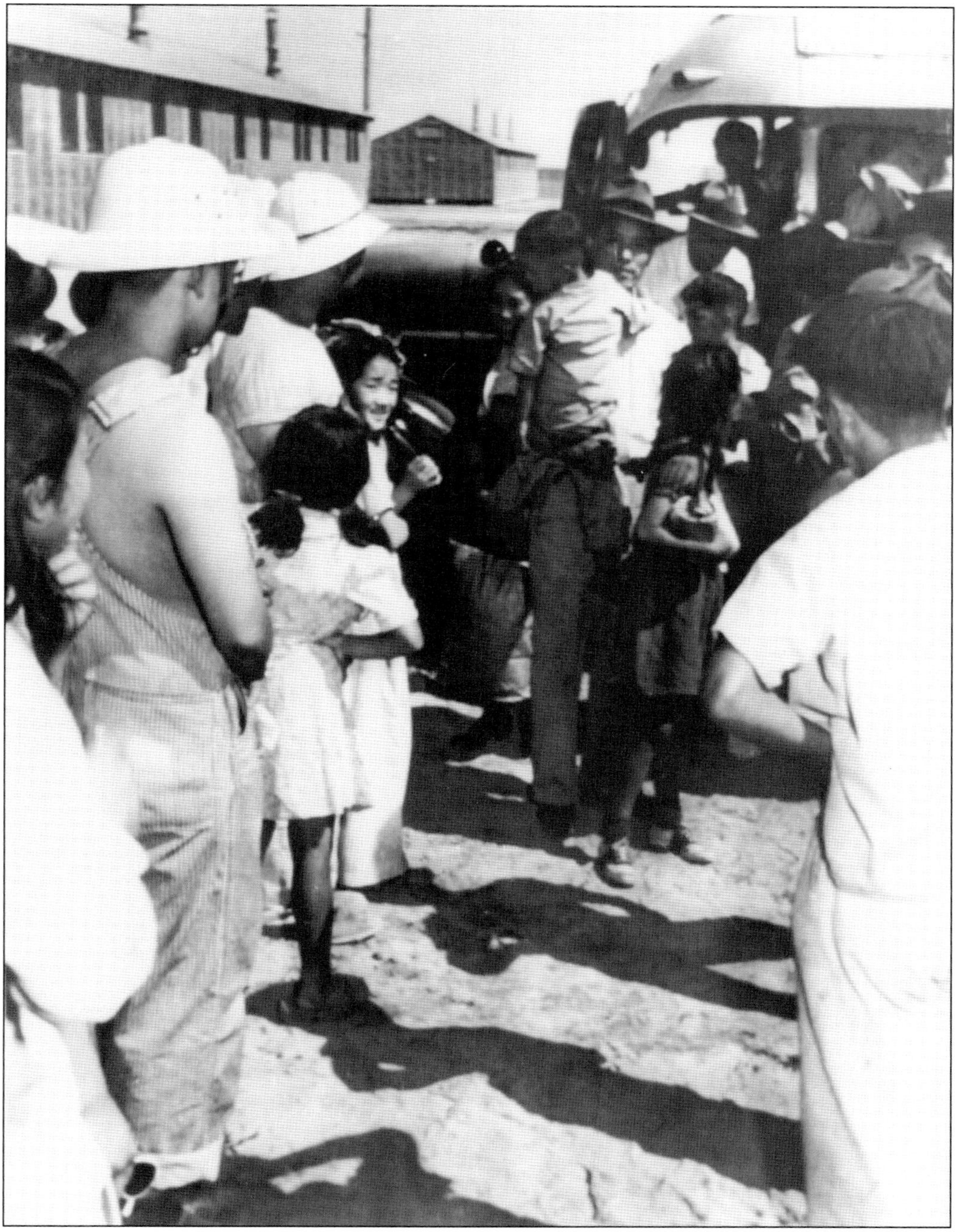

The Hunt Camp residents arrived in Jerome on the train and were transferred to the camp on school buses. When they left their homes in Washington and Oregon, they could only bring two suitcases for each person, and they had to carry those. Small childrens' and babies' items were carried in their parents' or older siblings' suitcases. While at the camp, they made useable items from leftover wood crates and the rocks and sagebrush surrounding the camp. When they left, many household items were left in the barracks to be retrieved by locals. Some of these items were donated to the Jerome County Historical Society and are on display at the in-town museum and at the Idaho Farm and Ranch Museum.